Motion Encoding in Language and Space

Edited by
MILA VULCHANOVA
AND EMILE VAN DER ZEE

OXFORD
UNIVERSITY PRESS

OXFORD
UNIVERSITY PRESS

Great Clarendon Street, Oxford, OX2 6DP,
United Kingdom

Oxford University Press is a department of the University of Oxford.
It furthers the University's objective of excellence in research, scholarship,
and education by publishing worldwide. Oxford is a registered trade mark of
Oxford University Press in the UK and in certain other countries

First Edition published in 2013

Impression: 1

British Library Cataloguing in Publication Data
Data available

ISBN 978–0–19–966121–3

Printed in Great Britain by
MPG Books Group, Bodmin and King's Lynn

Contents

Preface vii
The Contributors viii
Abbreviations xii

1 Introduction 1
Emile van der Zee, Mila Vulchanova

Part 1: Motion encoding across languages: multiple methods and applications

2 Distinctions in the linguistic encoding of motion: evidence from a free naming task 11
Mila Vulchanova, Liliana Martinez, Valentin Vulchanov

3 The encoding of motion events in Estonian 44
Renate Pajusalu, Neeme Kahusk, Heili Orav, Ann Veismann, Kadri Vider, Haldur Õim

4 Verbs of aquamotion: semantic domains and lexical systems 67
Yury Lander, Timur Maisak, Ekaterina Rakhilina

5 Spatial directionals for robot navigation 84
Andi Winterboer, Thora Tenbrink, Reinhard Moratz

6 The role of structure and function in the conceptualization of direction 102
Alexander Klippel, Thora Tenbrink, Daniel R. Montello

Part 2: Granularity

7 Granularity in taxonomy, time, and space 123
Jeffrey M. Zacks, Barbara Tversky

8 Granularity in the cross-linguistic encoding of motion and location 134
Miriam van Staden, Bhuvana Narasimhan

9 Granularity, space, and motion-framed location 149
Mark Tutton

10 Path and place: the lexical specification of granular compatibility 166
Hedda R. Schmidtke

11 The lexical representation of path curvature in motion expressions: a three-way path curvature distinction 187
Urpo Nikanne, Emile van der Zee

References 213
Index 233

Preface

The chapters that appear in this book are based on ongoing empirical research by the authors. Some of this research has been reported at conferences in Germany, the UK and Norway addressing topics in the encoding of motion in spatial language comprehension and production. We would like to thank the participants in these events for the active and stimulating discussions which have resulted in further refining the data presentations and analyses in the chapters which follow.

This book is dedicated to the memory of Uta Sassenberg, a wonderful friend and colleague.

Mila Vulchanova and Emile van der Zee
Trondheim/Lincoln, September 2012

The Contributors

Neeme Kahusk is a researcher in language technology in the Institute of Computer Science, University of Tartu, Estonia. His main research focus is upon computational semantics. He is specifically interested in computer lexicons: framenets and WordNets, but also word sense disambiguation.

Alexander Klippel is Assistant Professor for GIScience at the Geography Department of Pennsylvania State University. He is directing the Human Factors in GIScience lab as part of the GeoVISTA Center. His research interests focus on cognitive processes at the interface of language, graphics, and environmental space.

Yury Lander is a research fellow at the Institute of Oriental Studies, Moscow. His primary interests include North Caucasian languages, Austronesian languages, the typology of noun phrases, polysynthesis, and lexical typology.

Timur Maisak is Senior Research Fellow at the Institute of Linguistics/Russian Academy of Sciences (Moscow). His main research interests concern Caucasian languages and typology of grammatical categories.

Liliana Martinez is a PhD student in the Department of Modern Languages at the Norwegian University of Science and Technology. Her research interests are in the field of categorization and the linguistic encoding of motion. She is currently completing a dissertation on the semantics of motion verbs.

Daniel R. Montello is Professor in the Department of Geography, and Affiliated Professor in the Department of Psychology, at the University of California, Santa Barbara. His research interests are in the areas of spatial, environmental, and geographic perception, cognition, affect, and behaviour; cognitive issues in cartography and GIS; and environmental psychology and behavioural geography.

Reinhard Moratz is Associate Professor of Spatial Information Science and Engineering at the Department of Spatial Information Science and Engineering, University of Maine, Orono, USA. His research is centred on the development of a unified theory for the representation of spatial knowledge. This unified theory integrates sensory perception of a space, action within a space, and communication over a space.

Bhuvana Narasimhan is Assistant Professor at the Department of Linguistics at the University of Colorado, Boulder, USA. She specializes in first language acquisition of verb argument structure, with a focus on Hindi and Tamil.

Urpo Nikanne is Professor in Finnish Language and Literature at Åbo Akademie University in Turku, Finland. He works in the area of Conceptual Semantics, focusing on how natural language semantics builds on conceptual representations.

Haldur Õim is Professor Emeritus at the University of Tartu, Estonia, and Senior Researcher at the same university. His research interests include linguistic semantics and pragmatics, and in addition, modelling these topics in computer systems, following the Artificial Intelligence and Language Technology study lines.

Heili Orav, PhD, is researcher in the Department of General Linguistics, University of Tartu, Estonia. She is interested in computer linguistics and Cognitive Linguistics.

Renate Pajusalu is Professor of General Linguistics at the University of Tartu. Her main research interests are pragmatics (especially deixis), semantics, and language acquisition.

Ekaterina Rakhilina is Professor and Head of the Linguistic Programme at the Higher School of Economics (Moscow) as well as Senior Research Fellow at the Vinogradov Institute for Russian Language/Russian Academy of Sciences (Moscow). Her research interests include general and Russian semantics, lexicography, lexical typology, and corpus linguistics.

Hedda R. Schmidtke is Assistant Teaching Professor at Carnegie Mellon University in Rwanda. Her main research interests are in applications and theory of contextual reasoning on lightweight distributed computing platforms. She publishes in the areas of Ubiquitous/Pervasive Computing, Artificial Intelligence, Knowledge Representation and Reasoning, Geographic Information Systems, and Cognitive Science. Until 2011, Dr Schmidtke was Research Director of the TecO group at the Karlsruhe Institute of Technology (KIT), Germany. From 2006 to 2009, she was Research Fellow and Research Professor at the Gwangju Institute of Science and Technology (GIST) in South Korea. She holds a doctoral degree in computer science from the University of Hamburg, Germany.

Thora Tenbrink is a researcher at the Faculty of Linguistics at Bremen University, Germany and a principal investigator in two projects in the collaborative research centre SFB/TR 8 Spatial Cognition. Her main research interest concerns the relationship between cognitive processes and linguistic representations, in particular spatial language usage across situational factors.

Mark Tutton is a lecturer in English Linguistics at the University of Nantes, France. He was awarded his PhD in linguistics in 2010 for a thesis which examines how speakers of English and French use both speech and gesture to express static locative relationships. His research interests include the encoding of locative semantics cross-linguistically and the use of speech and gesture in social interaction.

Barbara Tversky is Professor Emerita at Stanford University and Professor of Psychology and Education at the Teacher's College, Columbia University, New York, USA. Her research on memory and cognition has focused broadly on spatial thinking and event cognition, how they are communicated through language, depiction, and gesture, and how they are applied to design.

Emile van der Zee works as Principal Lecturer in the School of Psychology at the University of Lincoln, UK. He studies the interface between spatial representation and language.

Miriam van Staden works as an advisor in the Academy of Government Communication, Ministry of General Affairs, The Netherlands. As a linguist she works on event reports and complex constructions in Papuan and Austronesian languages.

Ann Veismann is a Research Fellow in general linguistics at the University of Tartu, Estonia. Her research relates to Cognitive Linguistics, and her main research interests are semantics of adpositions and adverbs, space and time expressions in Estonian, and empirical methods in semantics.

Kadri Vider is a researcher in language technology in the Institute of Computer Science, University of Tartu, Estonia. Her research interests focus on computational linguistics and lexical semantics. She is more specifically interested in computer lexicons as thesauri and WordNets, but also word sense disambiguation.

Valentin Vulchanov is a Senior Researcher at the Department of Modern languages at the Norwegian University of Science & Technology (NTNU). His research is in the area of language and cognition, the development of figurative language, language in developmental disorders, diachronic syntax, and Slavic languages.

Mila Vulchanova is a professor at the Department of Modern Languages at the Norwegian University of Science & Technology (NTNU), and Director of the Language Acquisition and Language Processing Lab. Her research encompasses linguistic theory, language acquisition, language processing, spatial categorization and language, cognitive development, language in developmental deficits, language talent, and diachronic syntax.

Andi Winterboer is a scientific consultant at VDI/VDE-IT, Berlin, Germany, where he is responsible for analysing, supporting, and organizing innovation and technology for clients with political, research, and industry backgrounds. Before returning to Germany, he received a PhD from the University of Edinburgh, UK, and worked as a postdoctoral researcher at the Intelligent Systems Lab (ISLA) of the University of Amsterdam, NL. His general research interests are in the areas of human-computer interaction, cognitive science, and artificial intelligence.

Jeffrey M. Zacks is in the Departments of Psychology and Radiology at Washington University in Saint Louis, USA. Research in his laboratory focuses on higher cognition using behavioural methods, neuroimaging, and clinical neuroscience.

Abbreviations

ABL	ablative case
ACC	accusative case
ACT	active voice
ADE	adessive case
AdvP	adverbial phrase
AG	agent marker
ALL	allative
AOR	aorist
APART	active participle
ASP	aspectual participle
ART	article
ATR	attributive
CAUS	causative
CLR	classifier
CNV	converb
CONJ	conjunctive participle
CONT	continuous
COP	copula
DAT	dative
DECL	declarative
ELA	elative case
ERG	ergative
ESS	essive case
ESTWN	Estonian WordNet
EXCL	exclusive
F	raw frequencies
F	feminine
FUT	future
GEN	genitive
GIST	Gwangju Institute of Science and Technology
GL0	Grain level 0 verbs

GL1	Grain level 1 verbs
GL2	Grain level 2 verbs
GPS	navigational systems
ILI	Interlingual Index
ILL	illative case
IMPERF	imperfective
INDIR	indefinite direction
INE	inessive case
INF	infinitive
INF1	1st infinitive
INF2	2nd infinitive
INF3	3rd infinitive
INS	instrumental case
IPF	imperfective
ISLA	Intelligent Systems Lab of the University of Amsterdam, NL
KIT	Karlsruhe Institute of Technology, Germany
LOC	locative
M	masculine
MoM	Manner of Motion verbs
NOM	nominative case
NP	noun phrase
NTNU	The Norwegian University of Science & Technology
PAR	partitive case
PART	participle
PERF	perfective
PL	plural
POSTLAT	postlative
PP	prepositional phrase
PR	possessor
PRS	present tense
RDP	reduplication
PST	past
PTCL	particle
PRTCPL	participle
REFL	reflexive
REL	relative marker

SG	singular
ST	stative
SPART	stative participle
TOP	topic
TRA	translative case
VT	verbal theme
WSD	Word Sense Disambiguation Corpus of Estonia

1

Introduction

EMILE VAN DER ZEE, MILA VULCHANOVA

Why is motion encoding an interesting issue to consider in relation to language? There are many possible answers to this question, but we consider two answers here that cover a wide range of issues. In the first place, motion detection and identification play a salient role in human life, evolution, and communication. Among other things, motion recognition and understanding underlie such diverse abilities as navigation and action anticipation. Our ability to communicate about these things has clear evolutionary and social advantages, and is also linked to potentially advantageous applications in robotics, navigational systems (GPS), etc. Motion thus permeates language, and its encoding in language is linked to all sorts of advantages for individuals, the groups they belong to, and the species they represent.

A second reason why motion encoding is interesting in relation to language is that it is accepted in different linguistic traditions, for instance in Conceptual Semantics (Jackendoff 1983, 1997, 2002) and in Cognitive Linguistics (Lakoff 1987; Langacker 1987, etc.), but also in psychology (see e.g. Zacks and Tversky, this volume), that the encoding of space—including motion—is central to our cognitive and linguistic functioning. Notions relating to space are taken as an analogical model or a metaphorical source for other kinds of semantic relations, such as possessive constructions, temporal expressions, and so on. Whether we utter 'The car goes from Amsterdam to Paris', 'Paul gives a bottle of champagne to Pascal', or 'The meeting will take place from 4 o'clock till 5 o'clock', there is an underlying similarity in the core situational descriptions—an entity going or extending from a point A to a point B. In other words, linguistic motion encoding can be expected to play a central role in various other non-spatial domains in language.

A reason why motion encoding is specifically interesting when studying spatial language is that it is not always possible to understand descriptions of static situations without considering notions of movement. Consider the following examples in English:

(1) *The hotel is right behind the church.*
(2) *You will find the red lamp post before the tower.*
(3) *He jumped in the pool.*

Although terms such as *behind* typically locate a static Figure in relation to a static Ground, the use of *behind* as part of a set of route directions as in (1) can only be understood from a dynamic perspective: here *behind* defines a region of space based on the direction of motion of a protagonist. In contrast, an originally dynamic preposition, such as *before*, can be used to describe the location of a static Figure—deriving its meaning from a context in which the speaker or listener is (virtually) moving around in a scene. The example in (3), in turn, highlights the fact that, cross-linguistically, many prepositions are underspecified for a direction/location semantic component, and are only felicitously interpreted in the context of verbs denoting motion, such as *jump*. These examples thus illustrate that the locative and dynamic aspects of situation descriptions overlap in language, and that they should be studied in conjunction.

This book investigates how motion is encoded in spatial language. Spatial language refers to those parts of natural language that describe aspects of perceived space (see also Carlson and van der Zee 2005). Much research in linguistics, psychology, and computer science has been devoted to how languages manage the encoding of motion—the way in which languages encode how an entity (e.g. an object or an object part) changes position in relation to another entity. Research in the area of motion encoding in spatial language ranges from how languages encode path roles (e.g. the encoding of goals and sources of motion; see Bennett 1975; Gruber 1965; Jackendoff 1983; Johnson 1987; Lakoff 1987; Langacker 1987; Miller and Johnson-Laird 1976; Talmy 2000; Zwarts 2005), and manner of motion, such as running and hopping (e.g. Talmy 2000), to how languages encode causality (e.g. Jackendoff 1990 and Nikanne 1990). Recent research has also addressed how path features constrain grammatical encoding (Bohnemeyer 2003; Nikanne 1990), how languages represent path shape (van der Zee 2000), and how motion is represented in iconic gestures, not only in spoken language, but also in sign language (Kita and Özyürek 2003; Talmy 2003). This book does not pretend to cover all of these aspects of motion encoding. Part 1 presents interesting new insights into the parameters that play a role in the expression of motion (see also Levinson and Wilkins 2006), and new empirical research in the representation of direction in language (see also van der Zee and Slack 2003), while Part 2 addresses a topic that has so far received very little attention in the linguistic literature: the different levels of spatial resolution (or grain, or scale) at which languages represent motion.

The chapters in Part 1 update recent insights about the parameters that play a role in motion encoding, including directed motion, by presenting new research on Estonian, English, Norwegian, Bulgarian, Italian, German, Russian, Persian, and

Tamil. This research also ventures into two relatively unexplored areas of motion encoding, by considering the parameters that play a role in biological motion encoding (Chapter 2; for example, *to walk*), and the parameters that play a role in aquamotion (Chapter 4; for example, *to swim*). The last two chapters in Part 1 extend current research by considering how directional terms are used for instructing robots or human beings where to go in a constrained (grid-like) environment. The chapters in Part 1 are also connected in another sense: they display a wide variety in the methods used to research motion encoding in spatial language. Although traditionally linguists have worked with linguistic examples to illustrate theoretical notions, or to support any claims made, Chapter 2 uses a free naming task in combination with statistical methods to detect patterns or parameters referring to motion. The data in Chapters 3 and 6 are based on corpus analyses, and Chapter 5 uses instructions produced by participants as data. Chapter 4 in Part 1 together with all of the chapters in Part 2 use examples in the more traditional sense to study individual languages or cross-linguistic variation.

Part 2 contains a unique collection of chapters exploring the grain levels of spatial encoding in language, starting with a review paper by Zacks and Tversky on how the concept of 'granularity' plays an important role in human cognition, and then continuing with chapters that build on this work to link the issue of granularity to motion encoding in language. In the remainder of this Introduction we introduce each of the Parts of this book with their chapters in more detail.

The chapters in Part 1 of this book explicitly focus on the possible parameters that play a role in the encoding of motion in language. Recent insights into the parameters that play a role in motion encoding mainly draw on Talmy's (1985, 2000) influential work; in particular, the awareness that linguistic expressions of motion are constrained by schemas consisting of sets of elements encoding Motion, Path, Manner of Motion, Figure, and Ground. Depending on whether Path is commonly expressed in verbs or in what Talmy calls satellites to the verb (for example, verb particles or verb prefixes), languages fall into verb-framed and satellite-framed categories respectively. This widely used typology has not remained unchallenged, however, in recent theoretical, but mainly, empirical research (cf. Zlatev and Yangklang 2004; Croft et al. 2010; Beavers et al. 2010, to mention a few).

Chapter 2 presents the results of an exploratory free naming study of how biological motion is encoded in five different languages: Bulgarian, Russian, English, Norwegian, and Italian. The first four languages are satellite-framed languages, while Italian is a verb-framed language. A cluster analysis of the data in this chapter shows that all the languages in the sample behave similarly and make a clear distinction between non-supported high velocity high energy gaits (running), and supported slow-to-normal velocity motion (walking), and that they display greater variation in the latter domain. Dimitrova-Vulchanova, Martinez, and Vulchanov propose among other things a fine-grained feature analysis for the representation of biological motion descriptions that is based on the following parameters: the medium traversed; the species involved; the characteristic limb use, speed, orientation, posture, and psychological state of the Figure; the motion vector orientation (goal, source); and the path shape. This chapter thus contributes to an identification of parameters that play a role in biological motion encoding across languages previously assumed to belong in different typological groups (satellite vs. verb-framed languages, Talmy 1985, 2000).

Work by Pajusalu, Kahusk, Orav, Veismann, Vider, and Õim in Chapter 3 considers the motion parameters Goal, Source, and Path in Estonian while contrasting these motion parameters with the way in which Location is specified. The analyses in Chapter 3 are based on a representative corpus of the language with the relevant verb frequencies specified. Special attention is paid to the distinctions made in the Estonian Case system between Allative and Illative, Elative and Ablative, and Inessive and Adessive expressions in encoding Goal, Source, and Location, respectively. The Estonian verbal lexicon is introduced in the format typical of WordNet descriptions in terms of interrelations between lexical items organized into synonym sets with a special focus on relations of hyponymy. This leads to two words being at the top of the hierarchy of motion verbs: the intransitive verb *liikuma* (move, change position), and the derived causative transitive verb *liigutama* (make move, cause to move). The authors provide a comprehensive picture of the central motion verbs common to Estonian with their typical collocations (NPs, adverbials, and adpositions). As in other languages, the most common and frequent locomotion verbs also appear to be highly polysemous, such as *käima* (walk, visit), *minema* (go), while other notions are only restricted to motion senses, such as *lendama* (fly) and *keerama* (turn).

Chapter 4 considers the possible features for a semantic typology in the domain of aquamotion (e.g. swimming) by looking at languages such as Russian, German, (standard) Indonesian, Persian, and Tamil. In this chapter, Lander, Maisak, and Rakhilina give arguments for a division of event types for verbal lexemes in the domain of aquamotion into swimming, sailing, and floating. Depending on the presence of these distinctions, and finer distinctions based on this tri-partition, the authors distinguish between rich, poor, and 'middle' systems of aquamotion. They argue that Russian and German represent poor systems, that (standard) Indonesian is an example of a rich system, and that Persian and Tamil are instances of 'middle' systems. The chapter also discusses interesting shifts and extensions of the semantic divisions due to the fuzziness of the boundaries among these divisions.

The focus of the next two chapters is on directed motion and the way in which directions are encoded in spatial language. In Chapter 5, Winterboer, Tenbrink, and Moratz consider the use of prepositions, such as *to the left of* and *in front of* from a dynamic perspective. They show that participants use these prepositions as directional instructions to a robot moving around in a scene. The authors discuss a series of experiments in which a robot was instructed to reach a goal. The speakers were free to use any kind of instructions, and were thus not asked to keep to a list of specific instructions that might be part of the robot's inbuilt lexicon. The authors show in their chapter that people spontaneously use more direction instructions (e.g. *go left*) compared to goal-based descriptions (e.g. *go to the black cardboard box*), and that the efficiency of their direction-based instructions improved when some basic changes were made to the robot's lexicon and its possibilities for moving around, thus allowing the robot to recognize more expressions and allowing the instructions to be briefer.

In Chapter 6, Klippel, Tenbrink, and Montello analyse the verbal output of native English speakers who describe how an imagined cyclist would go along a route on a map. They consider—among other things—how direction changes at decision points are described in terms of the prepositions and verbs used. One of their interesting findings is that at complex junctions participants do not use prepositions with modifiers (e.g. *go slightly left*), but that participants use ordering concepts (e.g. *take your second left*). These findings contrast with findings relating to object location, where participants use modifiers in order to locate a Figure in relation to a Ground object (e.g. *It is left behind y*).

Part 2 of this book looks at the way in which spatial scale or granularity plays a role in the encoding of motion in language. The relation between spatial scale and language has received attention in AI and Geography (e.g. Montello 1993; Bennett and Cristani 2003; Schmidtke and Beigl 2010), in psycholinguistics for descriptions of static relations (e.g. Burigo and Coventry 2010; Carlson and Covey 2005; Morrow and Clark 1988; van der Zee et al. 2009), and even in sociology (Schegloff 2000). However, up until quite recently, the relation between spatial scale and motion encoding in language has received surprisingly limited attention (see Tenbrink and Winter 2009; van der Zee et al. 2010). This is surprising, since if we are interested in the relation between spatial language on the one hand, and the spatial representations that language refers to on the other (Jackendoff 2010), we can see how strongly felicitous interpretation depends on the correct level of representation in the presence of polysemy in this area. For example, Krüger and Maaß (1997) observe that the phrase *past the houses* may be a correct description of path A, path B, or path C in Figure 1.1, depending on such factors as the size of the objects involved, the speed of the Figure, the field of visual attention, and the communicative situation.

Part 2 starts with Zacks and Tversky's chapter on 'Granularity in taxonomy, time and space'. This chapter gives a comprehensive overview of the notion of granularity in several areas of cognition, but at the same time relates the notion of granularity to language. Zacks and Tversky argue in Chapter 7 that cognitive processing in many areas of cognition is influenced by the grain level that is in focus. For example, when asked to list object properties on a coarse taxonomic scale people tend to refer to an object's function (e.g. that furniture makes one comfortable), when asked to list such

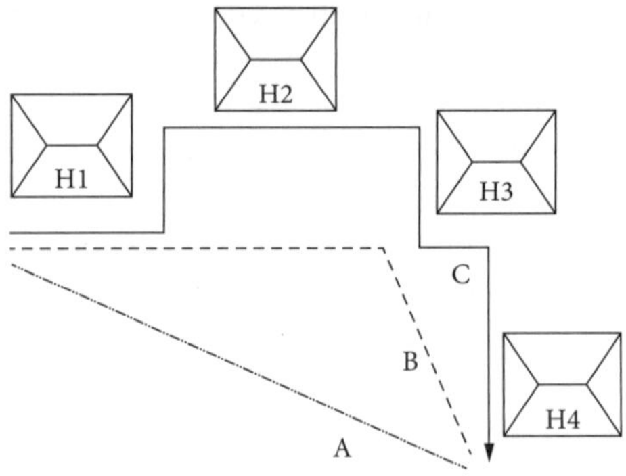

FIGURE 1.1 The phrase *past the houses* may correspond to path A, path B, or path C (from Krüger and Maaß 1997).

properties on an intermediate taxonomic scale people tend to refer to object parts (e.g. that a chair has legs, a seat, etc.), and when asked to list such properties on a fine-grained taxonomic scale people tend to refer to colours and materials. Zacks and Tversky thus argue that cognitive processing is not scale invariant.

Using Zacks and Tversky's work, van Staden and Narasimhan distinguish between three different notions of granularity in Chapter 8: (a) the encoding of event boundaries at the clausal level, (b) the expression of elements within an event, and (c) the level of specificity at which the elements in (b) are expressed. Van Staden and Narasimhan look, for example, at events of caused motion into containment (e.g. a ball being put into a box), and consider how such events are encoded in a selection of languages in terms of (a) through (c). One of the conclusions they draw is that the grammatical and lexical resources of a language to some extent reflect the default or basic level of granularity at which an event is encoded. They argue that, for instance, serial verb constructions allow for the encoding of 'wider' event boundaries in a single chunk than languages in which such constructions are not available.

Building on the two previous chapters in Part 2, Tutton shows in Chapter 9 that dynamic prepositions referring to object motion, such as *before* and *after*, can be used to talk about object location. And, what is more, Tutton shows that such prepositions demand a coarse level for the interpretation of the spatial scene, and do not tolerate a fine level of spatial granularity (e.g. it is possible to say that *The train station comes before the cathedral*, but it is not acceptable to say that ?*The table comes before the sofa*). Tutton furthermore shows that static prepositions that correspond to their dynamic counterparts, such as *in front of* and *behind*, do accept both coarse and fine grain levels at which a situation is represented (e.g. it is both possible to say that *The train station is in front of the cathedral* and that *The table is in front of the sofa*). Tutton's work thus shows an asymmetry in the use of static and dynamic prepositions that can be attributed to two different levels of spatial resolution at which these classes of prepositions tolerate an interpretation of a situation.

In Chapter 10, Schmidtke interprets spatial granularity as referring to grain size (i.e. as referring to sizes and distances), but also as referring to the level of detail of a representation (i.e. as representational granularity), and like other authors in Part 2 adopts the terms 'coarse' and 'fine-grained' to refer to different levels of granularity. Focusing on German she presents several formal tools for representing granularity-dependent notions such as 'point-like' or 'proximity'. She shows how the developed formalism can be used to encode compatibility restrictions of spatial granularity in expressions referring to object location and route instruction. She argues that the German adverbial use of *entlang* ('along') demands an interpretation of a reference object that is extended, whereas the use of *vorbei* ('past') demands an interpretation of a reference object that is atomic, and illustrates how her formal framework works by combining these different adverbials with German *an* ('at/on/by'), which denotes close proximity or contact. Schmidtke shows that her model of lexically specifying granular compatibility can explain why certain expressions are not acceptable for a native speaker.

In Chapter 11, Nikanne and van der Zee consider the different levels of granularity at which path curvature can be represented in the Finnish and Dutch grammars. They argue that the motion verbs in these languages may represent path curvature neutrally, globally, or locally. Their three-grain-level hypothesis is then used to formulate language-specific constraints on the way in which motion is encoded in Finnish and Dutch. In a similar fashion to Schmidtke in Chapter 10, their work thus shows that considering motion encoding at different levels of spatial resolution contributes to a further understanding of speakers' acceptability judgments in language.

A thematic organization of chapters in an edited book such as this runs the risk of leaving some general issues underexposed. It is therefore good to point out that, despite the differences in perspective or methodology employed, there is an important recurrent theme that unites the chapters in the current volume. This is the parameters and features that constrain the encoding of motion categories in language, and the ways in which research can approach and predict linguistic variation and analysis. From a methodological point of view, the uniting theme is how coarse or fine representation or encoding can be. For example, the distinctions made in the chapters in Part 2 concerning granularity can be considered to apply directly to parameters in motion encoding, as addressed in Part 1.

The chapters in this book provide new explorations in motion encoding in language. The examples provided in this area are not exhaustive, and the conclusions are not final, but we hope that you enjoy the journey through the landscape that is offered by the authors.

Part 1

Motion encoding across languages: multiple methods and applications

2

Distinctions in the linguistic encoding of motion: evidence from a free naming task[1]

MILA VULCHANOVA, LILIANA MARTINEZ, VALENTIN VULCHANOV

In this chapter we present and discuss the results of an exploratory free naming study of how biological motion is encoded in five languages: Bulgarian, Russian, English, Norwegian, and Italian. The cluster analysis of our data reveals interesting patterns of similarity as well as differences across all five languages. These patterns suggest that the linguistic encoding of motion may be based on a system of conceptual features, which reflect physical parameters, acknowledged to influence motion categorization both in visual perception and in linguistic semantics. We propose that some of these features are *medium*, *phase*, *velocity*, *posture*, *method of propulsion*, *species*, *path orientation*, and *figure orientation*. Our findings are in accordance with ideas expressed in recent work by Malt and colleagues (Malt et al. 2010), who propose that the mapping of conceptual structure to language is constrained, but flexible. The mapping tends to be clearer/more constrained for clear discontinuities in nature (e.g. suspended vs. supported motion), while less clear discontinuities (e.g. different subtypes of supported motion) tend to be represented more flexibly across languages, with variation both in what features are lexicalized in a particular language, and how these features are bundled. While all the languages in our sample make a clear distinction between non-supported high-velocity high-energy gaits (running), and supported slow-to-normal velocity motion (walking), they display greater variation in the latter domain, as well as in other types of motion (crawling, climbing). In addition, our study has revealed an interesting function of

[1] We want to thank Enrico-Filippo Cardini, Ekaterina Rakhilina, and Timur Maisak for collecting the data for Italian and Russian. We are also grateful to Thomas Brox Røst and Ole Edsberg who developed the multiset clustering algorithm and helped us apply it to our data.

modifiers of the verb not observed previously. We dub this function the *non-default explication function* and suggest that its role is to signal non-default settings of the perceptual parameters characterizing motion scenes.

2.1 Background

It has been widely acknowledged that schematization is one of the key principles of how humans categorize the world through language. Schematization is a process that involves the systematic selection of certain aspects of an object or a scene to represent the whole, while disregarding the remaining aspects (Talmy 2000). Particularly interesting from this point of view is *biological motion*, because it encompasses a wide spectrum of experientially relevant physical parameters that are good candidates for being included among the aspects foregrounded under linguistic categorization. The notion of biological motion, as we use it throughout this work, covers self-agentive translational motion by live organisms, which involves complex patterns of internal motion of the body and limbs, the function of which is to cause translation.

Many linguistic studies about the parameters that play a role in motion encoding mainly draw on Talmy's (2000) influential work; in particular, the awareness that linguistic expressions of motion are constrained by schemas consisting of a limited set of elements, such as Motion, Path, Manner of Motion, Figure, and Ground. Motion-event typology focuses on how these elements are encoded cross-linguistically. According to this scheme, verbs referring to biological motion (e.g. *run*, *spring*, *trot*, *walk*, *strut*, etc.) have been all lumped together as 'Manner verbs'—verbs in which the element of Motion is conflated with Manner (a '*...subordinate event [that] can be held to constitute an event of circumstance in relation to the macro-event as a whole and to perform the functions of support in relation to the framing event...*'; Talmy 2000: 220). In their capacity as Manner verbs, biological motion verbs have been placed in an opposition with 'Path verbs' (e.g. *enter*, *exit*, *arrive*, *depart*)—verbs in which the element of Motion is conflated with Path ('*the path followed or the site occupied by the Figure object with respect to the Ground object*'—Talmy, 2000: 25).

Recently, it has become clear that Manner and Path are pre-theoretical terms, and may be further decomposed into conceptually relevant features. Path, for instance, can be represented in different ways (e.g. as an axis or as a vector; see Zwarts 2003), and subsumes parameters as diverse as frames of reference, direction, distance, shape, reference objects, and relations defined on the basis of the spatial or functional properties of these, etc. (see van der Zee and Slack 2003). The notion of Manner can be also decomposed into a number of independent parameters pertaining to various aspects of the motion scene (cf. Dimitrova-Vulchanova and Weisgerber 2007). Moreover, Path and Manner may overlap, if not defined properly (see

Nikanne and van der Zee, this volume; Martinez 2009). Many verbs which actually encode *path shape* are traditionally defined as manner verbs (e.g. *zig-zag*, *spiral*, *curve*). *Path orientation* (depending on whether the motion is along the vertical or horizontal axis) may define distinctions within the verbal lexicon which also pass for Manner. Thus, *climb* specifies vertical motion, while walking verbs, by default, encode horizontal motion. Quite often, what is meant by manner is the specific pattern of limb movement during locomotion, but it can be as remote as, for example, referring to the speed of motion. Likewise, many so-called 'Manner verbs' lexically encode both a Manner and a Path component. We consider lexically encoded information in the sense of Koenig et al. (2003) to mean 'information which is immediately activated upon accessing the word'. For motion verbs like *run*, for instance, the manner can be specified primarily in terms of the high velocity of the locomotion. However, in addition there is a path traversal component, which is inherent in *run* (cf. 'to **move along** with quick steps lifting each foot off the ground before the other one touches the ground'[2]) and which can license the use of directional prepositional phrases which specify aspects of this path (e.g. path beginning/end; path length). In this respect, *run* contrasts with other motion verbs, like *dance*, where such a component is absent. For this reason, prepositional phrases in the context of *dance* can only denote a location (e.g. *She was dancing* ***in the room***).[3] Thus, *run* encodes both the specific Manner of locomotion and Path traversal, while *dance* only encodes Manner.

In current work (Dimitrova-Vulchanova et al. in press), we have proposed that the verbal lexicon of languages should be addressed from the point of view of conceptual granularity (Zacks and Tversky, van der Zee and Ninanne, and Staden and Narasimhan, this volume) reflected in the encoding of locomotion in terms of a *basic level* (*walk*, *run*, *climb*), a *superordinate level* (*go*, *come*, *move*), and a *specific level* below the basic one (i.e. verbs referring to subtypes of the motion pattern described by the basic level verbs, for example *strut*, *stroll*, *sprint*, *canter*, etc., which are different kinds of walking and running). Since the verbs belonging in those three levels reflect different levels of detail in describing the locomotion pattern, an adequate model of motion encoding should consider and reflect the difference in their contribution to the motion template. Thus, verbs from the superordinate group never encode pattern of locomotion due to the coarse level of granularity, but they may encode path direction (*come*, *go*, *ascend*, *descend*, *enter*), while verbs at the specific level are only manner verbs (*strut*, *amble*, *perambulate*). Like *run*, most verbs at the basic level combine Manner and Path lexically.

[2] Cambridge Dictionaries Online.

[3] Lexical encoding excludes the possibilities made available by grammatical constructions, such as e.g. the way-construction in English, as in *She danced her way through the corridor*. Observe, that many languages do not allow this type of resultative at all (Bulgarian, Greek; see Dimitrova-Vulchanova 2003; Stavrou and Horrocks 2003).

The task of current research is to map out the parameters of importance for the linguistic categorization of biological motion. Results from recent empirical and experimental work (Slobin 2006; Dimitrova-Vulchanova et al. in press; Malt et al. 2008) demonstrate that, regardless of cross-linguistic variation, languages not only systematically encode some basic parameters that are perceptually salient in locomotion scenes, but are also constrained in their lexicons by the biomechanical distinctions that characterize locomotion. Studies by Malt and colleagues (Malt et al. 2008, 2010) and others (Khetarpal et al. 2009, 2010) show that spatial terms reflect near-optimal spatial categories, that is, objectively observable distinctions in the physical world allowing humans to make experientially relevant distinctions. The results of these studies do not allow us to make precise predictions concerning the composition of the motion lexicon and inventory of motion expressions of individual languages. However, they suggest that the likelihood of lexicalization for experientially based semantic features may be placed on a continuum from most to least likely. Features corresponding to more readily observable discontinuities in nature are more likely to play an important role in the linguistic categorization of motion. Malt et al. demonstrate this for the features *velocity* and *phase of motion* (*suspended* versus *supported*; cf. definitions of these terms in the next section) for human gaits.

In this chapter we want to explore the importance of a wider set of features relevant for the linguistic categorization of biological motion. For our purposes, we adapt methods for data gathering and data analysis already used in previous studies (Strömqvist and Verhoeven 2004; Majid et al. 2008; Malt et al. 2010), and our data come from five languages: two Germanic (English and Norwegian), two Slavic (Bulgarian and Russian), and one Romance (Italian). We are interested in what perceptual aspects of observed biological motion affect its lexical encoding in the languages in our sample. The exposition has the following structure: section 2.2 lays out our proposal for a system of features, based on independent studies in the fields of biomechanics and linguistics. Section 2.3 describes a free naming experiment we designed for the purpose (section 2.3.1), the methodological issues connected with analysing the data (section 2.3.2), some facts about motion verb systems in some of our target languages (section 2.3.3), and the results for the individual languages (section 2.3.4). Cluster analysis is used to show how the stimulus scenes are grouped by the motion verbs occurring in their descriptions. In addition, some observations are made about how the occurrence of modifiers can be used as an indicator of the default feature values in verbs (section 2.3.5). Section 2.4 summarizes the biological motion categories lexicalized in the target languages, and compares how biological motion verbs are related based on the physical parameters of motion. It compares the results to the set of features proposed in section 2.2, and discusses their relative importance within and across the languages.

2.2 Features of relevance for the linguistic categorization of motion

So far, it transpires that the linguistic encoding of motion needs to be described by a more refined system, which looks at how Path and Manner can be decomposed for the purposes of capturing salient cross-linguistic patterns. We propose a fine-grained feature analysis for the representation of biological motion based on parameters independently argued to apply in the identification and categorization of motion in biomechanics (Alexander 1982; McMahon 1984), research on visual perception (Thornton and Vuong 2004; among others), and in linguistic semantics (Dimitrova-Vulchanova 2004a, b; Dimitrova-Vulchanova et al. in press; Weisgerber and Geuder 2007). Evidence of the relevance of such parameters comes from different sources.

A viable hypothesis of the factors that play a role in biological motion categorization can draw on the classification of biological motion from the perspective of biomechanics (cf. seminal works in the field like Alexander 1982, 1996; McMahon 1984; and Hildebrand 1985). Although the descriptions and classifications of locomotion patterns in the literature involve a multitude of anatomical, mechanical, kinematic, kinetic, etc. details that are not likely to be of importance for the purposes of linguistic encoding, there are some parameters that seem to tie in well with the biological motion categories found in non-technical language. Such parameters are: ***posture*** (position of the body relative to the terrain: perpendicular vs. parallel; presence of contact, as in crawling, vs. absence of contact, as in walking, running, and jumping), ***stance*** (position of the legs relative to the body—e.g. *sprawling/bent,* as in lizards, vs. *semierect*, as in crocodiles, vs. *erect*, as in mammals or birds), ***use of limbs*** (*bipedal*, such as walking, running, or skipping, vs. *quadrupedal*, as in pacing, trotting, and galloping), ***temporal spacing of footfalls*** (*symmetrical*, as in walking, trotting, running, vs. *asymmetrical*, as in jumping, hopping, cantering, galloping), ***phases*** of the gait (*supported* gaits, in which at least one foot touches the terrain at all times, as in walking and crawling, vs. *suspended* gaits that have an airborne phase, as in running, vs. *aerial* gaits, in which the airborne phase is especially prolonged, as in jumping).

A feature which is very difficult to define is ***velocity***. Applying categories such as 'fast', 'normal', and 'slow' is relative, both to the performer and to the gait (the speed of translation in fast walking is not the same as the speed of translation in fast running or fast crawling, in the same way as a fast human moves at a different speed from a fast snail). For the sake of analysis, it is more useful to use terms like ***relative stride rate*** (from low in walking and jumping to high in running and galloping) and ***relative stride length*** (short in walking vs. longer in running vs. longest in jumping). For comparing velocity across different gaits and species, Alexander (1982) defines the principle of dynamic similarity: *'Motions are said to be dynamically similar if they could be made identical by the uniform changes of the scales of length and time'.*

Thus, two gaits are identical if the ratios of stride-length-to-leg-length are identical. Velocity is inextricably intertwined with the anatomy of the moving organism, and the surrounding environment. A measure that reflects this is the Froude number,[4] which establishes the interrelation between velocity, leg length, and the force of gravity. Animals ranging from small rodents to horses and elephants use similar gaits and equal values of stride-length-to-leg-length at any given Froude number. Gait transitions tend to occur at particular Froude numbers (McMahon, 1984).[5] Moreover, what is normal/default speed for a species is also defined by biomechanical factors. For example, for humans, the normal or default locomotion pattern is walking (in which the posture and limb movements are adjusted so as to save energy by maximally utilizing the force of gravity to achieve forward displacement; see Alexander 1999).

The importance of these and other features is confirmed by evidence from research in visual perception. As it turns out, the human mechanisms of biological motion recognition are extremely robust. Biological motion can be recognized from severely impoverished stimuli, for example when the moving figure is reduced to a point-light display (classical experiment in Johansson 1973; Sigala et al. 2005). Furthermore, motion categorization is learning-based, perspective-dependent, and selective (ibid). Giese and Poggio (2003) argue that the robustness of motion categorization resides in two neural pathways, each of them representing motion in a specific way: a form-pathway recognizes biological motion as a sequence of 'snapshots' of the figure in motion, and a motion-pathway recognizes biological motion as a sequence of optic flow patterns. While human action perception seems to tolerate substantial variation in form features (Sigala et al. 2005), motion patterns seem to be specific to particular types of actions, which explains why biological motion can be recognized only through the motion-pathway and in the absence of form information (e.g. in point-light displays). This theory of motion recognition enables us to hypothesize which criteria will be relevant in the categorization and linguistic encoding of biological motion. Criteria related to the form-pathway of recognition are *body shape and proportions* (e.g. bulky vs. slim body; short vs. long legs), *characteristic use of limbs* (e.g. biped vs. quadruped; the isolated movements of the limbs) and, by extension, also *species* (e.g. human vs. non-human). The series of 'snapshots' in a particular temporal order is what we will call the *cycle* of a particular type of biological motion. Relevant factors, related to the motion-pathway of recognition, will be *path* (the presence vs. absence of translational motion), and

[4] $F = \frac{V}{\sqrt{gh_m}}$ where V = velocity, g = force of gravity, h = limb length.

[5] The Froude number of 0.6 corresponds to a change from bipedal walking to bipedal running or jumping, and from quadrupedal walk to faster quadrupedal gaits (e.g. trot or pace). The Froude number of 2.3 corresponds to a change from symmetrical quadrupedal gaits to faster asymmetrical gaits, such as gallop or bounding (McMahon, 1984).

velocity (defined as the ration between stride rate and stride length). The view dependence of motion recognition will predict that factors like *figure orientation* (e.g. front forwards vs. front backwards, head up vs. head down), relative *path vector orientation* (towards vs. away from vs. left-to-right vs. right-to-left) will play a part also in categorization, and possibly in lexicalization (cf. Jellema et al. 2002, for a bias for left-to-right human walking recognition in the macaque). Thornton et al. (2002) demonstrate that the identification of locomotion relies on both top-down and bottom-up processing, and that local low-level feature information is highly relevant and more robust, in that it is not affected by dividing attention. Furthermore, this research in the visual perception of motion has shown that manipulating features of the display, such as figure orientation, inversion, or vector orientation, may influence recognition strongly (Shipley 2003). In a learning experiment, Jastorff et al. (2006) demonstrate that learning speed and accuracy for human movements are quite similar to those obtained for completely artificial articulated patterns generated using individual features otherwise present in human locomotion. This study shows that familiarity or biological relevance of the underlying kinematics or skeleton does not seem to be critical for the visual learning process, as would be the case if processing was exclusively top-down/gestaltic, and not based on features and feature-decomposition.

Some pointers to physical properties that may be useful for the analysis of linguistic categorization can be found also in the linguistic literature. The notion of *path*, which is here defined as the presence vs. absence of translation (progression in space), offers a rich inventory of potential further specifications (such as *start point*, *end point*, *path length*), which have been studied extensively in the linguistic literature (see Jackendoff 2002 for a recent discussion of types of *path*). Different values of path direction and various relations with the reference objects can be specified in verbs such as *enter*, *leave*, and boundary-crossing verbs cross-linguistically. Luganda has a highly specialized verb, *fubutuka* (Ndiwalana 2005), which means 'to dash forth quickly', specifying exclusively and only the starting point of the path, but not the end. The latter verb shows also the importance of the temporal characteristics of the motion event as a whole (e.g. the sudden onset encoded in *dash off* vs. the steady progression encoded in *run*). Speed has been recently addressed in work by Gries (2006), Stefanowitsch (2008), and Malt et al. (2008) in connection with the characterization of *run* verbs, showing that languages distinguish between high-velocity motion and normal/slow-velocity motion in their lexicons. Locomotion medium is targeted by contrasts, such as *swim* vs. *fly* vs. terrestrial locomotion such as *walk*. As it happens, languages may have highly elaborate vocabularies reflecting such distinctions (see Lander et al. this volume). We would like to go further, by suggesting a more detailed and more systematized set of features, based on all that has been mentioned in this section so far. These are listed in (1):

(1) a ***Locomotion medium*** (e.g. terrestrial vs. aquatic vs. air)
b ***Gait phase*** (e.g. suspended vs. supported vs. aerial)
c ***Posture and stance*** (e.g. upright vs. low body; erect vs. sprawling legs)
d ***Temporal spacing of footfalls*** (symmetrical vs. asymmetrical)
e ***Figure orientation*** (front-forwards vs. front-backwards vs. head-up vs. head-down)
f ***Velocity*** (fast vs. normal vs. slow)
g ***Method of propulsion***—the use of body and limbs (no limbs/body undulation vs. bipedal vs. quadrupedal)
h ***Species*** (human vs. non-human)
i ***Path*** (presence vs. absence of translational motion)
i ***Reference object*** (type of relation to reference object)
ii ***Vector orientation*** (horizontal: towards vs. away from vs. left-to-right vs. right-to-left; vertical: up vs. down)
iii ***Path shape*** (circular, zigzag)

All of these features can in theory combine on all of their values, potentially yielding a host of possible motion scenes. Walking covers supported symmetrical gaits, usually involving upright posture and 'normal' speed. Running applies to quick suspended motion. Crawling is slow supported motion, with the body close to the ground, and (in limbed creatures) sprawling/bent limbs. Climbing covers motion where the figure performs a locomotor pattern in order to propel itself along a vertical axis. Jumping is an asymmetric aerial gait in which there is high force of ejection, and relatively big vertical displacement, but not necessarily horizontal displacement. In many cases, specific parameter values will tend to co-occur in nature. For instance, human terrestrial motion is by default bi-pedal, head-up, a fact reflected among other things in inverted point-light displays being processed more slowly, if at all (Shipley 2003; Reed et al. 2003; Loucks and Baldwin 2009). This is in line with the theory of Rosch et al. (1976), who proposed that humans use features that naturally co-occur in experience to assign objects to categories, and to determine how good an example an object is of a category.

Not all features are equally relevant for categorization in all cases. Languages may have lexical items encoding each basic type, but this is not necessarily so. For example, for the verb *swim*, which is a basic level verb, the manner in which the swimmer uses her limbs or body does not play any role whatsoever. Rather, the aquatic medium and whether motion is self-propelled or not are important, as in *swim* vs. *float* or *sail* (Geuder and Weisgerber 2006; Lander et al. this volume). However, the specific pattern of limb/arm movement can be crucial below the basic level, where we find a host of verbs denoting types of swimming (crawl, breast-stroke, butterfly). Moreover, not all languages have the same categories. For example, Ewe has only one verb *dzò*, for *jump*, *hop*, and *fly*, while Asante does not have verbs corresponding to *run* and *fly* (Dzidzorm 2007). A similar situation obtains in Mandarin Chinese (Lejiao Liu, personal communication).

This chapter discusses the results of an exploratory study of how biological motion is encoded in five languages: Bulgarian, Russian, English, Norwegian, and Italian. Italian is a Romance language which, despite being classified as verb-framed according to Talmy's (2000) typology, has a number of biological motion verbs and verb use patterns typical of satellite-framed languages (Iacobini 2009). Russian and Bulgarian are Slavic languages, and English and Norwegian are Germanic languages, all four languages having been previously classified as satellite-framed according to Talmy's typology. However, there are differences in how they describe motion events. The mechanism of verb-prefixation, which serves a variety of purposes in Slavic languages, makes it much harder to make an absolute distinction between manner verbs and path verbs (Croft et al. 2010; Sinha and Kuteva 1995; Smith 2006; Dimitrova-Vulchanova et al. under revision). Moreover, Bulgarian displays an interesting deviation from the rest of Slavic in the domain of motion words, most likely as the result of sustained contact with the other Balkan languages (Smith 2006; Dimitrova-Vulchanova 2009). Likewise, English is also not a typical Germanic language, because of the Romance component in its vocabulary.

Our intention is to explore the verb inventory for encoding terrestrial biological motion of the five languages. We want to compare how the target languages categorize terrestrial biological motion. In particular, we are interested in the features comprising 'manner' and we intend to investigate whether naming preferences depend on the variation of different parameters, for example *phase*, *posture*, *method of propulsion*, *spacing of footfalls*, *species*, *figure orientation*, *path vector orientation*, *presence vs. absence of translation*, etc.. In order to accomplish our goals, we conducted an experiment in which native speakers of the five languages provided free descriptions for a number of biological motion scenes played on a computer screen. The scenes we selected display locomotion as performed by humans as well as other species, and are all set in natural environments. This design allows us to test for the motion expressions native speakers are most likely to use when talking about motion.

2.3 The experiment

2.3.1 Method: materials, participants, and procedure

The participants were adult native speakers of the respective languages: sixteen for Bulgarian, sixteen for Norwegian, twelve for English, eighteen for Italian, and eighteen for Russian. Each of them watched a sequence of video clips on a computer screen and was asked to provide a free description in their native language of the action in each clip. The clips were viewed in a single session, preceded by detailed instructions on the screen. Participants were advised to provide the first word/description that came to mind and were allowed to work at their own pace. Each clip was shown only once and could not be played back for reference. Participants were then prompted to type in their responses in a text box that appeared under the image and proceed to the next clip.

The stimuli were selected from documentaries or created by the experimenters with the aim of providing a range of biological motion scenes performed in natural settings by animate beings (humans, non-human primates, other mammals, reptiles, insects, etc.). A full list of the twenty-nine target scenes can be found in Appendix A. The clips showed five full cycles of the action, or, for slower actions, a time interval of approximately five seconds. The scenes were shown in a pseudo-randomized order, to ensure that similar scenes were not presented close to each other. Scene selection was determined by the features in (1). The stimulus scenes covered variations with respect to **method of propulsion** (e.g. crawling on all fours, crawling on one's stomach, bipedal walking, quadrupedal walking, bipedal running, quadrupedal running, quadrupedal trotting), **phase** (supported: walking, crawling vs. suspended: trotting, running, galloping), **spacing of footfalls** (symmetrical: walking, bipedal running, and trotting vs. asymmetrical: quadrupedal galloping), **species** (e.g. human, ape, bird, cat, dog, insect, snake, etc.), **age** differences among the actors (baby vs. adult), **velocity** (slow vs. default/normal vs. fast), **translation vs. non-translation** (regular running vs. running on the spot or running on a treadmill), **path vector orientation** (horizontal: towards vs. away from camera; vertical: up vs. down), **figure orientation** (front forwards vs. front backwards; head up vs. head down), **path shape** (straight, circular), **type of substrate** (ground vs. branch vs. leaf; smooth vs. grassy surface). Since we wanted to elicit preliminary responses to a variety of instances, the scenes presented in the experiment were not matched with respect to environmental setting, physiological characteristics of the agents, and viewing angle. It would have been impossible to cover the full variation within each feature or the full range of possible combinations of values between the features. For this reason, we chose to restrict ourselves to gaits relatively familiar to humans—only scenes of terrestrial motion, but excluding aerial gaits (jumping, hopping, prancing) which in humans are not often used in translational motion. Our purpose was not to control for all value combinations, but to find general indications of their role and potential significance in motion categorization and naming, and thus help to direct attention to specific features for further research. We are aware that the results should be interpreted accordingly.

2.3.2 *Methodological issues in the analysis*

Since the verb is considered to be the locus of event encoding, our analysis concentrates on how verbs were used in the scene descriptions. The results were analysed in the following way: for each answer, we isolated the verb used to describe the action in the respective scene. Our aim was to investigate whether the patterns of verb use in the target languages would show grouping according to particular characteristics of the locomotion pattern. We wanted also to see how the groups and their defining features would compare between the languages. Therefore, for each language, we performed cluster analysis on group the twenty-nine target scenes according to the motion verbs occurring in their descriptions.[6] Cluster analysis has proved to be useful in revealing patterns of grouping in collections of objects, and thus potential similarity (cf. the seminal work by Tversky, 1977), and is specifically popular in the field of matching perceptual stimuli to lexical items to reveal patterns of lexical preference, as shown in Majid et al. (2007). The distance of branching in the dendrogram (cluster tree) shows the degree of similarity between scenes, and gives an idea as to whether a scene is central or peripheral within its cluster. The method we used in our analysis was hierarchical agglomerative clustering with average linkage. We employed a *multiset* distance measure (explained in detail in Appendix B), which takes into account the frequency of occurrence of verbs in the description of each scene. Our preference for the multiset distance measure over the Jaccard distance measure used by Majid et al. (2008) is motivated by the fact that the coded representation of a video clip is a multiset (a set in which each verb may be present multiple times). This allows our analysis to reflect not only the naming strategies being used, but also the relative degree of preference for each of them.

For each language we also calculated Simpson's diversity index, which is a measure used to determine the variation in categorical data. The index is calculated individually for each scene in each language, and reflects the diversity in the descriptions of that particular scene. The index for each language is the average of all per-scene indices for that language, and shows how diverse scene descriptions are on average. Values near zero correspond to high diversity/heterogeneity (i.e. many different lexemes per scene), and values near one correspond to high homogeneity (i.e. fewer lexemes per scene). As applied to our data, this measure suggests the degree of variation in lexical items used for the naming of the target scenes. Russian and Norwegian have the highest average Simpson's index values ($D = 0.66$ and $D = 0.61$, respectively), which suggests that they display the greatest degree of homogeneity (consistency of verb choice across participants for the same scene). Bulgarian is the most diverse (with average Simpson's index $D = 0.38$), and English and Italian are intermediate (0.56 and 0.49, respectively).

Since this was an exploratory study, it is important to underline that our results cannot be used to prove or falsify a hypothesis, but should rather be taken as the source for hypotheses that have to be tested in more specific controlled experiments.

[6] Verbs not expressing motion (e.g. *look around, search, hunt, attack, ambush, play*) were not included in the analysis.

In hierarchical agglomerative clustering, it is impossible to determine the precise number of clusters, because it depends on how high up we are in the dendrogram. Therefore, we have to define criteria for deciding what clusters are of importance in the analysis. Since our task is to find the connection between locomotion verbs and observable properties of the target scenes (the features/values defined in (1)), we are especially interested in subtrees in which all scenes possess the same values of a particular feature or group of features, distinguishing them from the scenes in the remaining subtrees. Because we are using the multiset measure, the membership in the subtrees is determined at least to some degree by the proportions of verbs occurring in the scene descriptions. Therefore, it makes sense to look into the proportion of verb usage for each meaningful (in terms of features) subtree. If a meaningful subtree is connected to a particular verb or verbs, we may surmise that there is a connection between the underlying feature of the subtree and these verbs. The dendrogram of each of the five languages (Figures 2.1–2.5, see the respective language sections) has to be examined individually to try to establish such connections. In what follows, the results are described language by language, covering the number of meaningful subtrees, the scenes participating in each subtree, and the most frequent verbs in the verb multiset corresponding to the subtree (sections 2.3.4.1–2.3.4.5). In addition, we discuss the use of verb modification to express non-default values (section 2.3.5). This is followed by a comparison of the five sets of clusters and their corresponding verbs, in order to draw a conclusion about the internal structure of the biological motion domain across languages (section 2.4).

2.3.3 *Verb pairs in some of the languages*

Before giving the details of how verbs of motion are used in the descriptions of the target scenes, it is necessary to mention some facts about the motion verb lexicons of three of our target languages. In Norwegian, there are two verbs of running, *løpe* and *springe*, distinct in terms of register. The verb *løpe* belongs to the formal Bokmål variety, while *springe* is more informal, being typical of particular dialects, where it is employed consistently instead of *løpe*. Since both verbs do not usually coexist within the active vocabulary of the same speaker (that is, depending on dialect, a person would use either one or the other), the two verbs were conflated in one representative form (*løpe*) in the analysis.

In Russian, there are fifteen pairs of motion verbs that have two separate imperfective forms, which, while referring to the same type of motion (walking, running, crawling, swimming, flying, carrying, leading, dragging, etc.), give different information about the circumstances of performing the motion. In the literature, this distinction has been referred to as definite vs. indefinite or determinate vs. indeterminate (Foote 1967). Definite/determinate verbs of motion (e.g. *idti* 'walk', *bežat'* 'run', *polzti* 'crawl', *lez't'* 'climb') refer to motion that has a locus in time, and is specific, non-iterative, directed, and usually has an underlying sense of purpose. Indefinite/indeterminate verbs (e.g. *xodit'* 'walk', *begat'* 'run', *polzat'* 'crawl', *lazit'* 'climb') refer to motion in general (e.g. in root modal contexts), to motion that has no direction (covering iterative and habitual motion events), and motion with no underlying purpose. Not all of the individual uses (e.g. metaphorical or extended uses) of each member of a pair are paralleled by equivalent use of their partner in the pair, but both verbs share a basic sense. The occurrence of specific verb forms and the circumstances thereof will be acknowledged in the analysis below.

In Bulgarian, there are pairs of synonymous verbs of walking (*xodja/vŭrvja*), running (*tičam/bjagam*), and crawling (*pŭlzja/lazja*), which in standard Bulgarian dictionaries are listed with very similar, and even overlapping, definitions. Quite often, one of the verbs is used to explain the meaning of the other, and native speakers may experience problems in explaining the potential difference between the two verbs in the pair, as confirmed in interviews with the participants right after the experiment. Although we are aware that each verb in a pair has specific collocational restrictions, there is no experimental or even descriptive research to confirm this. By observing the distribution of these six verbs in the scene descriptions, we can check whether there is evidence about differences in terms of how the verbs refer to the perceptual features included in our stimuli.

2.3.4 *Results and discussion*

2.3.4.1 *Bulgarian* In Bulgarian (Figure 2.1), there are four meaningful subtrees: a subtree containing nine scenes of running (suspended, relatively quick, and energetic terrestrial motion); a subtree containing two scenes of climbing/clambering up (upwards motion on a vertical substrate); and two somewhat related (in the sense that they are nearer to one another than they are to the running- and climbing-up-subtrees) subtrees of supported motion on a horizontal substrate, with normal-to-slow speed. One of these subtrees contains eight walking scenes (terrestrial supported motion performed with upright posture at 'normal'/default speed). The other one contains eight crawling scenes (relatively slow motion performed in a low, sprawling posture). For the sake of brevity, these subtrees will be called from now on the run-, climb-up-, walk-, and crawl-subtrees. There are also scenes that are 'outsiders'—a scene of two monkeys walking in a circle around a tree, which is remotely related to the run-subtree, and a scene of a sloth of climbing down a tree/branch, which is remotely related to the walk/crawl-subtree.

Of the answers for the run subtree, 37.5 per cent contain the verb *tičam* 'run', and 30.6 per cent contain the verb *bjagam* 'run'. There are also other motion verbs occurring in the descriptions, but they occur infrequently and with no specific pattern across scenes. The majority of these verbs refer to a more specific type of running (e.g. *podtičvam* 'half-run, run along someone who determines the speed',

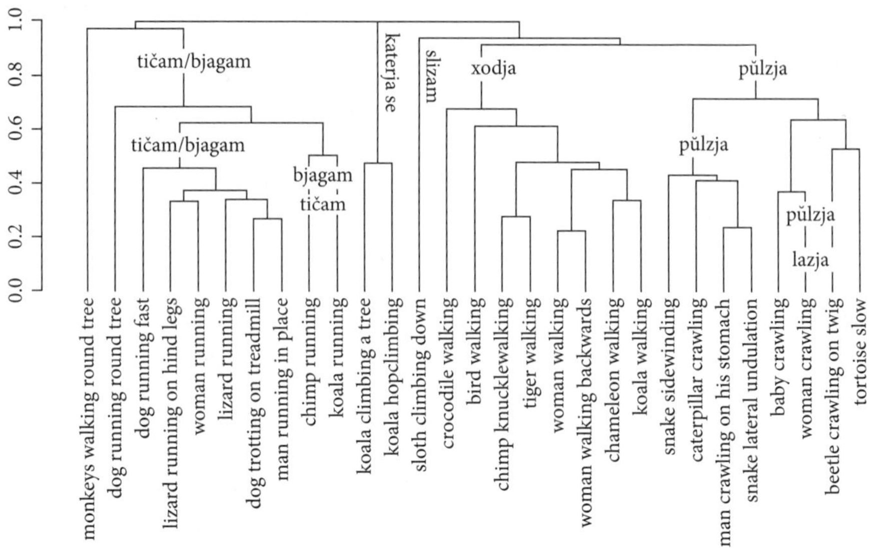

FIGURE 2.1 Dendrogram for Bulgarian. Meaningful subtrees are named after the verb or verbs that are most prominent in their descriptions. The major subtrees in Bulgarian are *tičam/bjagam* 'run', *xodja* 'walk', *půlzja* 'crawl', *katerja se* 'climb/clamber up', and *slizam* 'climb down'. In the *tičam/bjagam* subtree there is a further subdivision between scenes that are described predominantly by the verb *tičam*, and scenes that are described predominantly by *bjagam*. In the *půlzja* subtree there is a further subdivision between scenes that are described predominantly by the verb *půlzja*, and scenes that are described by both *půlzja* and *lazja*.

prepuskam 'gallop', *pripkam* 'trip', *tŭrča* 'run (col.)'), but also verbs describing jumping (e.g. *podskačam* 'hop'), intrinsic motion (e.g. *tancuvam* 'dance'), and tandem motion (e.g. *gonja* 'chase', *presledvam* 'pursue') have been used. This points to the conclusion that, in its lexicon, Bulgarian distinguishes the category of running (fast suspended motion, performed by ejecting oneself from the ground using repeated limb cycles—cf. Dimitrova-Vulchanova 1999), which is consistently represented by the two verbs *tičam* and *bjagam*.

Judging by the relative height of branching in the run-subtree, there are six scenes that are more similar to one another, and three marginal scenes, two of them closer together. The core group is characterized in 44.8 per cent of the cases by the verb *tičam*, and 28.1 per cent of the cases by the verb *bjagam*. The subgroup of two peripheral scenes is characterized in 50 per cent of the cases by the verb *bjagam*, and in only 18.8 per cent of the cases by the verb *tičam*. Examining the scenes for perceptual features distinguishing the core group from the peripheral group shows that the scenes in the core group all show a side view of the motion, while the scenes in the peripheral group show motion towards or away from the camera (see representative images of the scenes in Appendix A). On the basis of this, we can surmise that the meaning of the verb *bjagam* involves deictic direction, while the meaning of *tičam* does not involve such an element. However, this has to be studied further before drawing a definitive conclusion.

The third peripheral running scene shows a dog running in repeated quick circles around a tree. The only major biological motion verb in the descriptions of this scene is *tičam* (31.3 per cent), with only occasional uses of the verbs *bjagam* and *tŭrča* 'run (col.)'. What is particular here is that the answers contain an extremely high number of non-motion verbs (31.1 per cent),[7] and some verbs referring to the shape of the trajectory (*obikaljam* 'go around' and *vŭrtja se* 'turn, spin'). We can only surmise that the presence of a relatively unusual pattern of behaviour in this scene shifts the focus away from the locomotion pattern. How this will be verbalized depends on what the speaker chooses to highlight—for example, the specific behaviour (in this case, the circular trajectory of motion) or its cause (e.g. purpose or mental state). This surmise is supported by the outsider status of the other scene of circular motion (monkeys walking around a tree), whose descriptions do not contain any verbs of biological motion, but are characterized by the verbs *obikaljam* 'go around' (43.8 per cent) and *vŭrtja se* 'turn, spin' (12.5 per cent), both related to path shape.

The predominant verb in the descriptions of the eight scenes in the walk-subtree is *xodja* (50.8 per cent), followed at a distance by *vŭrvja* (14.1 per cent). More specific biological motion verbs, whose occurrence in the descriptions is more sporadic, are *krača* 'pace', *pristŭpvam* 'step', *razhoždam se* 'stroll', *šljapam* 'splash along', and *tŭtrja se* 'drag oneself'. There are also isolated occurrences of verbs belonging to other biological motion categories (*pŭlzja* 'crawl' and *pritičvam* 'run a short distance to a target'). There are also verbs of general motion (*dviža se* 'move') and directed motion without a 'Manner' component (such as *minavam* 'pass', *vrŭštam se* 'return', *otivam* 'go', *zapŭtvam se* 'set off', and *napuskam* 'leave'). Thus, we can say that, in its lexicon, Bulgarian distinguishes the category of walking (supported terrestrial motion performed with an upright posture, and at a 'normal' speed) through the verb *xodja* (and also *vŭrvja*). The results from this experiment cannot give us more information about the distinction between the two verbs, and further research must be conducted to determine their relation.

The walk-subtree is structured around six scenes (featuring the motion of humans and other mammals) that are more similar to one another, and two peripheral scenes (featuring a crocodile and a long-legged bird). Comparing the proportions of verbs

[7] 'Non-motion verbs' is a diverse category including verbs/phrases encoding primarily intentions, mental states, or other aspects of the action, not related to pattern of locomotion per se, for example *ludeja* 'to act like crazy', *vdetenjavam se* 'to act in a childish way', *mŭrzeluvam* 'to be lazy', *gledam* 'to watch'. The cumulative proportion of such verbs for a particular subtree does not bear equal importance to the proportion of a single verb, because it does not reflect a single conceptual category. As mentioned in section 3.3.2, such verbs are not included in the input data for the cluster analysis.

that occur in the core versus the periphery shows that the descriptions of the six 'core' scenes are centred around the verb *xodja* (57.3 per cent), and to a lesser degree *vŭrvja* (16.7 per cent), with other verbs occurring in much smaller proportion (usually only once or twice). Only 31.3 per cent of the descriptions of each of the peripheral scenes contain the verb *xodja*. The crocodile scene is also described by the verb *dviža se* 'move' (18.8 per cent) and by a variety of manner verbs (*šljapam* 'splash', *tŭtrja se* 'drag oneself', *lazja* 'crawl', etc.), which indicates that inconsistency in naming this scene may be due to divergence from the default features of walking (upright posture). In the descriptions of the bird scene, there is a relatively high and consistent occurrence of verbs referring to more specific types of walking (18.8 per cent *krača* 'pace', 18.8 per cent *razhoždam se* 'stroll'). This indicates that the bird scene may diverge from the core walking scenes because of the great salience of features that fit better with categories expressed by more specific verbs available in the language (see the section on Norwegian for similar results in running scenes).

The most frequent verbs occurring in the descriptions of the crawl-subtree are *pŭlzja* 'crawl' (52.3 per cent) and *lazja* 'crawl' (18 per cent). Other verbs occurring in the descriptions are various verbs expressing extrinsic non-biological motion (*mŭkna se* 'drag oneself', *promŭkvam se* 'sneak'), biological motion (*xodja* 'walk', *kačvam se* 'ascend'), intrinsic motion (*izvivam se* 'wriggle, twist oneself'), general motion (*dviža se* 'move'), and directed motion of various sorts (*izbjagvam* 'escape', *presledvam* 'chase'). There are two subgroups of crawling scenes. The first one involves not only low posture with the body parallel to the ground, but also contact between the body and the ground, and a minimal use of appendages to propel oneself (as in the motion performed by snakes, worms, caterpillars, and humans when they are dragging themselves along on their stomach). This subcluster is described by *pŭlzja* in 71.9 per cent of the cases, and by *lazja* in only 6.3 per cent. The second subgroup involves also slow motion performed in a low posture, but involving the use of appendages to propel oneself (for example, the motion of insects, tortoises, or humans crawling on all fours). It is represented by *pŭlzja* in 32.8 per cent of the cases, by *lazja* in 29.7 per cent, and by *xodja* in 12.5 per cent. This shows that there is a difference between the verbs *pŭlzja* and *lazja* with respect to the specification of body cycle. While *pŭlzja* is the basic-level verb for slow, supported biological motion performed in a low or supine posture, *lazja* has the additional requirement for the use of limbs to propel oneself. The presence of *xodja* here and of *lazja* in the descriptions of one of the peripheral walking scenes shows that the categories of walking and crawling overlap.

The climb-subtree contains only two scenes of motion upwards, which are described by the verbs *katerja se* 'clamber up' (75 per cent), and *kačvam se* 'ascend, go up' (15.6 per cent). There are no other motion verbs in the descriptions. The only climbing-down scene among the stimuli shows more similarity to walking and crawling scenes than to climbing-up scenes. It is characterized by the verbs *slizam* 'go down (using limbs)' (43.8 per cent) and *spuskam se* 'descend, go down' (25 per cent), and the occasional use of verbs from the walk and crawl categories (*xodja* 'walk', *pŭlzja* 'crawl', *lazja* 'crawl'). This shows that Bulgarian splits the domain of vertical biological motion into two categories—those of upwards and downwards motion—and that the category of upwards motion is more crystallized/independent. It shows as well that, in vertical motion, path orientation is much more salient than in horizontal motion, and tends to be foregrounded much more frequently during verbalization by the use of dedicated lexical items.

2.3.4.2 English In English, there are five meaningful subtrees (Figure 2.2). The major split points to the distinction between a subtree of nine scenes of fast suspended motion (running), and the remaining scenes, all of which show supported motion. Within the scenes of supported motion, we can distinguish a subtree of nine scenes of motion performed mostly with upright posture and at 'normal' speed (walking), a subtree of vertical motion (climbing) scenes, and two subtrees of scenes showing motion with low/sprawling posture (crawling).

The run-subtree is the most tightly knit one, with no obvious core. This subtree is characterized by the verb *run* in 71.3 per cent of the cases. There are also some other motion verbs whose frequency is very small in comparison. These include verbs referring to different types of running (*bound, gallop, jog, lollop, scurry, sprint, trot*),

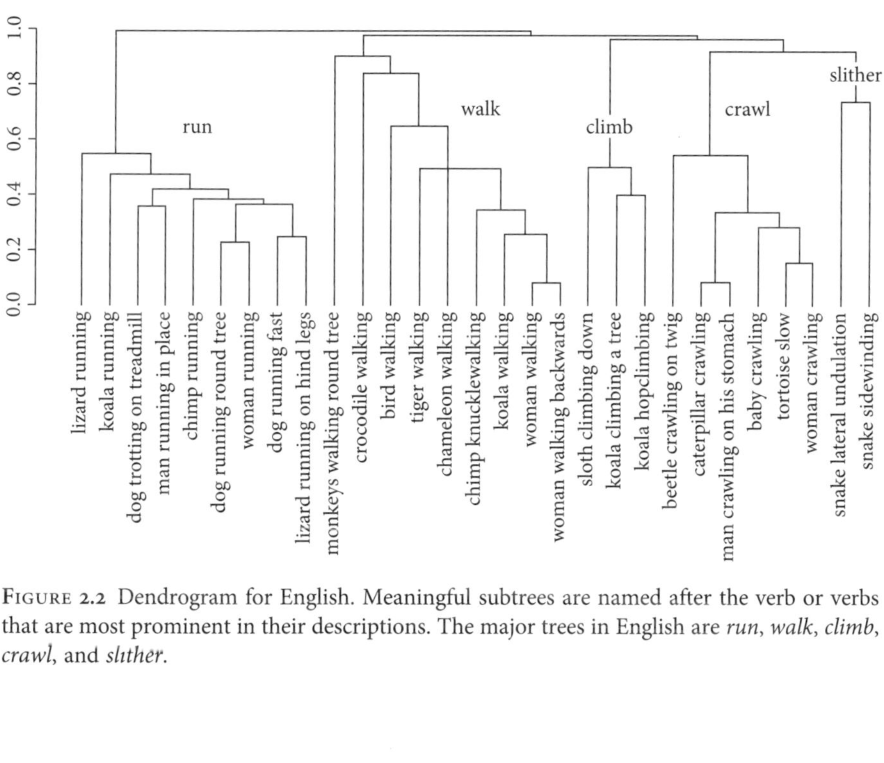

FIGURE 2.2 Dendrogram for English. Meaningful subtrees are named after the verb or verbs that are most prominent in their descriptions. The major trees in English are *run, walk, climb, crawl*, and *slither*.

jumping (*hop, gambol*), walking (*walk*), velocity (*race*), tandem motion (*chase*), and general motion (*move*). From this, we can conclude that, in its lexicon, English distinguishes a category of suspended translational motion represented by the verb *run*.

The walk-subtree has a core consisting of two scenes of humans walking, which can be taken as evidence of the anthropocentricity of the category. The most characteristic verb for this subtree is *walk* (used in 63 per cent of the cases), which leads to the conclusion that this verb represents the category. Other verbs, which have much smaller frequencies in the descriptions, refer to different types of walking (*lumber, pace, pad, paddle, prowl, slope, stalk, step, stroll, strut, waddle*), other biological motion categories (*crawl, lope*), tandem motion (*chase, follow*), and general motion (*move, make one's way*).

The three scenes in the climb-subtree are characterized by the verb *climb* in 77.8 per cent of the answers. Therefore, we can say that English distinguishes in its verbal lexicon a category of biological motion in contact with a vertical substrate, without distinguishing between upwards and downwards motion. Other verbs used to describe climbing scenes are the general motion verb *move*, the directed motion verb *descend* (obviously applying specifically to the climbing-down scene), and some verbs specifying the manner of upwards propulsion in the climbing-up scenes (*walk, crawl, hop*).

In the domain of supported motion performed with a low posture, and at low speed, English exhibits a split on the basis of species, with two snake scenes belonging to a separate subtree. The other scenes of slow motion in a low/sprawling posture are characterized by the verb *crawl* in 77.8 per cent of the descriptions, with the occasional occurrence of other biological motion verbs (*creep, mosey, walk, scurry, climb*) or general motion verbs (*move, make one's way*). The most characteristic verb for the two snake scenes is *slither* (50 per cent), although there are other motion verbs used too (*crawl, sidewind, ripple, slide, move*).

3.4.3 Italian The subtrees for Italian (Figure 2.3) are not as clearly articulated. The most clearly distinguishable meaningful subtree contains the same nine scenes that constituted the *run* categories for English and Bulgarian. The most prominent verb in the descriptions of these scenes is *correre* 'run' (59.9 per cent). We can therefore conclude that it is the representative verb in Italian for the *run* category. Other verbs occurring in the descriptions refer to various types of running (*scattare* 'shoot, spurt'), jumping (*fare skip* 'skip', *saltare* 'jump', *saltellare* 'hop, skip'), tandem motion (*fuggire* 'escape', *inseguire* 'chase', *rincorrere* 'run after, chase', *scappare* 'escape', *seguire* 'follow'), walking (*andare* 'go', *camminare* 'walk', *passeggiare* 'stroll'), rotation (*girare* 'turn, rotate'), and general motion (*muoversi* 'move').

The 'core' of the very loose subtree of supported motion consists of two scenes of a human walking (forwards and backwards), joined at some distance with a scene

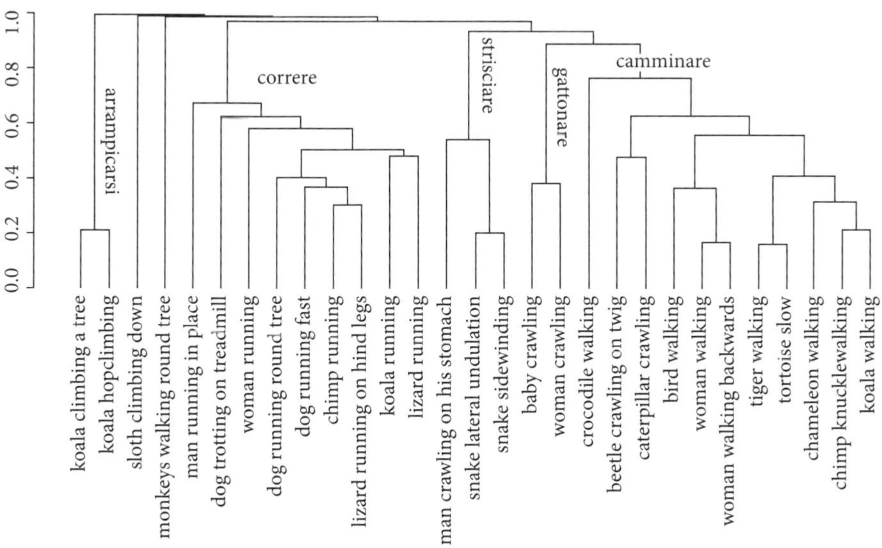

FIGURE 2.3 Dendrogram for Italian. Meaningful subtrees are named after the locomotion verb or verbs that are most prominent in their descriptions. The major trees are *camminare* 'walk', *correre* 'run', *gattonare* 'crawl on all fours (for a human)', *strisciare* 'crawl, slither', and *arrampicarsi* 'climb/clamber up'.

showing a walking bird. These three scenes are described by the verb *camminare* 'walk' in 81.5 per cent of the cases, which shows that the prototype of the walking category in Italian is anthropocentric bipedal motion. A subtree of five scenes showing the default mode of walking for a tiger, a chimpanzee, a koala, a chameleon, and a tortoise (that is, supported non-human quadrupedal motion at normal speed) is the nearest neighbour to the central walk-subtree, but it is described by *camminare* in only 52.2 per cent of the cases, with verbs of general motion (*muoversi*, *spostarsi*, both meaning 'move') occurring in 27.8 per cent of the answers, which may indicate insecurity in naming due to increased distance from the default features of walking (e.g. species: human, use of limbs: bipedal).

In the dendrogram for Italian, there is no subtree corresponding to a general (basic-level) crawl category, as reflected in the labels on the subtrees in Figure 2.3. However, there are a couple of narrow categories of biological motion related to very specific features. One of them is a category of supported motion where the body has maximal contact with the terrain, and there is friction between the body and the terrain (characterized by the verb *strisciare* 'slither' in 72.2 per cent of the answers for three scenes that had this feature). There is also a category of human motion on all fours, characterized by the verb *gattonare* in 55.6 per cent of the descriptions of the two scenes that had the respective feature. Between these two categories and *camminare*, there are various degrees of removal from the human-upright-bipedal prototype. In the description of the three intermediate scenes (which describe the motion of insects or reptiles), the verb *camminare* is used in approximately 30 per cent of the descriptions.

The scene of monkeys walking around a tree is an outsider for the supported motion subtree. Its description includes 27.8 per cent rotation verbs (*girare* 'turn, rotate' and *ruotare* 'rotate, spin'), 55.6 per cent non-motion verbs, and some verbs of tandem motion (*inseguire* 'chase', *rincorrere* 'chase, run after'), but no biological motion verbs. As in the case of Bulgarian, this leads us to surmise that in some languages, a salient path shape may compete with manner of propulsion and displace it during verbalization.

The two climbing-up scenes are grouped together (characterized by the verb *arrampicarsi* 'climb/clamber up' in 80.6 per cent of the cases, and *salire* 'ascend' in 11.1 per cent of the cases), separate from all others. The climbing-down scene (characterized in 94.4 per cent of the cases by the verb *scendere* 'descend') does not belong to any subtree, which suggests that Italian, like Bulgarian, distinguishes in its lexicon upwards from downwards motion. Moreover, there is a dedicated biological motion verb only for upwards supported motion, while downwards motion is covered by a more general directional verb.

2.3.4.4 Norwegian In Norwegian (Figure 2.4), the first large meaningful distinction is between a subtree of nine running scenes familiar from the previous languages, and all other scenes. Therefore, the main distinction is again between suspended and supported motion. Within supported motion, the first category that splits away is that of vertical motion, containing both upwards and downwards motion. There is a relatively clearly defined subtree of eight scenes of supported motion at normal speed; however, there is no clear distinction between upright and low-posture/sprawling motion.

The run-subtree contains eight relatively closely related scenes, characterized by the verb *løpe* 'run' in 80.5 per cent of the descriptions, and one 'outsider' scene (man running on the spot), which is predominantly characterized by the verbs *jogge* 'jog' (68.8 per cent) and *løpe* (31.2 per cent). Other motion verbs used to describe running scenes refer to different subtypes of suspended motion (*galoppere* 'gallop', *ile* 'hurry', *pile* 'scurry', *sprinte* 'sprint', *spurte* 'spurt'), jumping (*hoppe* 'jump, leap', *sprette* 'bound, jump'), walking (*gå* 'walk, go', *lunte* 'trot, stroll'), directed motion (*flykte* 'flee', *jage* 'chase'), and general motion (*bevege seg* 'move'). However, *løpe* is the only verb whose occurrence is pervasive in the descriptions of all nine scenes, and it can therefore be considered representative of the category of suspended translational motion, which Norwegian distinguishes in its lexicon. *Løpe* can be displaced by more specific verbs of running when there are salient features evoking a more specific category (for example, in the peripheral scene in the run-subtree, the viewers most probably surmise that the purpose is not traversal of space but working

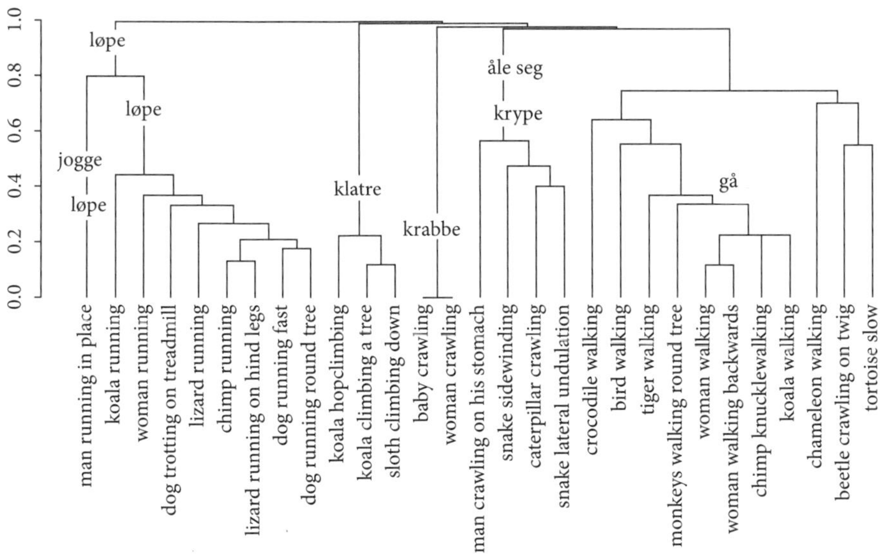

FIGURE 2.4 Dendrogram for Norwegian. Meaningful subtrees are named after the verb or verbs that are most prominent in their descriptions. The major subtrees in Norwegian are *løpe* 'run', *gå* 'walk', *klatre* 'climb', *krabbe* 'crawl on all fours (for a human)', and *åle seg* 'wriggle'/ *krype* 'creep'. Within the *løpe*-subtree, the majority of scenes are described by that verb, but one scene is described predominantly by *jogge* 'jog', and in a much lesser degree by *løpe*.

out). At present this is all that the dendrogram can reveal. A more detailed analysis of *løpe* and its status in the Norwegian motion lexicon may be established by future studies.

The next clearly distinguished category of biological motion is that of propelling oneself along a vertical substrate by the effortful use of limbs. This category encompasses both upwards and downwards motion, with the verb *klatre* 'climb, clamber' occurring in 91.7 per cent of the cases.

In Norwegian, there is no single category for slow supported motion in a low/sprawling position. However, there are two subtrees which seem to contain scenes distinguished on the basis of degree of contact with the terrain, the use of limbs, and the species of the moving individual. The first subtree includes two scenes showing humans (a baby and an adult) crawling on all fours, which are described by the verb *krabbe* (similar to the Italian verb *gattonare*) in 100 per cent of the cases. The second subtree includes four scenes featuring the motion of snakes, caterpillars, and humans crawling on their belly, whose descriptions vary a great deal. The most commonly occurring verbs for these scenes are *åle seg* '(lit.) eel oneself' = 'wriggle like an eel' (43.8 per cent), *bukte seg* 'curl, wriggle, meander' (12.5 per cent), and *krype* 'creep' (23.4 per cent). The former two refer to intrinsic motion of the body, rather than to translational motion. The latter refers to the motion of insects, which can be characterized as 'small scale' motion, with body close to the ground and sprawling legs. Other verbs used to describe the scenes from this subtree are *krabbe* 'crawl', *kravle* 'crawl', *slange seg* '(lit.) snake oneself' = 'wriggle like a snake', *smyge* 'sneak', and *snike seg* 'sneak'. Thus, it seems that this subtree does not correspond to a single clearly crystallized category of translational biological motion, and that low-posture/sprawling supported motion (excluding the scenes covered by *krabbe*) can be covered by a number of verbs describing motion on different levels (intentions, intrinsic motion, translational motion, etc.) depending on the interpretation of the action under specific circumstances.

There is a clearly distinguishable subtree of eight supported motion scenes showing the gait most typical of humans and mammals (walking). This group also contains scenes showing a walking bird and a walking crocodile, but these scenes are more peripheral in the subtree than the scenes showing mammals (that is, the scenes showing mammals are more similar to one another with respect to the verbs used to describe them). The predominant verb in the descriptions of the eight scenes is *gå* 'walk' (75 per cent), although there are other less frequently occurring motion verbs, such as verbs referring to different types of walking (*lunte* 'stroll', *rusle* 'stroll', *tusle* 'shuffle', *luske* 'sneak, slink', *marsjere* 'march', *spankulere* 'walk with a proud, stiff bearing', *spasere* 'stroll', *sprade* 'strut', *stavre* 'totter', *wagge* 'rock, sway from side to side', *vralte* 'waddle'), and running verbs (*løpe* 'run', *trave* 'trot'). The nearest neighbour of the walk-subtree is a small subtree consisting of three scenes showing the motion of a chameleon, a beetle, and a tortoise. The verbs occurring most frequently in the descriptions for these scenes (*gå* 'walk, go' 35.4 per cent, *krabbe* 'crawl' 14.6 per cent, *krype* 'creep' 22.9 per cent, but also the verbs *snike seg* 'sneak', *spasere* 'stroll', *stavre* 'totter', *luske* 'sneak, slink' and *kravle* 'crawl') show that the motion this subtree represents is a 'grey zone', on the fuzzy edges of the Norwegian walk and crawl (*krabbe*) categories. Thus, the representation of low-posture/sprawling terrestrial motion in the Norwegian lexicon is similar to that of Italian: in the centre of this domain is the most characteristic gait of humans and mammals, but the boundaries of the category are very fuzzy, and the variation in naming preferences depends on how far removed a scene is from the centre. In Norwegian, this may have a bilateral dependence with the polysemy of the verb *gå*, which, in addition to describing walking, can be extended to refer to directed motion in general (as in *toget/bussen går* 'the train/the bus goes'), or to various abstract meanings (for example, *tiden går* '(lit.) the time goes').

2.3.4.5 Russian In Russian (Figure 2.5), the main meaningful distinction is again between suspended and supported motion, distinguishing the familiar set of nine running scenes from all other scenes. The next big meaningful distinction is between seven walking scenes (showing mainly the most characteristic gait of humans and

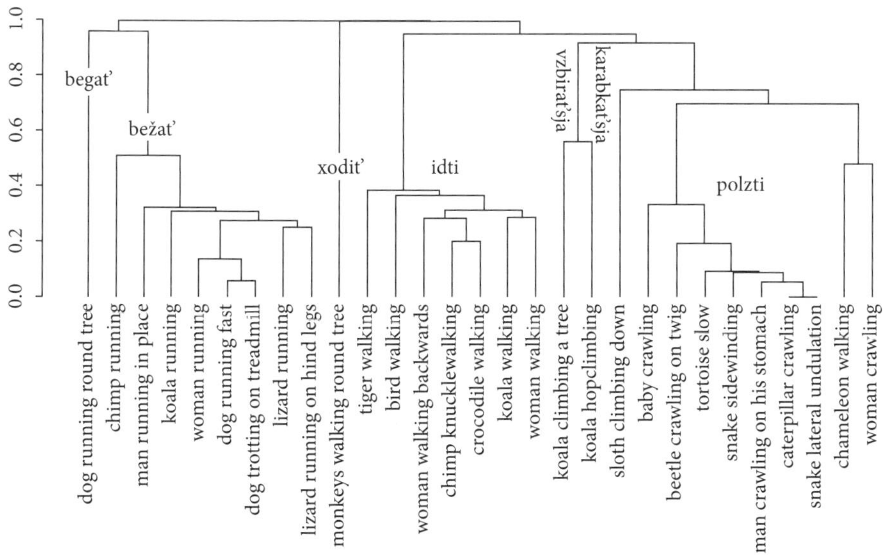

FIGURE 2.5 Dendrogram for Russian. Meaningful subtrees are named after the verb or verbs that are most prominent in their descriptions. The major subtrees in Russian are *idti* 'walk (def.)', *bežat'* 'run (def.)', *polzti* 'crawl (def.)', and *karabkat'sja/vzbirat'sja* 'climb/clamber up'.

other mammals, performed with an upright posture, and at 'normal' speed), and the remaining supported motion scenes. Within the latter, the next two groups to be distinguished are two loosely related climbing-up scenes. In the remaining ten scenes, there is a subtree of seven scenes with low-posture, low-speed supported motion that stands out as central, while the remaining three scenes are more peripheral.

Within the run-subtree, there are eight scenes that are relatively close, and are described by the verb *bežat'* 'run (definite)' in 79.9 per cent of the answers. Other verbs occurring in the descriptions of these scenes more infrequently include the partner of *bežat'* from the definite indefinite pair (*begat'*), several more specific running/jumping verbs (*skakat'* 'bound', *semenit'* 'scurry, patter', *podprygivat'* 'skip', *ubegat'* 'run away'), and some verbs referring only to speed (*nestis'* 'race (definite)') or general motion (*dvigat'sja* 'move'). The ninth running scene (dog running in circles) is very dissimilar to the remaining scenes with respect to naming pattern. The predominant verb in the descriptions of this scene is *begat'* 'run (indefinite)', but there is also a high occurrence of the verb *nosit'sja* 'race (indefinite)' (22.2 per cent), and of non-motion verbs (16.7 per cent). Thus, the main distinction between the core scenes and the peripheral scene is not in terms of manner of propulsion, but in terms of aspectual properties of the event—the dog scene shows repeated cycles of circular motion, which explains the preference for indefinite verb forms.

The walk-subtree is relatively tightly knit, with no scene standing out as central. The seven scenes in the subtree are characterized predominantly by the verb *idti* 'walk (definite)' (81 per cent). Other verbs that occur in the descriptions are the partner of *idti* from the definite–indefinite pair (*xodit'*) and verbs referring to different types of walking (*defilirovat'* 'parade', *guljat'* 'stroll', *krast'sja* 'sneak', *šagat'* 'pace', *pjatit'sja* 'walk backwards'), directed motion (*podxodit'* 'approach', *vozvraščat'sja* 'return'), and other types of translational biological motion (*polzti* 'crawl (definite)'). This establishes *idti* as the most representative of the overarching category of supported motion performed with upright posture at normal speed. It is interesting to compare this subtree to the scene of monkeys walking around a tree, which is an outsider to all the subtrees in the tree. This scene is predominantly described by the verb *xodit'* 'walk (indefinite)' (83 per cent), which shows that its distance from the other walking scenes is not due to difference in propulsion pattern, but due to different aspectual properties of the situation.

The last big subtree covers seven scenes displaying slow low-posture supported motion, and it seems that the scenes with closer contact between the body and the substrate (featuring the motion of snakes, caterpillars, and humans crawling on their belly) constitute the core of the subtree. At a greater distance from the core are scenes showing motion with low posture that is less near the substrate (for example, a chameleon, or humans crawling on all fours) or with non-default orientation of the axis of motion (climbing down). The seven core scenes are described by the verb *polzti* 'crawl, creep (definite)' in 92 per cent of the cases. Other verbs occurring in the descriptions are *polzat'* 'crawl (indefinite)', *idti* 'walk (definite)', *xodit'* 'walk (indefinite)', *izvivat'sja* 'wriggle', and *dvigat'sja* 'move'. The two scenes exemplifying motion which is more removed from the substrate are described by *polzti* 'crawl, creep (definite)' in 41.7 per cent of the cases, and by *idti* 'walk (definite)' in 33.3 per cent of the cases. Thus, it seems that Russian distinguishes in its lexicon a category of slow low-posture supported motion represented by the verb *polzti*, which has a fuzzy border, with the walk category represented by *idti*.

Although all scenes showing vertical motion are related to some degree to the crawl-subtree, climbing-up scenes are more independent from crawling scenes than climbing-down scenes. Downwards supported motion does not have a dedicated verb. The most predominant verbs used to describe it are *polzti* 'crawl (definite)' (38.9 per cent) and *spuskat'sja* 'descend' (33.3 per cent). The former foregrounds the manner of propulsion and downplays the vertical orientation of the substrate, while the latter foregrounds the vertical orientation and the direction of motion, but abstracts away the propulsion pattern. Climbing-up scenes are predominantly described by the verbs *karabkat'sja* 'clamber up (onto/into)' (36.1 per cent) and *vzbirat'sja* (*zabiratjsja*) 'climb up (onto/into)' (38.9 per cent). Thus, it seems that Russian distinguishes in its lexicon supported biological motion on a vertical substrate from that on a horizontal substrate, but this distinction appears systematic only for upwards motion. However, in the latter case, there is no single biological motion verb to represent this category.

2.3.5 Additional observations on the default features of lexicalized biological motion categories, based on the use of modifiers

Although all facts point to an organization of the meaning of biological motion verbs around bundles of features that co-occur frequently in nature, sometimes these verbs are used to describe motion events that deviate from the default features. We ran a separate analysis of how often and what verb modifiers are used in the answers, in order to check whether language resorts to compensating strategies that explicate deviation from the default. By modifiers, we mean adverbial phrases within the VP, which include (but are not restricted to) Talmy's satellites (cf. Beavers et al. 2010). The phrases included here may refer to direction (with or without reference to a landmark—*up*, *up a tree*, *towards the sea*), location/substrate of motion (*in the grass*, *on a twig*, *on a treadmill*), speed (*quickly*, *slowly*), figure orientation (*head down*, *sideways*, *backwards*), etc.. We use the presence of such modifiers as an indicator that a feature of the main verb needs to be set to a non-default value or is simply not expressed overtly. We propose *non-default explication function* as a preliminary label for this tendency. On the whole, the average frequency of occurrence of modifiers per scene was 31 per cent for Bulgarian (range 94 per cent – 0 per cent), 43.4 per cent for English (range 100 per cent – 8 per cent), 44.8 per cent for Italian (range 94 per cent – 11 per cent), 49.1 per cent for Norwegian (range 100 per cent – 13 per cent), and 25.5 per cent for Russian (range 72 per cent – 0 per cent). When the relative ranking of scenes according to the frequency of modifier use is examined, we can see that the following five scenes are distinguished by the presence of modifiers in more than 50 per cent of their descriptions for all five languages, or at least four out of five languages:

- Woman walking backwards – 94 per cent in Bulgarian, 100 per cent in English, 94 per cent in Italian, 100 per cent in Norwegian, and 60 per cent in Russian
- Man running on the spot – 75 per cent in Bulgarian, 100 per cent in English, 61 per cent in Italian, 94 per cent in Norwegian, and 72 per cent in Russian
- Sloth climbing down a tree head down – 56 per cent in Bulgarian, 83 per cent in English, 94 per cent in Italian, 88 per cent in Norwegian, and 61 per cent in Russian
- Dog running around the tree – 69 per cent in Bulgarian, 83 per cent in English, 61 per cent in Italian, 94 per cent in English, and 44 per cent in Russian
- Koala climbing a tree – 56 per cent in Bulgarian, 33 per cent in English, 56 per cent in Italian, 56 per cent in Norwegian, and 61 per cent in Russian

All the modifiers used for the scene with backwards motion refer to the non-default orientation of the moving figure (figure-orientation in our terminology). In the following enumeration, the languages will be indicated by their initial: B for Bulgarian, E for English, I for Italian, N for Norwegian, and R for Russian. Such modifiers are B *nazad, zadnishkom*, E *backwards*, I *all'indietro*, N *baklengs, bakover*, R *nazad, zadom* (*napered*). Most modifiers used in the descriptions of running-on-the-spot scenes explicate the absence of translational motion (for example, B *na mjasto*, E *on the spot, in place*, I *sul posto, da fermo*, N *på stedet*, R *na meste*). The modifiers accompanying the two climbing scenes refer mostly to direction (B *nadolu*, E *down(wards)*, I *in giù*, N *ned, nedover*, R *vniz*), substrate (for example, B *po dŭrvoto*, E *down the tree*, I *dall'albero*, N *nedover treet*, R *po derevu*), and in the descriptions of the climbing-down scene, also to the non-default orientation of the moving individual (for example, B *nadolu s glavata*, E *head down*, I *a testa giù*, N *med hodet ned*, R *vniz golovoj*). Most modifiers in the dog-running-around-a-tree scene refer to circular motion, by either using an *around*-PP in the respective language (B *okolo*, E *around*, I *intorno*, N *rundt, omkring*, R *vokrug*), or by aligning the trajectory with a shape (circle). The high frequency of modifiers in the descriptions in these five scenes, and the type of modifiers used, show that backwards motion, motion head down, and the lack of translation are deviations from the default for biological motion.

2.4 Biological motion categories and their distinctive features as revealed in the analysis

Our aim in this chapter has been to map out the lexical encoding of biological motion from the point of view of what perceptual features are likely to affect speakers' choices in a sample of five languages. We have shown that those languages may pattern similarly on certain parameters, but also display differences which cannot be explained trivially by genealogy (e.g. Germanic vs. Slavic languages). Both the similarity and difference patterns can be accounted for in terms of conceptual features that reflect independently attested biomechanical and perceptual aspects of biological motion.

Our results are strikingly similar to the findings in recent work by Malt and colleagues (Malt et al. 2010; Wolff and Malt 2010), who argue that the cross-linguistic encoding of motion is constrained by the physical properties of the world (reality), but is flexible and language-specific at the same time. Our results give a tentative confirmation of the importance of most of the features we proposed in section 2.2 in the linguistic categorization of biological motion. At the same time, it became clear that features differ with respect to their pervasiveness and constancy in defining biological motion categories between our five target languages. As suggested at the beginning, following works like Giese and Poggio (2003), Sigala et al. (2005), and Malt et al. (2010), some features are more robust than others, both with respect to their uniform occurrence across our target languages, and with respect to the constancy of scenes in whose categorization they play a role.

The categories of terrestrial translational biological motion represented in the verbal lexicons of our target languages are very similar, but not identical. In all languages there is a clear divide along the feature ***phase*** between *supported* (normal speed to slow) and *suspended* (high-velocity) terrestrial biological motion, and a less clear distinction in the domain of supported motion with respect to ***posture*** (*normal/upright* vs. *low/sprawling* posture), and **velocity** (*normal* vs. *slow*). Another relatively robust distinction is made with respect to the feature ***path vector orientation*** (*vertical* vs. *horizontal* substrate of motion), which, for some of the target languages, is restricted to supported motion. This is most probably due to the mechanical nature of suspended motion, which, under normal circumstances, is impossible on the vertical axis due to the force of gravity.

In the domain of fast suspended motion (running) all languages distinguish within their lexicons a single overarching category. In English, Norwegian, and Italian, this category is represented by a single verb (*run*, *løpe*, and *correre*, respectively), while Bulgarian and Russian have verb pairs (*tičam/bjagam* and *bežat'/begat'*, respectively) that differ with respect to ***path direction***, but not with respect to the method of propulsion expressed by the verb. The inclusion of other scenes (for example, scenes showing different kinds of jumping, bounding, and leaping gaits, or running scenes for which there are strictly specified terms, such as *gallop*) could have brought a different outcome in the clustering. The occasional presence of jumping verbs in the descriptions of running scenes in all target languages suggests that the domain of suspended motion may be organized similarly to the domain of supported motion (see below), with a number of loosely related subcategories with fuzzy boundaries.

The categories of supported motion (walking, crawling, and climbing) found in the analysis partially overlap within languages, but there is some variation in how many and what biological motion categories are distinguished in the lexicons of the five target languages. The most stable across languages is the category of walking (the default gait of humans and mammals, characterized by upright posture and normal speed), represented in English, Norwegian, and Italian by a single verb (*walk*, *gå*, and *camminare*, respectively), and by a pair of verbs (*idti/xodit'*) in Russian. In Bulgarian there are also two walk verbs, but one of them, *xodja*, has a much higher frequency than the other (*vurvja*), and the distinction between the two cannot be explained by our results.

Bulgarian (with the verb *pulzja*), Russian (with the verbs *polzti* and *polzat'*), and maybe English (with the verb *crawl*) are the only languages that have a unified category of slow low-posture terrestrial motion. However, this category shares a fuzzy boundary with the category of walking, and it is impossible to determine its precise span. In the remaining two languages, there is no 'basic level' category of crawling, but there are various more specific categories, which vary cross-linguistically with respect to the defining criteria. One of these criteria is ***species***—as in Italian *gattonare* and Norwegian *krabbe*, which refer exclusively to human motion on all fours, Norwegian *krype*, which is used for crawling by non-human species (e.g. insects), or English *slither*, which is exclusively used for snake motion. Another criterion is the ***method of propulsion*** (use of limbs, which is important for the Bulgarian verb *lazja*). Yet another criterion is ***body contact with the substrate*** (as in English *slither* and Italian *strisciare*).

In the domain of vertical motion, two of our languages (English and Norwegian) have a single category for upwards and downwards supported motion, represented by the verbs *climb* and *klatre*, respectively. Bulgarian has separate biological motion verbs for upwards and downwards supported motion (*katerja se* and *slizam*, respectively). Russian and Italian have dedicated biological motion verbs only for upwards supported motion (*karabkat'sja/vzbirat'sja/zabirat'sja* and *arrampicarsi*, respectively), and rely on verbs that express only path orientation or only manner of propulsion irrespective of path orientation.

Some of the features proposed in section 2.2 did not appear to be reflected in lexical items at the basic level of biological motion in our five languages. Such features are *spacing of footfalls* (symmetric vs. asymmetric—both symmetric bipedal running/quadrupedal trotting, and asymmetric gallop were likewise described by basic level run-verbs), *species* and *bipedal* vs. *quadrupedal* gait (they were categorized as walking or running on the basis of phase/velocity), *figure orientation* (both walking forwards and walking backwards were described as walking, however walking backwards is non-default, see section 2.3.5) or *presence vs. absence of translation in space* (both translational running and running on the spot were described as running). However, the verb modification patterns reported in section 2.3.5 demonstrate that these features do play a role in the linguistic categorization of biological motion. There is a difference between necessary, fully specified features, and underdetermined features in a verb's conceptual structure (cf. Dimitrova-Vulchanova 2004a, b). While a certain value for the feature *phase* (supported vs. suspended) would be vital for being able to apply such verbs as *run, walk*, or *crawl* to a motion pattern, and a vertical path vector is necessary to be able to call a motion climbing, there are features for which a certain value is the default, but is by no means the only possible one. While default values are the ones understood when a motion verb is used without any additional specifications, non-default yet acceptable values are marked and have to be specified explicitly. In our specific case, this mechanism for non-default specification is used to supply marked values for the following features: figure orientation with respect to the back–front axis (the default orientation is front forwards), figure orientation with respect to the up–down axis (the default value is head-up), the presence vs. absence of translation/path (the default value is presence of translation/path), path shape (the default value is a straight path), and path orientation (the default value is horizontal). All these features and their default values seem to be experientially motivated by the locomotion patterns that most naturally occur in nature (on the experiential motivation of language see Rosch et al. 1976; Barsalou 1999; Tyler and Evans 2003; Mandler 2004, among others).

We find similar naturally motivated groups also in the patterns of co-occurrence of the necessary/defining features that were listed above. It is not possible to separate the moving individual from the *phase* of motion (*suspended* vs. *supported* gaits) and their *posture* from the features of *velocity* and *propulsion pattern* (the way the agent moves her limbs and body in order to achieve translational motion). This observation corresponds to the established facts from biomechanics (Alexander 1989, 1996) that we reported in section 2.2. Our results also confirm the findings in Malt et al. (2008, 2010) that clear discontinuities in nature (e.g. suspended (high velocity) vs. supported motion, or vertical vs. horizontal substrate) tend to correspond to clear distinctions and more stable/invariable categories across languages, while less clear distinctions (in our case, the distinction between different types of horizontal supported motion) are more irregularly represented, both in terms of category granularity, and in terms of the selection of category-defining features.

In conclusion, we have to say that this is a study of limited scope, and our conclusions are based strictly on the results of our free elicitation experiment, with all the reservations we initially made about the limited choice of stimuli, and the chosen method of analysis. Our work's contribution is that the current findings combine insights and support hypotheses from several disciplines. They also establish a foundation for future research, which may endeavour to study the domain of biological motion in depth using a wider variety of elicitation tasks with a balanced design and data from more diverse languages.

Appendix A

This appendix contains still images of the twenty-nine target scenes used in the analysis.

1 Chimpanzee running

2 Koala running

3 Dog running fast

4 Dog running in circles

5 Dog running on treadmill

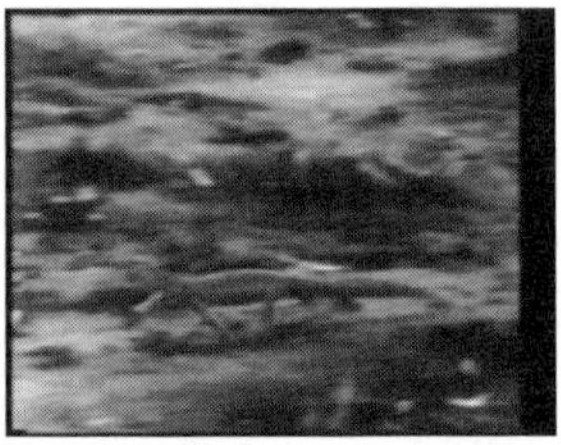

6 Lizard running

7 Lizard running on hind legs

8 Man running on the spot

9 Woman running

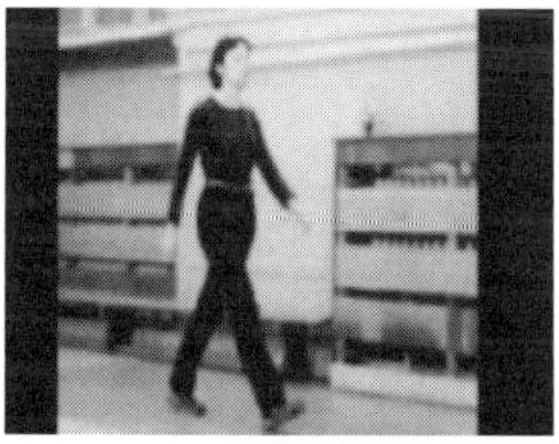

10 Woman walking

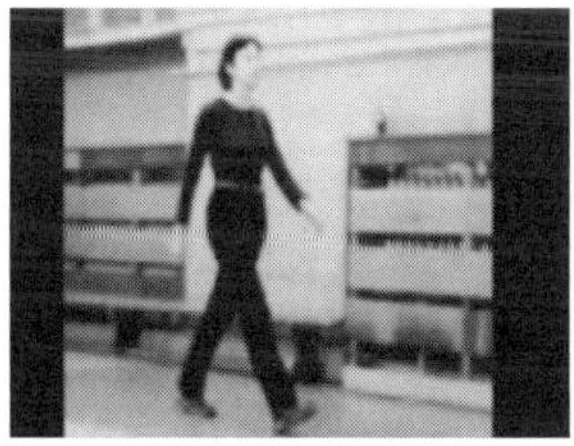

11 Woman walking backwards

12 Chimpanzee walking

13 Long-legged bird walking

14 Crocodile walking

15 Monkeys walking round a tree

16 Tiger walking

17 Koala walking

18 Chameleon walking on twig

19 Baby crawling

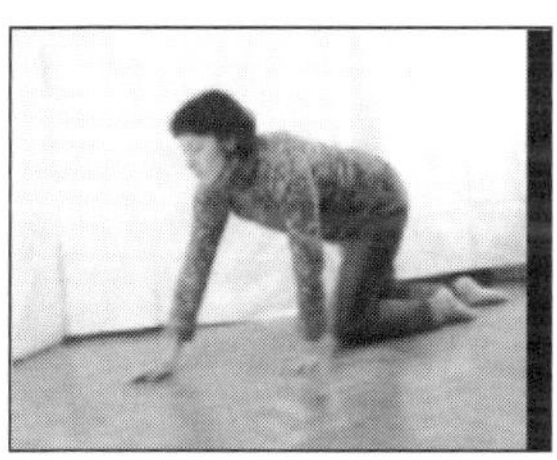

20 Woman crawling

21 A slow tortoise

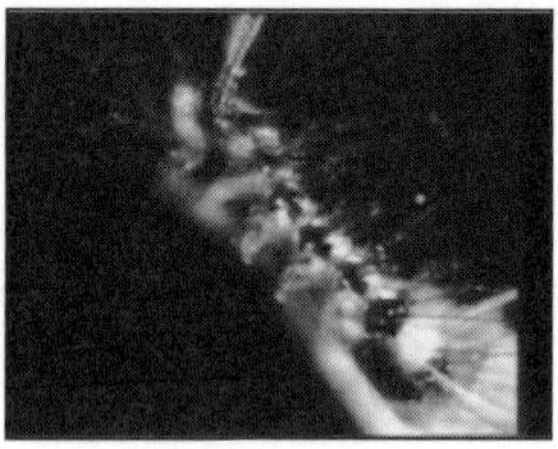

22 Caterpillar crawling

23 Beetle crawling on twig

24 Man crawling on his stomach

25 Snake crawling

26 Snake sidewinding

27 Koala climbing a tree

28 Koala climbing a tree in small hops

29 Sloth climbing down a tree

Appendix B

Distance measures

We wanted to measure the distance (dissimilarity) between two scenes, with respect to the verbs that the participants used to describe those scenes in a given language. Majid et al. (2007) used the Jaccard distance for this purpose. Given two scenes a and b, the Jaccard distance between them is defined as

$$d_J(a, b) = 1 - \frac{|A \cap B|}{|A \cup B|},$$

where A is the set of verbs the participants used to describe scene a, and B is the set of verbs they used to describe scene b.

Because the Jaccard distance uses sets, it takes into account only the presence or absence of a verb in the collected descriptions for a scene, not the number of occurrences. To rectify this, we devised a new distance measure analogous to the Jaccard distance but using multisets in the place of sets. A multiset is like a set, but allows multiple membership. We define the Multiset distance between two scenes a and b as

$$d_M(a, b) = 1 - \frac{\sum_{\in V} \min(n(v, a), n(v, b))}{\sum_{v \in V} \max(n(v, a), n(v, b))},$$

where V is the set of verbs involved in the study as a whole, and $n(v, x)$ is the number of times verb v occurs in the multiset of verbs used by the participants to describe scene x.

Simpson's diversity index

Simpson's D for a given verb list was calculated with the formula

$$D(a) = \frac{\sum_{v \in V} n(v, a) \times (n(v, a) - 1)}{N(a) \times (N(a) - 1)},$$

where V and $n(v, x)$ are as above, and $N(x)$ stands for $\sum_{v \in V} n(v, x)$.

3

The encoding of motion events in Estonian

RENATE PAJUSALU, NEEME KAHUSK, HEILI ORAV, ANN VEISMANN, KADRI VIDER, HALDUR ÕIM[1]

3.1 Introduction

This chapter is an introduction to a major research project which aims to identify how motion events are encoded in the Estonian language. The main objective of the chapter is to find out which regularities prevail in the structuring and categorization of the spatial characteristics of motion events in Estonian. We are looking at the ways Estonian expresses space and motion, and hoping to address in this research the question how the speakers of Estonian think about them, in vein of Slobin's 'thinking for speaking hypothesis' (Slobin 1996a).

The chapter focuses mainly on the regularities in the occurrence and functions of phrases other than the verbal phrase itself (NP, PP and AdvP); verbs are only briefly dealt with (for a more detailed analysis of motion verbs, see, for example, Weisgerber 2008). Estonian is a satellite-framed language according to Talmy's (2000 and previous) classification (Veismann and Tragel 2008). This means that in Estonian there should be a higher degree of description of Path of motion than in verb-framed languages (Slobin 1996b; Cadierno and Ruiz 2006). We aim to show which components of motion events are usually encoded in Estonian and which means are used to encode them. This means that our chapter is language-centred and deals with the categorization of experience of motion situations (Zlatev et al. 2010) or conceptual typology of motion events (Pourcel 2010) only as much as these are expressed in language.

On the other hand, our research project does not focus purely on linguistics, but also entails application of the results in language technology, for example. One of the

[1] The study was funded by grants No 7492 and No 5534 of the Estonian Science Foundation and Estonian Government Target Financing projects SF0180056s08 and SF0180078s08. We are very grateful to Jane Klavan and anonymous reviewers for their helpful comments on earlier versions of this chapter.

outputs of the project is a computer program which conducts a semantic analysis of Estonian sentences describing motion events. The computational analysis of sentential semantics is a relatively new field in language technology despite the fact that it has a wide range of applications (in the case of sentences describing motion events, in robotics, for example). At the moment there is a version of the program that analyses Estonian simple sentences describing motion events out of context, but the aim is to develop it into a program that processes integrated texts (cf. Orav et al. 2010, Õim et al. 2010). This, however, presupposes the existence of a conceptually developed theoretical model; in this case that of motion events.

One of the main methodological problems in giving a sufficient description of any semantic area is the polysemy of linguistic units: we cannot find all the appropriate sentences from corpora by searching for lexical or morphological categories, because they are too polysemous. We have a rather unique semantically disambiguated corpus of Estonian that gave us the opportunity to find sentences expressing motion on a semantic basis. This automatically-generated sub-corpus of sentences containing verbs of motion served as research material for finding the main categories of motion expressed by satellites (see below). The chapter only deals with actual movement; thus, all the cases where a verb of motion is used metaphorically remain beyond the scope of the present research.

We use the following terms for describing components of motion events: MOVING AGENT (a self-moving agent of motion), CAUSAL AGENT (initiator of motion which does not itself move), and OBJECT (entity that is moved by the MOVING AGENT or the CAUSAL AGENT). These components are included in our model because we are specifically interested in motion events and not in 'pure' motion: there cannot be any motion event without a moving object and—in the case of caused motion—without a cause. Space-related aspects comprise a separate group of components of motion events. The well-known chart (see e.g. Levinson 2003: 100) presented in Table 1 served as the basis for studying space. The Estonian case system encodes LOCATION (inessive and adessive), GOAL (illative and allative), and SOURCE (elative and ablative) (for a detailed overview of the Estonian case system, see Viitso 2003: 32–5). In each pair the first member generally describes three-dimensional and the second member two-dimensional space. In addition, the Estonian language has the terminative case, which encodes the place that the MOVING AGENT reaches. The Estonian cases have many meanings and uses that are not included in this simplified chart. It is impossible to treat them all in the present chapter. The most important feature is that the adessive, allative, and ablative also, and actually more often, occur as the indirect object[2] in constructions denoting getting, giving, and owning. The above

[2] The Estonian reference grammar does not consider the indirect object as a part of the sentence because its form does not differ from the adverbials. Discussion concerning the existence of the indirect object is still on the agenda in Estonian linguistics.

TABLE 3.1. **Prototypical Estonian cases and postpositions in the domain of space**

	LOCATION	GOAL	SOURCE
1 Dimension	*juures* 'at'	*juurde* 'to' terminative (*-ni*)	*juurest* 'from'
2 Dimension	*peal* 'on' adessive (*-l*)	*peale* 'onto' allative (*-le*) (terminative)	*pealt* '(from) off' ablative (*-lt*)
3 Dimension	*sees* 'in' inessive (*-s*)	*sisse* 'into' illative (*-sse*) (terminative)	*seest* '(from) out of' elative (*-st*)

cases also have many different uses in time expressions, which are not dealt with in the present chapter.

In addition to cases, Estonian has a number of postpositions and a few prepositions that are sometimes almost synonymous with the cases, but usually denote meanings that cannot be expressed by them (e.g. for one-dimensional space). The most prototypical postpositions in the domain of space are presented in Table 3.1. Locational postpositions may form triplets of local cases that correspond to the following categories: LOCATION, GOAL, and SOURCE (e.g. *juurde* 'to', *juures* 'at', *juurest* 'from–at', *peale* 'onto', *peal* 'on', *pealt* 'from–on').

PATH in the sense of Jackendoff's conceptual semantics (e.g. 1990: 43) includes the starting point (SOURCE) and the end point (GOAL in our sense), and VIA (route) as its components. Besides SOURCE, GOAL, and LOCATION, described in Table 3.1, ROUTE is another important component of motion events. It can be expressed in Estonian by some specific pre- and postpositions (*üle* 'across', *mööda* 'along', etc.) that are fairly common and form a separate semantic group. Thus, spatial aspects of motion events can be characterized by a conceptual field which consists of four basic spatial notions (SOURCE, GOAL, LOCATION, ROUTE). As one can see, this coincides more or less with the four semantic roles of Fillmore's case system (Fillmore 1977). It was not our primary goal to follow the Fillmorean system, but at the present stage of research our main interest lies in the syntax-semantics interface rather than in the deep semantic/conceptual representation of events in the spirit of, for example Talmy or Jackendoff—this would be our next step (for discussion of the differences of the treatments, see e.g. Talmy 2000: 26).

Examples (1–3) are provided to clarify the categories.

(1)
Poiss	*läks*	***kodu-st***	***kooli***	***mööda***	***tänava-t.***
boy	go.PST	home-ELAT	school.ILL	along	street-PART
MOVING AGENT	MOTION	SOURCE	GOAL	ROUTE	

'The boy went **from home to school along the street.**'

(2)

Poiss	*jooks-is*	***põllu-l***	*kuni*	*jõud-is*	***metsa-ni.***
boy	run-PST	field-ADE	until	reach-PST	forest-TERM
MOVING AGENT	MOTION	LOCATION	MOTION		GOAL

'The boy ran **in the field** until he reached **the forest**.'

(3)

Poiss	*viska-s*	*palli*	***korvi.***
boy	throw-PST	ball.PART	basket.ILL
CAUSAL AGENT	MOTION	OBJECT	GOAL

'The boy shot the ball **into the basket**.'

The manner of motion (e.g. *fast*, *jumping*, etc.), instrument of motion (*driving*, *riding*, etc.), and time are also important when describing motion events, but the present chapter does not discuss them.

A considerable number of the phrases that denote SOURCE, LOCATION, GOAL, or ROUTE function syntactically as locative adverbials. The Estonian reference grammar divides locative adverbials into five groups:

1) lative adverbial (GOAL);
2) locative adverbial (LOCATION);
3) separative adverbial (SOURCE);
4) terminative adverbial (motion towards a place, GOAL);
5) prolative adverbial (ROUTE). (Erelt et al. 1993: 71–2)

It is also possible to express spatial meanings of motion events by using constituents other than adverbials; the present chapter discusses some of the possibilities, but further research is needed.

The chapter has the following structure. First, we will introduce the data followed by a short overview of the verbs of motion that occurred therein. Then sections on SOURCE, GOAL, ROUTE, and LOCATION will follow; separate sections are devoted to the verb *käima* 'go to and from'.

3.2 Data: method and corpus

This chapter is based on a sub-corpus of 1,168 sentences which were automatically extracted from the Word Disambiguation corpus of Estonian by using Estonian WordNet (EstWN).

Our research is based on the assumption that the predicate verb acts as the nucleus of the sentence and determines the situational type of the whole sentence. When we deal with the interface between syntax and semantics where the (input) syntactic category is a sentence and the (output) semantic category an event, then the predicate verb is the unit which on the syntactic level determines the sentence structure, and on the semantic level the possible event structure: which participants can participate in which semantic roles in the event referred to by the predicate verb.

If the core sense (i.e. literal meaning) of a verb is related to motion, it can be considered a verb of motion. However, motion can be expressed by a verb the literal meaning of which is not motion at all. For example, the verb *punuma* has the core (literal) meaning of 'to enlace, entwine, interlace, intertwine, lace, twine, twine together, twist together', but *punuma* can also be used in the sense 'to move rapidly, scamper, scurry, scuttle, skitter'.

It is possible to automatically identify the meanings of verbs in Estonian by using the Estonian WordNet[3] (EstWN, see Orav and Vider 2005) where the word meanings are organized into synonym sets or synsets. In order to differentiate between word senses (meanings) and semantic units represented by synsets, the latter are usually called concepts.

Synsets are interconnected by various lexical or semantic relations. EstWN is a part of the EuroWordNet,[4] where eight different languages are interlinked by the Interlingual Index (ILI). The entries of the ILI mostly come from the original WordNet version 1.5 (Miller et al. 1990) created at Princeton University. WordNet is a unique database of semantic systems of different languages which can be used for semantic analysis in different ways (see Korhonen 2002 for an example dealing with motion verbs).

The most important semantic relation between the synsets is hyponymy (IS A or IS A KIND OF), which creates ontological hierarchies. Ontological hierarchies usually consist of nominal senses, but verb senses can also be classified into general and more specific senses. At the very top of a hierarchy is the synset that contains the most general concepts; the sub-hierarchies that contain narrower meanings are located at the lower levels. We focus on motion-related hierarchies and verb synsets. The top verbs of the hierarchy, which include almost all the senses of motion verbs, are the following:

1) liigutama(2) – *'make move, displace, move – cause to move'*[5] with 123 synsets in a subtree
2) liikuma(3) – *'move, change position'* with 223 synsets in a subtree.

Verbs as lexical units are more polysemous than nouns (Fellbaum 1990), and their senses are more dependent on the arguments and collocations with which they co-occur in a sentence. The verb senses under discussion include some of the senses of the highly polysemous and the most frequent verbs in Estonian—*käima* 'walk, visit', *minema* 'go', *ajama* 'drive', *andma* 'give', *panema* 'put'—as well as verbs the meanings of which are entirely related to motion—e.g. *lendama* 'fly', *sõitma* 'ride', *sagima* 'bustle around', *tuiskama* 'drift', *hõljuma* 'hover', *keerama* 'turn',

3 http://www.cl.ut.ee
4 http://www.illc.uva.nl/EuroWordNet///
5 Translation equivalent in English WN1.5.

viskama 'throw', *tirima* 'drag', *vedama* 'carry', *kerima* 'wind', *ringlema* 'circulate', *põikama* 'dodge', *vehkima* 'brandish'. Nevertheless, there are also verbs that are quite polysemous but rarely encode motion, for example *koguma* 'gather' in the synset <*kuhjama* 'pile up', *koguma* 'gather'>.

The top verbs of the hierarchies *liikuma* 'move' and *liigutama* 'cause to move' represent an important feature in Estonian verb derivation. Transitive verbs, often with a causative meaning, can be derived from the intransitive stem by adding the derivational affix *ta/da* to the verb. Similar derivational verb pairs denoting motion include *hajuma/hajutama* 'dissipate/cause to dissipate', *kerkima/kergitama* 'rise/raise', *kõikuma/kõigutama* 'rock/cause to rock', *veerema/veeretama* 'roll/cause to roll'.

The Word Sense Disambiguation (WSD) corpus of Estonian contains about 100,000 tokens from fiction texts of the 1980s that are annotated with the EstWN sense numbers. We extracted from the corpus those sentences that included any verb sense belonging to the MOTION hierarchy; this procedure resulted in a MOTION sub-corpus of 1,168 sentences. The sub-corpus includes only those sentences where the verb denoting motion was in the finite form. The sentences were then cut into finite clauses separated by punctuation marks or conjunctions. The finite clauses where the predicative verb denoted motion were analysed in greater detail.

3.3 Verbs of motion

The most frequent motion verbs in the corpora included *tulema* 'come' (two senses), *minema* 'go' (five senses), *käima* 'walk, go to, visit' (five senses), *tooma* 'bring' (one sense), *jõudma* 'arrive' (one sense), *sõitma* 'ride' (four senses), *astuma* 'step' (two senses), *viima* 'take, bring somewhere else' (one sense). As the synset is the elementary unit of WordNet, our data allows the identification of the most frequent synsets and the dominant members of the more frequent synsets. Table 3.2 presents the statistical data on the raw frequencies (F) of the members of the various synsets in the data and the most frequent verbs representing a synset.

Table 3.2 convincingly shows that all the synsets containing several members have a dominant member, which is twice as or even more frequent than the next member. It is a clear indicator that the concepts are centred around one prototypical representative.

3.4 SOURCE

The SOURCE of motion is usually expressed in Estonian by a separative locative adverbial. The starting point of motion is encoded by the following means:

a) NP in elative expressed by suffix *-st*;
b) NP in ablative expressed by suffix *-lt*;
c) PP, primarily a postpositional phrase;
d) adverb of place, incl. pro-adverb *sealt* 'from there' or *siit* 'from here';
e) supine construction, i.e. a non-finite verb form with the suffix *-mast* (e.g. *tuli söömast* '(lit.) came from eating': sööma 'to eat').

The elative and ablative cases usually have a synonymous postpositional phrase. For example, *pealt* 'from the surface' is almost equal to the ablative ending *-lt* (*laua pealt* = *laualt* 'from the surface of the table'), and *seest* 'from inside' has almost the same meaning as the elative ending *-st* (*kasti seest* = *kastist* 'from the inside of the box')—both are translated into English using the preposition 'from', and thus no difference can be made between them in translated texts. However, there are rather frequent constructions with local case forms that are not related to space and for which the synonymous PP is not a possible equivalent, as for example *rääkis kasti-st*

TABLE 3.2. **Frequent verb synsets and their members**

Synset F	Synset id and Interlingual Index equal synonym	F	Verb
113	51@v – arrive, get, come	68	tulema
		37	jõudma
		5	saabuma
		2	kohale_jõudma
		1	pärale_jõudma
98	718@v – travel away, depart, go away, go	98	minema
70	1550@v – come, come up	70	tulema
55	789@v – attend, go to (visit)	55	käima
46	679@v – bring, get, convey, fetch	46	tooma
46	47@v – walk, go on foot, foot, leg it, hoof, hoof it	21	kõndima
		10	sammuma
		8	astuma
		7	käima
31	5984@v – take, bring	31	viima
27	9363@v – step, take a step	27	astuma
25	976@v – sit down, sit	17	istuma
		8	istet_võtma
25	48@v – ride	25	sõitma
22	31@v – throw, project through the air	18	viskama
		4	heitma
22	880@v – leave, go forth, go away	22	kaduma
21	667@v – pull, draw by force	11	tõmbama
		5	tirima
		3	sikutama
		2	Kiskuma

('talked about box'). So it seems that the main difference between the two encodings is that the PP is more clearly related to the spatial meaning of locative expressions.[6]

3.4.1 *NP in elative case*

The words in the **elative** denoting SOURCE occurred eighty-five times in our data. Most of the cases represent a clearly defined three-dimensional space, for example *toast* 'from inside the room' in (4).

(4) *Ema* *tule-b* ***toa-st.***
mother come-3.SG room-ELAT
'Mother comes **from the room.**'

The elative case may also occur in Estonian if the referent is not only the starting point of motion, but when more complex semantic processes are involved. In such cases the PP as a synonymous equivalent is usually not possible. Example (5) refers to an institution rather than a location. The native speaker of Estonian understands that the music teacher had once studied at Peda (colloquial for Tallinn Pedagogical University); the starting of the motion is somewhat metaphorical, although the motion has actually taken place.

(5) *Mei-le* *tul-i* ***Tallinna*** ***Peda-st*** *laulu-õpetaja.*
1.PL ADE come-3.SG.PST Tallinn.GEN Peda-ELAT song.GEN-teacher
'A music teacher from **Tallinn Peda** came to us.'

3.4.2 *NP in ablative case*

SOURCE occurred in the **ablative** case twenty-four times and in our corpus typically denoted specific two-dimensional space; in (6), *kartulipõld* 'potato field'.

(6) *Vana-ema* *ja* *Mari* *tul-i-d* *kahekesi* ***kartuli-põllu-lt.***
Grand-mother and Mari come-PST-3PL in.pair potato-field-ELAT
'Grandma and Mari returned **from the potato field.**'

According to our data, two-dimensional SOURCE is less frequent than three-dimensional. Actually, as we will see in the conclusion (see Table 3.3), the same tendency occurs in other parts of motion events as well. According to our data, motion is most frequently encoded in three-dimensional space.

3.4.3 *PP*

Adpositional phrases denoting location and the starting point of motion were relatively infrequent in our data (PP related to the temporal aspect occurred often,

[6] There is evidence that the use of the Estonian adessive case and the adposition *peal* are not synonymous; the difference lies in the relation between Trajector and Landmark (Klavan et al. 2011). The same should be true according to other adpositions, but further research is needed.

but this issue is not discussed in the present chapter). The following postpositions were frequent in the description of motion events and denoted the starting point of motion: *alt* 'from-under' (eight times), *juurest* 'from-at' (four), *tagant* 'from–behind' (four), *vahelt* 'from–between' (four), *eest* 'from–front' (three), *kõrvalt* 'from–beside' (two), *pealt* 'from–on'(two).

In some cases, postpositions, such as *vahelt* (example (7)), *poolt*, *juurest*, and *kõrvalt* (example (8)) were related to the object the location of which was fixed in space and allowed the description of motion. They are in the transitional area between SOURCE and ROUTE. This clearly illustrates one of the problems with our approach: without taking into account the broader context of the situation it is often impossible to identify the proper function of an argument NP or PP. For instance, the postpositional phrase NP + *vahelt* (lit. 'from between NP') may express ROUTE (VIA), as apparently is the case in the examples below, but in the case of other kinds of objects denoted by NP it may refer to the starting point (SOURCE) of some motion as well. It depends on how far back one wants to go in fixing this starting point.

(7)

Praokile	*jää-nud*	***ukse***	***vahelt***	*siugle-s*	*kööki*
ajar	left-PRTCPL	door.GEN	from-between	snake-PST	kitchen.ILL

Mants	*ja*	*kurruta-s*	*tüdruku*	*jalu-s.*
Mants	and	purr-PST	girl.GEN	feet.PL-INE

'Mants snaked its way into the kitchen **through the door** left ajar and purred at the girl's feet.'

(8)

Läks	***kassa***	***kõrvalt***	*kaupa-de*	*poole.*
go.3SG.PST	cash register	from.side	good-PL.GEN	towards

'He walked **from the cash register** towards the goods.'

3.4.4 *Adverb*

The data revealed some **adverbs** related to SOURCE: *sealt* 'from there', *siit* 'from here', *kust* 'from where', *eest* 'from–front' and *väljast* 'from–out'.

(9)

Leeve	*tõi*	***välja-st***	*seina*	*äärest*	*mõlkis plekknõu.*
Leeve	bring.3SG.PST	from-out-ELAT	wall.GEN	from–side	dented can.GEN

'Leeve brought a dented can from the side of the wall outside.'

The most common adverb co-occurring with the noun in the elative case *välja* 'out' stresses the motion away from (and usually 'out of') a specific place or object to an unspecified location. Thus, the use of *välja* is similar to *ära* (see section 3.4.5), which denotes the disappearance of an object.

3.4.5 SOURCE *in combination with other categories*

In motion events SOURCE may serve as the starting point of motion, but it can also be interpreted as ROUTE, as was mentioned above. It is especially true of the verb *käima* 'walk', which will be discussed in greater detail in section 3.7. In (10), the verb determines that the adposition usually denoting SOURCE will be interpreted—because of the use of the elative case—as ROUTE: the motion first takes place towards the grave and then forwards. The example can also be interpreted so that both GOAL *haud* 'grave' and SOURCE *haud* 'grave' are encoded at the same time. But this can be considered a typical occurrence of ROUTE as well.

(10) *Käi-s* ***haua*** ***juure-st*** *läbi.*
walk-3SG.PST grave.GEN by-ELAT PERF.ADV.
'He (came and intentionally) stopped **at the grave** (and continued his walking route).'

A sentence may contain both SOURCE and GOAL, but in many cases they together denote a manner of motion that is characterized by repeated entrance and exit. In (11), the child moves several times from the lap (*sülest*) of SOURCE to the lap (*sülle*) of GOAL; as a matter of fact, different persons are involved. Again, in this case one may pose the question whether we are not actually dealing here with a case of ROUTE. If so, this means that the functions ROUTE and MANNER are mixed together (in particular, it seems that there cannot be a MANNER of motion when there is no ROUTE).

(11) *Laps* *rända-s* ***süle-st*** ***sülle.***
child travel-3SG.PST lap-ELAT lap.ILL
'The child moved **from lap to lap.**'

There is also a rather frequent phenomenon among the spatial characteristics of motion events which is expressed by adverbs *ära* 'away' and *välja* 'out', and is interconnected with the category of SOURCE. Our data revealed seventeen cases where disappearance of the SUBJECT from SOURCE was encoded by the adverb *ära* 'away' and sixteen cases of *välja* 'out'.

In such cases, the sentence does not encode in any way the concrete place to where the object moves, but only that it disappears from the SOURCE that is in focus. An adverb *ära* 'away' is polysemous and difficult to analyse. The main function of Estonian adverb *ära* 'away', like the equivalent adverb in many other languages, is a perfective particle, and in that function it is difficult to differentiate it from the adverb denoting disappearance from SOURCE. *Ära* co-occurred most often with the verb *minema* 'go' (e.g. *Ma läksin ära* 'I went away'), but it sometimes also co-occurred with other verbs of motion. In most cases, the adverbial that encoded SOURCE (*Hiiu õllesaal* 'Hiiu beer hall' in (12)) was also present in the same sentence; at the same time, GOAL was only expressed once and by means of an indefinite pronoun (*kuskile* 'somewhere' in (13)).

(12) *Just eile vii-si-me ta Hiiu õlle-saali-st* ***ära.***
only yesterday take-PST-1PL 3SG.GEN Hiiu beer-hall-ELAT away.
'It was only yesterday that we took him **away** from the Hiiu beer hall.'

(13) *Ole-ksi-n hea meele-ga kuski-le* ***ära*** *sõit-nud.*
be-COND-1SG good mind-COM somewhere-ALL away ride-PRTCPL
'I would have loved to go **away** somewhere.'

The data provided ten additional uses of *ära* 'away' where the SOURCE was not specified and *ära* expressed disappearance of the subject and/or perfectivity of the action. In these sentences, *ära* encodes GOAL rather than SOURCE. Metslang has pointed out how some Estonian particles (like *ära* 'away', *maha* 'down', *läbi* 'through', *välja* 'out', *üles* 'up') express perfectivity and at the same time function as directionals (Metslang 2001: 445; Erelt et al. 1993: 20–1). Rice and Newman have called the meaning related to the English particle *away* in expressions like *cut away, fade away* 'disintegration' (Rice and Newman 1994: 319). Veismann and Tragel (2008) have studied the connection between directional and aspectual meanings of Estonian particles.

3.5 GOAL

In our data, GOAL in fact covers two roles: DIRECTION and GOAL (i.e. the end-point of motion). As the cover category we will use GOAL, since GOAL presupposes DIRECTION but not vice versa.

The following means are used to convey GOAL/DIRECTION:

1) NP in the illative (i.e. an internal local case or a three-dimensional local case) with the ending *-sse*; fusional forms without an ending are rather frequent;
2) NP in the allative (i.e. an external local case or a two-dimensional local case) with the ending *-le*;
3) adpositional phrase;
4) supine construction, more precisely, supine with the illative expressed by the morpheme *-ma*;
5) locative adverb (either in the illative or allative), including the pro-adverb *siia* 'here';
6) NP in the terminative.

3.5.1 NP in illative

The **noun phrase in the illative** was the most common adverbial denoting direction (lative adverbial of location) in our data (see examples (14)–(15)). It occurred 232 times and it was one the most frequent means to express motion. As for motion, an adverbial in the illative accompanying the motion verb usually denotes a three-dimensional space/location towards which the motion takes place (and where it ends).

(14) *Läks* *rööki-des* ***koju.***
go.3SG.PST yell-INF home.ILL
'He went **home** yelling.'

(15) *Sealt* *saade-ti* *ta* *kunagi* ***Puiatu-sse.***
from.there send-PSS.PST 3SG once Puiatu-ILL
'From there he was once sent **to Puiatu.**'

3.5.2 NP in allative

The **noun phrase in the allative** was also rather frequent (ninety-one occurrences) in the data, but its functions were more diverse than those of the noun phrase in the illative. (16)–(19) illustrate the common usage of the allative expressing GOAL. In that case the adverbial denotes a location, which can be understood as a generic location (16) or a two-dimensional region of space (17). It could also be a functional area with a dominating (highlighted) dimension, as in (18) (where *tänav* 'street' is understood as a two-dimensional space, although it can be understood as three-dimensional as well) or the highlighted surface of the object, as in (19) (see Vainik 1995: 57–67).

(16) *Naabri-mees* *lõ-i* *käe-ga* *ja* *kihuta-s* *sooja-le* ***maa-le.***
neighbour-man hit-3SG.PST hand-COM and dash-3SG.PST warm-ALL land-ADE
'The next-door neighbour gave up and dashed to a warm **country**.'

(17) *Mehe-d* *veda-si-d* *kelku-de-ga* *nooda-d* ***jää-le.***
man-PL haul-PST-3SG sledge-PL-COM seine-PL ice-ALL
'The men hauled the seines **onto the ice** with sledges.'

(18) *Astu-si-n* ***tänava-le,*** *peatu-si-n* *hetke-ks.*
step-PST-1SG street-ALL stop-PST-1SG moment-TRANS
'I stepped **onto the street**, and stopped for a moment.'

(19) *Hoovi-s* *hüppa-s* *kõuts* ***prügi-tünni-le*** *ning* *sealt* *edasi*
yard-INE jump-3SG.PST tomcat dust-bin-ALL and from.there forward
kuuri ***katuse-le.***
shed.GEN roof-ALL
'In the yard the tomcat jumped **on the dustbin** and from there onto **the shed roof.**'

A noun phrase in the allative typically expresses the change of possession of the object, as in (20). Some researchers have claimed that the primary function of the external local cases in Estonian is to express possession rather than location (see Matsumura 1994).

(20)	*Noor-mees*	*süüta-s*	*sigareti,*	*andi-s*	*tiku-d*	***kaaslase-le.***
	young-man	light-3SG.PST	cigarette	give-3SG.PST	match-PL	companion-ALL

'The young man lit his cigarette and gave the matches **to his companion**.'

3.5.3 PP

There were relatively few **adpositional phrases** encoding GOAL in the data (149 tokens) by comparison with the noun phrases in the local case. As for the other components of motion events, PP and synonymous NP in the local case differ very little, if there is any difference at all. PPs are just more clearly spatial and usually cannot be used in non-spatial contexts as NPs in the local case can be. (On the synonymy of Estonian locative cases and adpositions see Klavan, in press.)

Example (21) presents a sentence that occurred in the data and a corresponding adpositional phrase, which has almost the same meaning.

(21)	*Ta*	*istu-s*	***trepi-le***	(cf. *trepi*	*peale*).
	3SG	sit-3SG.PST	stairs-ALL	stairs.GEN	on–to

'He sat down **on the stairs**.'

The most frequent postpositions for GOAL were *juurde* 'to', *poole* 'toward', *alla* 'under, down', *äärde* 'to (a border)', *taha* 'back', etc. ((22)–(23)) which have no synonymous NP-variants.

(22)	*Seepärast*	*astu-s*	*ta*	*ühe*	***tooli***	***juurde.***
	because	step-3SG.PST	3SG	one.GEN	chair.GEN	to

'That is why he walked up **to a chair**.'

(23)	*Naine*	*jooks-*is	***tiigi***	***äärde,***	*kükita-s*	*kalda-le*	*maha.*
	woman	run-3SG.PST	pond.GEN	to	squat-3SG.PST	bank-ALL	down

'The woman ran **to the pond**, and squatted down on the bank.'

There were also some prepositional phrases in the data, for instance (24).

(24)	*ja*	*sööst-si-d*	*tuule*	*ässituse-l*	*mehe-le*	*otse*	***vastu***	***nägu***
	and	dash-PST-3PL	wind.GEN	inciting-ADE	man-ALL	straight	against	face.PART

'and stirred by the wind dashed right **into** the man's **face**'

The grammaticalization of adpositions from lexical nouns is characteristic of Estonian; thus, it is not always possible to accurately identify whether one is dealing with an adposition or a noun phrase. For example, the word *äärde* 'to the border' (from the word *äär* 'border', see (23)) is considered to be grammaticalized, but the word *serv* 'edge' (see (25)) can be treated also as the local case of the noun.

(25)	*Ranna-papp*	*kohenda-b*	*süsi,*	*tõmba-b*	*halu*	***lõkke***	***serva.***
	coast-man	adjust-3SG	coal.PL.PART	pull-3SG	log	fire.GEN	edge.ILL

'The old man from the coast adjusts the coals and pulls a log **to the edge of the campfire**.'

3.5.4 *Supine construction*

The supine construction (a combination of the infinitive ending with *-ma* and a finite verb) as a locative adverbial can express destination by modifying verb forms (both transitive and intransitive) that denote the relocation of an entity (Erelt et al. 1993: 252). In addition to marking location, the supine usually also denotes purpose (ibid.). It is common to conceptualize an activity or a process as a location or an object. Metslang (1993, 1995) has discussed such supine constructions in Estonian in great detail. In (26) the agent goes to a place where he rests; here resting is thus an activity that can also be understood as a **goal**.

(26)	*ja*	*kui*	*Joona*	*isa*	*mõne*	*aja*	*pärast*	***puhka-ma***	***läks***
	and	when	Joona.GEN	father	some.GEN	time.GEN	after	rest-SUP	go.3SG.PAST

'and when Joona's father **went to have a rest** after a while'

3.5.5 *Adverb*

The lative adverbial can be expressed by **lative adverbs** (for example *ette* and *ligi* in 27–28).

(27)	*Tõmba*	*kohe*	*kardina-d*	***ette***!
	pull	at.once	curtain-PL	to.front

'Draw the curtains at once!'

(28)	*Mina,*	*ehtne*	*kratt,*	*hiili-n*	***ligi*** ...
	1SG	real	thief	sneak-1SG	to.close

'I, a real thief, sneak **close**...'

Lative adverbs were the most frequent ways to denote GOAL and DIRECTION in our data (251 tokens); *edasi* 'forward', *tagasi* 'back', *maha* 'down', *välja* 'out', and pro-adverbs *siia* '(to) here' and *sinna* '(to) there' were the most frequent adverbs denoting GOAL. It is noteworthy that the most frequent adverbs of direction can also function as aspectual markers. As Veismann and Tragel (2008) have pointed out, '*edasi* "forward" is a clear example of how spatial usage has taken on temporal (aspectual) meanings; in most cases it is ambiguous between the spatial and the aspectual reading'.

3.5.6 GOAL *in terminative*

As Estonian has the terminative case (*-ni*) to denote reaching a certain place or a boundary (see Erelt 2003), one can talk about a separate group comprising the relevant adverbials and assign them to the category GOAL. As for motion events, it is interesting to note that this GOAL is not specified with respect to dimensions presented in Table 3.1: the terminating point of motion can be at something, inside something, or on something. Furthermore, the adverbials can sometimes express only an intermediate stage, from where the motion continues. From the point of view of the event, it is important that reaching this intermediate point is encoded as an accomplishment, as in (29).

(29) *kuni jõud-si-d ühe-taoliselt kollase-ks krohvi-tud* ***maja-de-ni***
until reach-PST-3SG uniformly yellow-TRANS plaster-PRTCPL house-PL-TERM
'until they reached **the houses** that had been uniformly plastered in yellow'

The terminative as the marker of the end point of the motion event occurred nine times in the data. Some of them were borderline cases in respect to motion events; for example, one can argue whether *helid jõudsid minuni* 'the sounds reached me' can literally be considered a motion event.

NP in the terminative can encode the end point of motion also in a more complicated way. In (30), a woman walks into the water and the motion ends when she is *reiteni vees* 'thigh-high in the water'. The example shows how the encoding of a motion event depends on the point of view of the observer. If somebody walks into the water, it is usually not possible to say how far she went from the shore; what matters and can be described is the part of the body that the water reached.

(30) *Naine läks* ***reite-ni*** *vette.*
woman go.3SG.PST thigh-TERM water.ILL
'The woman went **thigh-high** into the water.'

3.6 LOCATION

LOCATION is usually expressed by a locative adverbial of place in Estonian.

The following means can be used to denote location:

a) NP in the inessive marked by the suffix *-s*;
b) NP in the adessive marked by the suffix *-l*;
c) PP;
d) adverb;
e) supine construction marked with the suffix *-mas*, which usually encodes at the same time both activity and the place where it is carried out.

The supine construction can in principle occur together with a variety of motion verbs, but in our data it was used only with the verb *käima* 'walk, go to–from', which will be discussed in section 3.7.

In the case of some verbs the grammatical object may denote a location where the activity takes place. This is the case with the verb *läbi jalutama* (+direct object) 'walk through, walk in everywhere', as well as with some other verbs with the adverbial component *läbi* 'through'. For instance, in (31), two people have walked through the whole republic, which is grammatically encoded as an argument of impersonal clause *terve vabariik* 'the whole republic'.

(31) ***Terve vabariik*** *nei-l kahe-l läbi jaluta-tud.*
whole republic 3PL-ADE two-ADE through walk-IMPERS.PRTCPL
'These two have walked through **the whole republic.**'

3.6.1 NP in adessive

The data contained thirty-three **adverbials in the adessive**. The word *tänav* 'street' or *tänavad* 'streets' were repeatedly mentioned as LOCATION; sometimes a specific and other times a generic street was meant, as *tänaval* 'in the street' in (32).

(32) *Meie käi-me* ***tänava-l*** *ja midagi meie-ga ei juhtu.*
1PL walk-1PL street-ADE and something 1PL-COM NEG happen
'We are walking **in the street** and nothing happens to us.'

An adverbial with a three-dimensional rather than two-dimensional meaning can also occur in the adessive case. In (33), the ground floor is considered to be space rather than a surface; nevertheless, it is expressed by means of the adessive. Actually, the word *tänaval* 'in the street' in the previous example is also regarded as space rather than a surface. Thus one can claim that the adessive often also denotes three-dimensional space that is defined by a certain surface: storey as space is defined through the floor and the street as space through the surface of the street.

(33) *Kola-si-me Lotte-ga veel* ***Schilleri maja alumise-l korruse-l.***
walk-PST-1PL Lotte-COM more Schiller.GEN house.GEN lower-ADE floor-ADE
'Lotte and I then walked around **on the ground floor of Schiller's house.**'

If the location is an NP encoded by the adessive, it denotes an entity through which the space is metonymically defined rather than the explored location. In (34), it is a wire on which the bird is sitting. The bird has literally not enough space on the wire; thus, one understands it as space that adjoins the wire and which is defined by the point of contact between the bird and the wire.

(34) *Pääsuke lenda-s üle me pea-de, teine kiiku-s*
swallow fly-3SG.PST over 1PL head-PL.GEN second swing-3SG.PST
rahutult ***traadi-l.***
restlessly wire-ADE
'A swallow flew over our heads, another was swinging restlessly **on the wire.**'

Example (35), where the letter was sent '(lit). on my address' *minu aadressil*, could be treated in a similar way; the address is an attribute of the place of residence rather than a location in its literal sense.

(35) *ja* *siis* *tule-b* *kauni-l* *sügis-päeva-l* *kiri,* *sealt.*
and then come-3SG beautiful-ADE autumn-day-ADE letter from.there
edasi ***minu*** ***aadressi-l***
forward 1SG.GEN address-ADE
'and then on a beautiful autumn day a letter arrives, and forwarded from there **to my address**'

LOCATION can also be defined deictically in respect to some person; for example, *vasakul* 'on the left' and *paremal* 'on the right' occurred in our data.

The material contained a single postpositional phrase (*vee peal* 'on the water') that expressed a two-dimensional LOCATION.

3.6.2 NP in inessive

There were sixty **adverbials in the inessive** that denote LOCATION (excluding the modifiers of the verb *käima* 'walk': see below). Most of them clearly expressed LOCATION, as in (36). Some sentences expressed a substance rather than a place; two of them were *õhus* 'in the air' (see (37)) and one *meres* 'in the sea'.

(36) *Vanasti* *kand-si-d* *niisuguse-d* ***veski-s*** *vilja-kotte* *või* *lossi-si-d*
in.old. times carry-PST-3PL such-PL mill-INE grain-sack or load-PST-3PL
sadama-s *laevu.*
harbour-INE ship.PL.PART
'In the old days such people used to carry sacks of grain **in the mill** or unloaded ships **at the harbour**.'

(37) *pall* *hüppa-s* ***õhu-s*** *nagu* *elektri-löögi* *saa-nud* *konn*
ball jump-3SG.PST air-INE like electricity-blow get-PRTCPL frog
'The ball jumped **in the air** like an electrocuted frog.'

There were also some metonymic cases where a certain location was referred to through an object with which it was in contact. In (38), the flag is fluttering not in the tower but outside of it. The phrase *pilved liiguvad lepaladvus* 'the clouds are moving in the tops of the alder trees' is not literally true; they seem to be in a region defined by the tops of the alder trees, as seen by the observer.

(38) *ja* ***Tartu*** ***raekoja*** ***torni-s*** *lehvi-s* *jälle* *punane* *lipp*
and Tartu Cityhall tower-INE flutter-3SG.PST again red flag
'and the red flag was once again fluttering **in the tower of the Tartu City Hall**'

The group includes four adverbials expressed by the inessive case that denote three-dimensional space in motion events; however, their meaning cannot be taken literally. Example (39) does not refer to the interior of *laud* 'table'; the illative form *lauas* '(lit.) in the table' is lexicalized in the meaning *laua juures istujate ja sööjate seas* 'among the people sitting at the table and having a meal'.

(39) **Laua-s** käi-si-d ringi foto-d.
table-INE walk-PST-3PL around photo-PL
'Pictures were passed **around at the table.**'

3.6.3 PP

Postpositional phrases with the meaning of three-dimensional space occurred nine times in the data. They include *ümber* 'around', *ees* 'in front of', *kohal* 'over, above', and *keskel* 'in the middle of'. Some of them (*kohal* and *keskel*) refer to their adessive origin, but clearly express three-dimensional space in present-day Estonian.

There were fifty-eight pre- and postpositional phrases that clearly denoted LOCATION (*vahel* 'in between', *all* 'under', *ees* 'in front of', *juures* 'at, near', *keset* 'in the middle of', *keskel* 'in the middle of', and *kohal* 'above'). The most frequent was *juures* (five times); however, it was rather rare compared to the word *juurde* 'to', which is derived from the same stem and denotes GOAL.

3.6.4 Adverb

Demonstrative adverb *siin* 'here' occurred four times in the data. The demonstrative adverbs are not differentiated with respect to their dimension, that is, *siin* 'here' and *seal* 'there' can theoretically be either two- or three-dimensional; all the instances of the deictic demonstrative *siin* 'here' that occurred in the data can be interpreted as three-dimensional.

3.7 Motion events expressed by the verb *käima* (lit. 'walk')

The Estonian verb *käima* is a highly frequent verb with a peculiar valency—the adverbial in the locative case instead of cases that usually express GOAL or SOURCE—and that is why it cannot be disregarded (see Pajusalu 2001: 181–4). The verb *käima* primarily means 'to walk', and in that case it is synonymous with many other verbs of motion. More often, however, *käima* means 'move to and back or away from somewhere, visit', and in that case it takes an adverbial of place in the inessive or adessive case. As the verb expresses motion to and back/away from the place marked by the adverbial, then from the perspective of the whole event the adverbial often denotes both GOAL and SOURCE at the same time (of different instances of motion, though). There were fifty-four such adverbials in the inessive (thirty-one), adessive (ten), or supine inessive (thirteen), that modified the verb *käima*. The adverbial denotes especially clearly GOAL or SOURCE in cases where the verb *käima* denotes repeated action: somebody moved to point X (in whatever manner, including driving) and returned. In (40), the photographer visited the house of the speaker, that is, he came and also left later.

(40)

Ühe-l	*sula-lumise-l*	*päeva-l*	*käi-s*	***mei-l***	*päevapiltnik.*
one-ADE	melt-snowy-ADE	day-ADE	walk-3SG.PST	1PL-ADE	photographer

'A photographer visited **us** on a day when the snow was melting.'

As for repeated action, the spatial meaning of the adverbial used together with the verb *käima* is not that clear. Rather, it covers GOAL, SOURCE, or LOCATION. It applies, for example, to the set phrase *koolis käima* 'go to school', which means both that the agent moves repeatedly to and from the school and that he attends school.

There were thirteen cases where the supine form of the inessive was used together with the verb *käima* 'walk, visit'. Such supine verb forms encode at the same time both the activity and the location where the action is performed (Pajusalu and Orav 2008). As a result of grammaticalization, the above verb form can also express the progressive (see Metslang 1993), but we are interested in the supine inessive primarily as a spatial characteristic of a motion event. In example 41, the phrase *teda vaatamas* '(lit.) seeing him' is a place adverbial of the verb *käima*, which shows that the GOAL of the motion event is to pay a short visit to the person denoted by the pronoun *teda* 'him'.

(41)

Innos	*käi-s*	*teda*	*kaks*	*korda*	***vaata-ma-s.***
Innos	walk-3SG.PST	3SG.PART	two	time.PART	see-SUP-INE

'Innos came to **see** him twice.'

The verb *käima* is often accompanied by an adverbial of place expressed by NP; in that case the purpose of the supine inessive is to encode the activity rather than GOAL (and SOURCE), but the latter cannot be completely ruled out (example 42).

(42)

Käi-si-n	*tehase*	*raamatukogu-s*	***toru-sid***	***paranda-ma-s.***
walk-PST-1SG	factory.GEN	library-INE	pipe-PL.PART	fix-SUP-INE

'I went to the factory library **to fix the pipes**.'

3.8 ROUTE

The ROUTE along which the motion proceeds from SOURCE to GOAL is an important component of motion events. As we have explained above, we mean by ROUTE just the route by which the motion proceeds. Treating the category ROUTE as a conceptual role category makes it possible (e.g. in the frames of Jackendoff's general Path category) to pick out and describe the details concerning the motion process of the moving entity between SOURCE and GOAL. There are specific linguistic means, namely pre- and postpositions, which highlight the ROUTE and not the starting or end point of the motion event. Estonian has no case form to mark ROUTE (as it has for GOAL, SOURCE, and LOCATION), and thus it is expressed either by the meaning of the verb itself or through grammatical words. As we are exploring parts of sentences other than the verb, we are primarily interested in the encodings of ROUTE expressed by grammatical words. Similarly to the other sections of the chapter, the syntactic problem is whether a grammatical word functions in the sentence as an adverb or a pre- or postposition. For example, *mööda* 'along' can be either a member of PP (*teed mööda* 'along the road') or an adverb (*ta kõndis mööda* 'he walked past'). In addition, the grammatical words encoding ROUTE in particular can occur both as pre- and postpositions. This topic needs to be analysed in greater detail;[7] here, we will only deal with the most common grammatical words that express pre- or postpositions: *mööda* 'along', *üle* 'across', *ümber* 'around', and *vastu* 'against'.

ROUTE was encoded in the data mostly with the words *mööda* 'along' (nineteen occurrences as a pre- or postposition) and *üle* 'across' (nineteen times as a pre- or postposition). Whether *mööda* 'along' denotes ROUTE directly or (additionally) an area where the motion takes place depends on the meaning of the accompanying An NP. If the NP expresses a road or some other long object (e.g. *mööda teed* 'along the road' or *mööda vaibajooni* 'along the carpet lines'), the meaning of ROUTE is clear. An NP used with *mööda* 'along' can also denote an area (*mööda linnaosa* 'along the district') or a surface (*mööda kive* 'along the stones'); in that case, the respective PP encodes LOCATION rather than ROUTE. All the *mööda*-phrases modifying motion verbs are treated as ROUTE in the statistics for the chapter because ROUTE is to a greater or lesser extent present in all of them.

The word *üle* 'over, across' is also highly polysemous (for a more detailed study, see Veismann 2004); its meaning becomes clear only together with the nominal part of the phrase. The motion can, for example, proceed *üle toa* 'across the room' or *üle jõe* 'across the river'; here ROUTE is encoded together with LOCATION. Sometimes the *üle*-phrase can be encoded as the end point of motion (*tõstis käed üle pea* 'he raised his hands over his head'); here ROUTE is combined with GOAL.

Another word that quite often expresses ROUTE is *ümber* 'around' (it occurred eight times as a pre- or postposition). *Ümber* 'around' encodes movement around some landmark (*ümber tule* 'around the fire' or *tema ümber* 'around her'); sometimes we are dealing with the result of the movement rather than the movement itself, and thus we can say that the respective PP encodes LOCATION rather than ROUTE. However, if a sentence contains a verb of motion, the co-occurrence of PP and a verb results in the encoding of ROUTE. Example 43 states that the scarf was tied *ümber tema tunkede* 'around his dungarees'; from the perspective of the moment when the sentence was uttered, the scarf was already fixed, and did not move any more. Nevertheless, all the *ümber*-phrases are here regarded as encoding ROUTE because only sentences containing verbs of motion were examined.

[7] Tuomas Huumo (2010) has analysed the differences between the uses of Finnish ROUTE-adpositions.

(43) ***Ümber*** *tema* ***tunke-de*** *oli* *mitmekordselt*
around 3SG.GEN dungaree-PL.GEN be.3SG.PST number.of.times
keera-tud *kitsas* *helepunane* *sall.*
tie-PRTCPL narrow bright-red scarf.
'A narrow bright red scarf was tied **around** his **dungarees** a number of times.'

The word *vastu* 'against' (seven instances as a pre- or postposition) also denotes ROUTE, but in a slightly different way from the previously discussed *mööda* 'along' and *ümber* 'around'. The word *vastu* 'against' expresses the end point of ROUTE and is thus a borderline case between ROUTE and GOAL rather than ROUTE and LOCATION (as *mööda* 'along' and *ümber* 'around'). At the same time, it is the ROUTE of motion that is clearly presented in motion events of sentences containing *vastu*-phrases; the ROUTE of motion is marked by the end point, not ROUTE itself. In (44), a man pushes a woman against the wall; the ROUTE along which the pushing occurs is highlighted, but it can also be interpreted as GOAL.

(44) *Siis* *lükka-s* *ta* *naise* ***vastu*** ***müüri.***
then push-3SG.PST 3SG woman.GEN against wall.PART
'He then pushed the woman **against the wall**.'

The material examined suggests that ROUTE can be expressed by various words in Estonian, but they all have multiple meanings. Therefore, first and foremost the construction of PP plus a verb is used to encode ROUTE.

3.9 Statistical conclusions

The objective of the chapter was to identify the most typical and common cases of the spatial characteristics of motion events, focusing on the nominal or adverbial components (arguments) in the event descriptions and not the verbs themselves. Here, we present some of the most important trends that we discovered in our data.

Table 3.3 is an overview of the statistical data on how the spatial characteristics of motion events are encoded by grammatical cases, adpositions, and adverbs. The modifiers of the verb *käima* 'walk' are presented separately.

Most importantly, Table 3.3 shows that in all categories of motion, three-dimensional local cases are more frequent than two-dimensional cases. We can also see that looking at three main special categories of motion event (SOURCE, GOAL, and LOCATION), it is GOAL that is most often encoded by a case-marked NP (mostly by illative or allative). This phenomenon (also called 'goal-bias') has been observed in many other languages as well (see, for example, Maisak and Rakhilina 1999 for an overview and Russian data). In addition, there is a separate case—the terminative—that marks GOAL; it does not occur very often, but increases the frequency of GOAL. On the basis of the material one can claim that GOAL is often encoded also by other

TABLE 3.3. **Number of instances where spatial characteristics of motion events were encoded by case, supine construction, postposition, preposition, or adverb among the 1,168 sentences of motion**

	SOURCE	GOAL	LOCATION	incl. *käima* 'go'
2-dimensional cases	24 (ablative)	91 (allative)	33 (adessive)	10 adessive
3-dimensional cases	85 (elative)	232 (illative)	60 (inessive)	1 illative 30 inessive
terminative		9		
supine constructions	1 (elative)	63 (illative)	13 (inessive)	13 inessive
postpositions	38	149	39	
prepositions	0	29	19	
adverbs	25	251	14	

means (PP and Adv). The most frequent GOAL-adverbs were *tagasi* 'back' (thirty-two occurrences), *ära* 'away' (seventeen), *välja* 'out' (sixteen) and *edasi* 'forward' (fifteen). Taking into consideration too that the verb *käima* 'walk, visit' denotes GOAL and SOURCE, then the number of sentences expressing GOAL rises still further. The expression of GOAL by the supine construction is especially common. Although Estonian has different supine constructions to denote GOAL as well as SOURCE and LOCATION, only one elative supine construction-encoding SOURCE occurred in the data (for further discussion of frequency of supine constructions in sentences which describe motion events, see Pajusalu and Orav 2008). As the inessive modifier of the verb *käima* is situated in the transitional area between GOAL, SOURCE, and LOCATION, we can claim that the supine construction typically expresses only GOAL and its peripheries in motion events. From Table 3.3 it can be concluded that as is characteristic of Estonian in general, mainly postpositions are used to express motion events, although prepositions sometimes do occur as well in expressions of GOAL and LOCATION.

3.10 Conclusions

The chapter focused on the means of encoding motion events in Estonian based on a sub-corpus containing 1,168 sentences with a finite form of verb of motion. The study identified both the verbs encoding motion and the means representing spatial characteristics of motion events.

Concerning the frequency of the motion verbs, one could identify a typical verb representing each semantic group; for example, for the synset 'arrive, get, come' it is *tulema* 'come', and *viskama* 'throw' is the typical verb for the synset 'throw, project through the air'.

The conceptual clarity of the Estonian categories varies. It is relatively easy to interpret SOURCE, GOAL, and LOCATION because they have their own grammatical cases. The major difficulties include:

a) explanation of the interaction of aspect and space. In the case of the perfect aspect the motion has already taken place and the AGENT or OBJECT has stopped moving;
b) interpretation of the arguments of the verb *käima* 'walk, visit'.

ROUTE, in the sense we adopted in our approach, is a category that is most difficult to interpret from the viewpoint of the interface between morphosyntax and semantics, as it does not have its own means of expression and because the adpositions that are typically used for expressing it are polysemous.

The categories of SOURCE, GOAL, LOCATION, and ROUTE proved to be important categories in our approach with regard to encoding spatial relations in a satellite-framed language such as Estonian; they all possess typical means of expression which are described in the chapter. Statistically, the following facts are of interest:

a) GOAL is most frequently encoded;
b) three-dimensional local cases are more frequent;
c) adverbs denoting GOAL are extremely frequent.

4

Verbs of aquamotion: semantic domains and lexical systems

YURY LANDER, TIMUR MAISAK,
EKATERINA RAKHILINA

4.1 Introduction[1]

It was argued during recent decades that the differences that languages show in their lexicon can often be described in a more or less consistent way (see Talmy 1985, 2000; Goddard and Wierzbicka (eds), 1994; Newman (ed.), 1997, 2002, 2009; Koptjevskaja-Tamm 2008 *inter alia*).[2] Nonetheless, the methodology of cross-linguistic comparison of lexicons is far from being well established. This chapter contributes to the discussion of possible approaches to this issue by presenting a framework based on distinguishing between typologically relevant semantic domains within a single semantic field.[3]

[1] This chapter is a revised version of our earlier manuscript entitled 'Domains of aquamotion', whose parts were presented at the 21st Scandinavian Conference of Linguistics (Trondheim, June 2005) and the 6th Biennial Meeting of Association for Linguistic Typology (Padang, July 2005), as well as in a number of smaller workshops. We are grateful to the audience of these conferences, Mila Vulchanova, and two anonymous reviewers for their valuable comments. All errors are ours.

The chapter resulted from the project 'Lexical typology of aquamotion', which involved a number of scholars, whose generous help we acknowledge: Maya Arad, Peter Arkadiev, Dagmar Divjak, Dmitry Ganenkov, Ekaterina Golubkova, Valentin Goussev, Elena Gruntova, Irina Makeeva, Liudmila Khokhlova, Victoria Khurshudian, Maxim Kisilier, Yana Kolotova, Maria Koptjevskaja-Tamm, Svetlana Kramarova, Julia Kuznetsova, Lee Su Hyon, Maarten Lemmens, Alexander Letuchiy, Solmaz Merdanova, Arto Mustajoki, Anna Panina, Irina Prokofieva, Ekaterina Protassova, Olga Podlesskaja (Shemanaeva), Alexander Rostovtsev-Popiel, Maria Rukodelnikova, Charanjit Singh, Anna Smirnitskaja, Natalia Vostrikova, Valentin Vydrine, Boris Zakharin. Most data of the project were published in Maisak and Rakhilina (eds) (2007) and at the website http://aquamotion.narod.ru. Additional literature on the topic includes Batoréo (2008) and Koptjevskaja-Tamm et al. (2010). This work was supported by RFFI (Russian Foundation for Basic Research) under grant No. 05-06-80400a.

[2] Much literature devoted to lexical typology was published in the late 2000s, that is, already after the first versions of the present chapter were prepared, so we could not consider all of it here.

[3] The terms 'semantic domain' and 'semantic field' are used here informally and refer to linguistically relevant ranges of meanings. These uses are not tied to any particular semantic theory.

We examine the expressions of motion/being in a liquid medium, called **aquamotion** henceforth (the term is owed to Philippe Bourdin). Despite the apparent simplicity of aquamotion, languages exhibit a great deal of variation in the ways they convey the relevant semantics: while English possesses no less than four basic aquamotion verbs (*swim, sail, float, drift*), there are languages like Turkish, which only have one verb of this kind, and languages like Indonesian, where the number of aquamotion verbs is extremely large. This diversity may be depicted as a kind of variation in **lexical (sub)systems**, that is, the types of correlations of semantic domains with their lexical representations.

Where does this diversity come from? How can we organize it and what parameters of cross-linguistic variation should we consider? We propose that this diversity is related in a large degree to a universal distinction between four semantic domains. This distinction can be taken as a basis for the comparison of this fragment of the lexicon in different languages.[4]

The rest of the chapter is structured as follows. Section 4.2 discusses certain general theoretical and methodological points we assume. Section 4.3 introduces the basic semantic domains of aquamotion. Section 4.4 illustrates how the proposed distinction between these domains works for a language with quite an extensive inventory of the verbs that convey the semantics of aquamotion, namely Standard Indonesian. In section 4.5 we outline the diversity shown by the languages of our sample in respect of the expression of aquamotion. Section 4.6 discusses a few complexities that may arise within our framework. The last section presents conclusions and perspectives on further research in the field.

4.2 Theoretical and methodological considerations

Following Talmy (1985),[5] we distinguish between several semantic components of the situations of motion, namely Figure, Ground, Manner, and Path. For example, the semantics of the clause *India is drifting into the continent Asia* can be 'dissected' in the following way: 'India (Figure) is moving (motion per se) into (Path) the continent Asia (Ground), and this movement is a kind of drifting (Manner)'. The same components minus Path are distinguished for posture situations.

An investigation into expressions of motion and location may focus on some of these components and/or the relations between them. For example, there has been quite a lot of study of the expression of Path and the interaction between Figure and Ground (see Fillmore 1983, 1997; Talmy 1985; Slobin 2004; Filipović 2007, among many others). Our study takes Manner as its subject.

[4] For the reasons of space, we restrict our exposition to the explication of basic points. A more detailed discussion can be found in Maisak and Rakhilina (2007).

[5] See also Talmy (2000).

Clearly, the diversity of Manner is much less predictable than the range of other parameters: the 'design' of this component is not well defined. This issue can be approached in two ways. First, the semantic parameters determining the variation can be formulated deductively, starting from our knowledge of the situation of aquamotion. Second, it may be possible to establish *tertium comparationis* inductively, by looking at the most frequent semantic distinctions found in languages. Below we follow the latter approach. It deserves mention here that the distinction between deductive and inductive approaches may not be as sharp as we present it. For example, we consider the approaches elaborated upon in Malt et al. (2008) (studying a distinction between walking and running) and Majid et al. (2008) (investigating the conceptualization of cutting and breaking) to be mainly deductive, since these studies provided parameters for the relevant distinctions beforehand. However, it is clear that the choice of these parameters was partly affected by the authors' pre-existing knowledge regarding conceptualization.

Languages may exploit different means for contrasting between different manners of motion in a liquid medium. Here we list only the most prominent of them.

(i) The use of different words is the clearest evidence for distinguishing between various manners of aquamotion. One of the simplest examples of such a distinction is that found in English between *swimming*, *sailing*, *floating*, and *drifting*, each of which reflects a certain manner of aquamotion. However, the words to be considered in this respect need not necessarily be dedicated aquamotion lexemes: numerous languages use general verbs of motion and location (such as 'go', 'come', or 'be') for some kinds of aquamotion.

(ii) Many languages distinguish between manners of aquamotion by using different morphosyntactic patterns. For example, the same verb can cover several kinds of aquamotion, yet it may have different subcategorization frames in different contexts. Thus, the Russian aquamotion verbs *plyt'/plavat'* can be used in many more contexts than any of their English translations (1)–(3).[6] However, the reference to Ground introduced by the preposition *po* 'along' is not found in the context of swimming (3). Moreover, only the sailing context admits reference to the means of sailing, which is introduced by the preposition *na* 'on' (2).

Russian

(1)	*Ja*	*plyl*	*kak*	*ryba.*
	I(NOM)	AM(PST:M)	like	fish(NOM:SG)

'I was swimming like a fish.'

[6] We gloss the aquamotion verb as AM (for 'aquamotion') in order not to impose its interpretation. The list of abbreviations used in glosses is given at the end of the chapter. The representation of the data for the most part follows our sources; the grammatical analysis is maximally simplified.

(2) *On* *plyl* *na* *plotu* *desjat'* *dnej* *bez*
he(NOM) AM(PST:M) on raft(LOC:SG) ten day(GEN:PL) without
vody *i* *edy.*
water(GEN:SG) and food(GEN:SG).
'He sailed on a raft for ten days without any water and food.'

(3) *Vot* *uže* *neskol'ko* *let,* *kak* *ja* *plavaju* *po* *Volge.*
PTCL already several year(GEN:PL) as I:NOM AM(1SG) along Volga
'I have already sailed (floated/*swum) along the Volga for several years.'

(iii) Probably the most unexpected criterion, which we nevertheless consider one of the most perfect and consistent, is the distribution of metaphorical extensions. Even when the two criteria mentioned above do not work perfectly, sometimes we find that only some meanings/uses of a given expression serve as a basis for a certain metaphor. For example, the idea of immersion is usually provided by verbs prototypically denoting swimming of animate beings (as in English *The meat is swimming in gravy*) and not by the verbs describing other kinds of aquamotion.

Notably, the criteria listed above represent 'anchors' that are frequently exploited for providing evidence for the relevance of some distinctions: the formal aspect, the syntagmatic (behavioural) aspect, and the paradigmatic aspect. In this sense, lexical typology does not need any specific methodology.

The conclusions presented in this chapter are based on the materials collected in the course of a project which involved scholars of various languages (see note 1). We conducted a questionnaire which covered various kinds of situation and could be used as a starting point for investigation of various lexical systems. Importantly, while the questionnaire relied on data from few languages, it was already much more detailed than these languages required it to be. The participants of the project could further broaden the questionnaire according to the peculiarities of their subject languages. The data were either taken from corpora (including Web sources) or obtained through elicitation procedures.

In total, we obtained information on conveying the idea of aquamotion from fifty languages, listed in Table 4.1. This language sample is a convenience sample, that is, it is not intended to represent all known genetic and geographic linguistic groupings. Still, we believe that it gives some impression of how languages differ in the expression of aquamotion. These data also allow us to formulate certain hypotheses on universal or near-universal distinctions found in the conceptualization of aquamotion. These are discussed immediately below.

4.3 The basic domains of aquamotion

The most basic distinction that we propose is that between the semantic domains of SWIMMING, SAILING, DRIFTING, and FLOATING. This distinction manifests itself in

TABLE 4.1. **Language sample**

Family	Languages
Afro-Asiatic	Standard Arabic, Modern Hebrew
Austronesian	Standard Indonesian
Dravidian	Tamil
Indo-European	Ancient Greek, Armenian, Bengali, Bulgarian, Dutch, English, French, German, Gujarati, Hindi, Italian, Latin, Lithuanian, Macedonian, Panjabi, Persian, Polish, Portuguese, Rajasthani, Russian, Serbo-Croatian, Spanish, Swedish
Niger-Congo	Maninka
Northeast Caucasian	Agul, Avar, Ingush, Itsari Dargwa, Karata, Lak, Lezgian, Standard Dargwa
Northwest Caucasian	Adyghe, Kabardian
Sino-Tibetan	Mandarin Chinese
South Caucasian	Georgian
Turkic	Karachay-Balkar, Khakas, Turkish
Uralic	Finnish, Komi-Zyrian, Nganasan, Selkup, Udmurt
Isolates	Japanese, Korean

most languages of our sample more or less consistently and is highly abstract, which makes it a convenient point of departure for studying the linguistic variation.

The SWIMMING domain is associated with self-propelled motion of an animate Figure. The predicates that serve for this domain presuppose much control and agentivity, and are the default expressions of aquamotion, at least for humans, certain animals, and fish.

SAILING predicates refer to motion of vessels or animates aboard. The situation denoted by predicates describing this domain also has a flavour of agentivity, yet this is not always the agentivity of Figure: examples like (4) represent this domain as well:[7]

(4) *But his seamanship skills were legendary; many of the passengers sailed on the Titanic because Captain Smith was in charge.*

The domains of FLOATING and DRIFTING cover the situations of 'passive', uncontrolled, and non-agentive aquamotion. Therefore, it is the verbs belonging to these domains that are commonly found with inanimate Figures, albeit such predicates usually allow animate Figures as well. The main difference between the two domains is that DRIFTING is associated with motion of Figure occurring due to the motion of the liquid, while FLOATING only profiles (in the sense of Langacker 1987) being in/on

[7] SAILING verbs may differ in whether they allow such contexts, but the most neutral of them normally do so.

the surface of liquid. The inclusion of FLOATING in aquamotion may seem debatable, since this domain is not even necessarily associated with motion proper. Yet, in many languages, it is expressed by aquamotion verbs. Note the following examples from Mandarin Chinese, which demonstrate the use of the same verb for the expression of FLOATING and DRIFTING:

Mandarin Chinese

(5)	*shù*	*yè*	*zài*	*shuǐ*	*miàn*	*shàng*	*piāo-zhe.*
	tree	leaf	in	water	surface	LOC	AM-STAT

'The tree leaves are floating on the surface of the water.'

(6)	*zhè*	*xiē*	*shùlín*	*shì*	*cóng*	*wǒ-men*	*zhè*	*lǐ*	*piāo-xià-qu*	*de.*
	this	CL	wood	COP	from	I-PL	this	LOC	AM-move.down-go.away	ATR

'This is the wood that drifted away from here.' (Rukodelnikova 2007: 602)

The fact that DRIFTING and FLOATING are often covered by the same lexical means could be an argument against the universal status of this distinction. But if we consider metaphors, we will find that DRIFTING and FLOATING give rise to very different extensions (Rakhilina 2007: 99–101). In particular, those expressions that describe DRIFTING are often used metaphorically for conveying the idea of unobstructed movement, which may further develop into expressions of slipping, flying, or expressions of the loss of form, loss of control, and penetration. At the same time, the expressions of FLOATING may evolve into expressions of emotional instability, unsteadiness, and random motion.

For reasons of space, we cannot provide all data suggesting the division between the four domains of aquamotion here—an interested reader is referred to the volume Maisak and Rakhilina (eds) (2007). But we will illustrate the proposed division for a single language, whose aquamotion lexicon is significantly distinct and more complex than, say, that of English.

4.4 An example: describing motion in a liquid medium in Indonesian

The subject language of this section is Standard Indonesian—an Austronesian language scattered across thousands of islands of the Malay archipelago.[8] Austronesians are known as navigators whose life depends closely on water. Not surprisingly, Standard Indonesian has a great number of aquamotion verbs. Some of them show restricted distribution, others are more common. But despite their diversity, Indonesian aquamotion verbs can be easily classified into four groups that correspond to the domains distinguished above, as is reflected in Table 4.1. The criteria

[8] Standard Indonesian is a variety of Malay that is used as the official language of Indonesia. Note that some other Malay varieties have markedly different systems of aquamotion expressions.

according to which these groups are distinguished are mainly semantic and include agentivity and control, constraints on the ontological status of Figure, and the presence/absence of interpretations related to directedness, as well as certain aspectual characteristics, in particular the ability of a verb to refer to the final stage of a situation; see Lander and Kramarova (2007) and Lander (2008) for details.

For example, the verbs derived from the root *renang* can only normally refer to controlled situations with animate Figures and usually presuppose the absence of means that keep Figure on the surface:

Standard Indonesian

(7) *Paus abu-abu jarang terlihat berenang hingga ke darat.*
whale grey rarely be.seen AM up.to to land
'Grey whales are rarely observed swimming up to the land.'

Similarly, *menyelam* 'swim under the water; dive' presupposes control and appears almost exclusively with animates, the only exception being its occurrence with submarines. Only *renang*-verbs and *menyelam* can easily refer to the final stage of a situation:

Standard Indonesian

(8) *Saya sudah berenang ke pantai ini.*
I ASP AM to beach this
'I have already swum up to this beach.'

The SAILING domain in Indonesian is quite rich, but all verbs belonging to it are derived from nominal roots (which describe either means or place of movement). These verbs can denote the motion of a person aboard a vessel, and almost all of them—with the exception of verbs specifying the means of motion—can refer to the movement of vessels:

Standard Indonesian

(9) *Di tengah laut, se-jumlah kapal dan perahu terlihat sedang berlayar.*
in middle sea one-number ship and boat be.seen ASP AM
'In the middle of the sea, one can see a number of sailing ships and boats.'

Some means-specified verbs show a further peculiarity: they require their Figure to control the motion and not simply to be a passenger; cf. the use of the verb *berakit* 'sail on a raft' in (10). This subclass of verbs may be less prototypical for the SAILING domain.

Standard Indonesian

(10) *Abang saya berakit ke sini.*
elder.brother I AM to here
'My elder brother sails here "driving" a raft.'

Finally, Indonesian possesses a number of aquamotion words that combine with Figures of almost any kind, which usually describe situations that do not presuppose any control and sometimes even imply its absence.[9] For these verbs, there are good reasons to distinguish between the verbs that usually denote uncontrolled situations and the verbs that necessarily do so. The first of these classes consists of the verbs derived from the roots *apung* and *ambang*. Such verbs may occur even when the situation is thought to be controlled, yet the control component is obscured, as in (11). In this example, though the floating of the ship is apparently controlled, what is profiled is only the fact that it remains on the surface and does not sink. Note that in (12), taken from a story of people having suffered a shipwreck, the appearance of the same verb is definitely motivated by the wish to emphasize the absence of control of the situation.

Standard Indonesian

(11) ...*para awak* *bekerja* *keras* *untuk* *men-jaga* *agar* *kapal*
crew work hard for ACT-watch.over so.as.to ship
tetap *terapung.*
permanently AM
'...the crew worked hard watching over the ship so it stayed afloat.'

(12) *Selama* *satu* *malam* *kami* *terapung* *di* *tengah* *laut*...
during one night we:EXCL AM in middle sea
'We were floating one night in the middle of the sea...'

The second subclass includes at least the verb *hanyut* 'drift (with the current)' (and possibly also *terombang-ambing* 'drift about (on water)') and always indicates the absence of control. It is also worth noting that it is *hanyut* that is typically met when the aquamotion is strongly dynamic and driven by the directed current:

Standard Indonesian

(13) *Puluhan* *batu* *gunung* *dan* *potongan* *kayu* *hanyut* *terbawa*
dozen stone mountain and piece wood AM be.carried
arus *sungai* *yang* *bergejolak.*
current river REL flare.up
'Dozens of mountain stones and pieces of wood were carried by the current of the growing river.'

It is conspicuous that the distinction between the two classes of 'passive' aquamotion verbs more or less corresponds to the distinction between FLOATING and DRIFTING proposed in section 4.3.

[9] Some of these verbs contain the prefix *ter-*, which explicitly marks the absence of control.

Finally, for motion of ships and other large Figures, Indonesian may exploit general verbs of motion, and in FLOATING contexts the language also displays verbs of existence/location:

Standard Indonesian

(14) *Ke mana kapal pergi, selalu kembali ke pelabuhan.*
to where ship go always back to harbour
'Whenever a ship goes, it always returns to (its) harbour.'

(15) *...keruh-nya air danau itu di-akibatkan oleh kotoran-kotoran*
turbidity-PR.3 water lake that PASS-give.rise AG garbage-RDP
yang ada di permukaan danau...
REL be in surface lake
'...the turbidity of the lake was due to the garbage that was on its surface...'

The Indonesian data demonstrate that the distinction between SWIMMING, SAILING, FLOATING, and DRIFTING is not based exclusively on English data and manifests itself as well in languages with more complex systems of aquamotion expressions.

4.5 Typology of aquamotion systems

Assuming that the contrast between SWIMMING, SAILING, DRIFTING, and FLOATING is universal, it can be taken as a basis for measuring the richness of the aquamotion fragment of the lexicon. In the following sections we will contrast between three types of aquamotion system, which we call 'middle' systems, 'rich' systems, and 'poor' systems. The main difference between them is the degree of the lexical elaboration of the aquamotion semantic field.

It is important for us that, unlike in simple classifications, there can be systems intermediate between types and that each type may serve as the subject of a separate study.

4.5.1 Poor systems

In a poor aquamotion lexical system, the distinction between SWIMMING, SAILING, DRIFTING, and FLOATING is obscured or made peripheral. However, such systems are not homogeneous. On the one hand, there are languages like Slavic, where a single root covers all of the four domains. To cite one example, Russian has only a pair of specific aquamotion verbs, *plyt'* and *plavat'*, which are (diachronically) morphologically related and differ roughly in iterativity and/or directedness of the process:

Russian

(16) a. *Sportsmen / lodka / brevno plyvët k beregu.*
sportsman(NOM:SG) boat(NOM:SG) log(NOM:SG) AM(3SG) towards bank(DAT:SG)
'A sportsman/boat/log is moving (in water) towards the bank.'

b. *Sportsmen / lodka / brevno plavaet nedaleko ot*
sportsman(NOM:SG) boat(NOM:SG) log(NOM:SG) AM(3SG) not.far from
berega.
bank(GEN:SG)
'A sportsman/boat/log is moving to and fro (in water) not far from the bank.'

Interestingly, however, in some systems similar to the Russian system, sometimes one observes more peripheral verbs associated with only one of the domains. This is the case, for instance, in German, where the verb *schwimmen* can operate in all four domains, yet it coexists with the verbs *segeln* 'sail', *treiben* 'be carried by water', and *driften* 'drift', which are more peripheral and restricted in use (Shemanaeva 2007). Similarly, in Lithuanian the whole range of aquamotion contexts can be covered by the pair *plaukioti* (non-directed)/*plaukti* (directed) (17)–(18), but within the DRIFTING and FLOATING domains we observe several verbs that are used on a par with *plaukioti–plaukyti, plūduriuoti* (19), and *būti* 'be':

Lithuanian

(17) *mes pamatėme, kad upe plaukia berniukas.*
we(NOM) see(PST:1PL) that river(INS:SG) AM(PRS:3) boy(NOM:SG)
'We saw that the boy was swimming/drifting along the river.'

(18) *žiūrime – laivas jau atsiskyręs nuo kranto*
look(PRS:1PL) ship(NOM:SG) already separate(APART.NOM:SG) from bank
ir plaukia Dauguva.
and AM(PRS:3) Daugava(INS:SG)
'We see the ship has already moved away from the bank and is sailing along the Daugava river.'

(19) *Upėje plūduriuoja rąstas.*
river(LOC:SG) AM(PRS:3) log(NOM:SG)
'There is a log floating in the river (where there is no stream).'
(Arkadiev 2007: 318, 321)

On the other hand, there are poor systems that do not neutralize the distinctions between all of the domains of aquamotion, but only single out one of them. Some systems of this kind are found in Northeast Caucasian languages, many of which usually exploit general verbs of motion and location for the description of aquamotion. However, in the SWIMMING domain of these systems we observe dedicated expressions of aquamotion that are essentially complex predicates:

Agul

(20) *gadaji lepe q'aa nac'un q:ireʁiqt:i.*
boy(ERG) wave do(IPF:PRS) river(GEN) edge(POSTLAT)
'A boy is swimming (lit. making a wave) towards the riverbank.'
(Maisak, Rostovtsev-Popiel, and Khurshudian 2007: 700)

The data from such languages as Agul suggest a non-trivial generalization: if a language only has one dedicated aquamotion expression, it can always be used to express of swimming. This, of course, reflects the general anthropocentricity of language.

4.5.2 Middle systems

We characterize an aquamotion system as 'middle' if it lexically distinguishes between SWIMMING, SAILING, and FLOATING/DRIFTING, optionally distinguishes between FLOATING and DRIFTING, but does not display any additional contrasts. We do not insist that a middle system contrast FLOATING and DRIFTING, because as we said earlier, these domains are often conflated. Moreover, we do not require that such a system have dedicated verbs for all of the distinguished domains.

Middle systems are by no means numerous. In our sample, there are only three languages that strongly distinguish lexically between three manners of aquamotion, among which two (Persian and Tamil) belong to the same Indo-Iranian area, but one (Maninka) is spoken in Western Africa. All of these languages have distinct lexical items for SWIMMING and FLOATING/DRIFTING, but for the SAILING domain they use general verbs of motion. Note the following Maninka examples:

Maninka

(21)	*À*	*bárá*	*à*	*námún*	*kà*	*nà*	*kánkún`*	*mà.*
	3SG	PERF	3SG	AM	INF	come	bank+ART	to

'He swam up to the bank.'

(22)	*Yírí*	*kúdún`*	*fún-nín*	*jí`*	*kàn.*
	wood	piece+ART	AM-SPART	water+ART	on

'A piece of wood is floating/drifting in the water.'

(23)	*Kúlún`*	*yé*	*nǎ*	*kàn*	*bá*	*kánkún`*	*mà.*
	boat+ART	IPF	come	CONT	river	bank+ART	to

'The boat is sailing/drifting towards the bank.' (Vydrine 2007: 732, 734, 736)

This is not likely to be a coincidence. Recall that in Indonesian the general verbs of motion such as 'go' and 'move' can also appear in expressions of aquamotion, and the preferred domain for them is SAILING. Presumably in Persian, Tamil, and Maninka we observe the same phenomenon. The only difference between these languages and Indonesian in this respect is that their systems lack additional contrasts, though general verbs of motion covering the SAILING domain contrast this domain with the other two.[10]

[10] Curiously, in Armenian, whose system resembles 'middle' systems, general verbs of motion are used mainly in the FLOATING domain, while both SWIMMING and SAILING employ dedicated verbs (resp. *loɣal* and *navel*).

In addition to languages showing trichotomy, we also observe languages that distinguish between all of the four basic domains. English, with its *swim* vs. *sail* vs. *float* vs. *drift* distinction, manifests a typical example of such a system distinguishing four manners of aquamotion. Of course, English may use other verbs for similar senses as well: as in many (if not most) languages, aquamotion is sometimes expressed with general verbs of motion such as *come* and *go*, although this time they are irrelevant for our typology because they do not specify any domain that is not specified by other lexical means. Further, English sometimes employs a Latin-based verb *navigate*, which was once associated primarily with aquamotion but does not seem to be so in the present-day language (cf. such examples as *We'll go in my car, and you can navigate*, which presumably need not be described as metaphorical). As in many other languages (such as Indonesian), the basic SAILING verb *sail* is derived from a noun, which possibly again points to the fact that it is not a native in the aquamotion system.

4.5.3 *Systems intermediate between the middle type and the poor type*

In addition to clear poor and middle systems, there are also systems that can be qualified as poor and middle at the same time. Such systems distinguish between the basic domains of aquamotion lexically, yet allow the most common aquamotion predicates to cover several domains.

The existence of systems that can be assigned to two types at the same time results from the fact that in some domains, several verbs may coexist and hence not be contrasted in any strict way. Then, like in a typical poor system, a single verb can be used for several domains, but for the expression of some manners of aquamotion it can appear on a par with other words. If this leads to a contrast between exactly three or four of the domains we proposed, the system can also be classified as middle.

An example of such a system is Georgian, which has a verb root *curva* serving for all of the four domains:

Georgian

(24) *bavšvebi* *cur-av-dnen* *mdinare-ši* *nap'ir-tan* *axlos.*
child(NOM:PL) AM-VT-IMPERF:3PL river-in bank-with near
'The children were swimming in the river near the bank.'

(25) *isini* *t'ba-ši* *navit* *da-cur-av-dnen.*
they lake-in boat(INS) INDIR-AM-VT-IMPERF:3PL
'They were sailing with a boat on the lake.'

(26) *mori* *mdinare-ši* *mo-cur-av-s.*
log(NOM) river-in HERE-AM-VT-PRS:3SG
'A log is drifting along the river.'

(27) *ak xomaldi ča-i-ʒir-a da amžamad narčenebi*
here ship(NOM) DOWN-REFL-sink-AOR:3SG and now remain(NOM:PL)
da-cur-av-s.
INDIR-AM-VT-PRS:3SG
'Here a ship went down, so now its remains are floating.'
(Maisak, Rostovtsev-Popiel, and Khurshudian 2007: 716–17)

However, in the SAILING domain it competes with general verbs of motion (28) (as well as with a peripheral dedicated sailing verb *naosnoba*), while FLOATING is regularly expressed by another dedicated aquamotion verb *t'ivt'iv-* (29):

Georgian
(28) *gemi navsadgul-ši še-mo-vid-a.*
ship(NOM) harbour-in IN-HERE-go-AOR:3SG
'The ship sailed in the harbour.'

(29) *xe c'q'al-ši t'ivt'iv-eb-s.*
wood(NOM) water-in AM-VT-PRS:3SG
'The wood floats (that is, it does not sink).'
(Maisak, Rostovtsev-Popiel, and Khurshudian 2007: 716)

A similar, yet different story is reported for Hindi by Khokhlova and Singh (2007). Here the verb *tairnaa* is found in the expressions of SWIMMING, SAILING, and FLOATING. However, in the SAILING domain it concurs with general verbs of motion, and in the FLOATING domain we also find the verb *utraanaa*. As regards DRIFTING, it is expressed by the third aquamotion verb *bahnaa*.

Qualifying such languages as belonging to two 'types' at the same time is justified as far as it adds additional perspectives and makes it possible to use data of these languages in recognizing generalizations concerning both poor and middle systems. However, we also admit the possibility that systems of this kind can be studied on their own.

4.5.4 *Rich systems*

Rich aquamotion systems also distinguish between at least SWIMMING, SAILING, and DRIFTING/FLOATING, but show additional lexical contrasts within at least some of the domains. The study of rich aquamotion systems is a study of these contrasts, which manifest linguistic diversity rather than any universal or near universal principles of categorization. Indeed, languages differ in which of the domains they elaborate and how many of them they elaborate.

In what follows, we will focus on those of the contrasts observed within SWIMMING, SAILING, DRIFTING, and FLOATING that seem most widespread or are of special theoretical interest.

The SWIMMING domain usually does not show much complexity. Given the anthropocentric nature of language together with the fact that human aquamotion (just as with any aquamotion of agentive species) is associated with this domain by default, one might expect to find a contrast based on humanness here. This expectation is only partly true, however: the human/non-human contrast is much more peripheral in the aquamotion field than in other fragments of the language. However, languages with SWIMMING verbs restricted mainly to human Figures exist. Thus, the Komi-Zyrian root *vartč'-* is used almost only for humans (and marginally for dogs),[11] while SWIMMING for most animals and fish is conveyed with a different verb *uj-*:

Komi-Zyrian

(30) *d'et'inka vartč'ə bereglan'.*
boy AM(PRS:3) bank(ALL)
'The boy is swimming to the bank.'

(31) *star'ik dorə ujis / *vartč'is č'eri i zavoditis šornitni.*
old.man edge(ILL) AM(PST:3) AM(PST:3) fish(NOM) and begin(PST:3) say(INF)
'The fish swam to the old man and began to speak.'
(Vostrikova 2007: 420–1)

In some other languages, there are verbs referring to SWIMMING whose subjects can only be human but whose use is restricted to the contexts related to sporting activities (e.g. *swuyeng hata* in Korean).

The contrasts observed within the SAILING domain are also few, yet most often they are easily recognizable. Some of them, namely those related to the specification of the location and means, have been already illustrated in section 4.2 with the Indonesian data. Other examples of verbs involving this kind of specification include the Nganasan verb *ŋəntə(u)-* 'sail on a wooden boat', the obsolete Portuguese verb *marear* 'sail the sea', and the Korean complex predicate *hanghay hata* 'sail the sea' (lit. 'navigation do'):

Korean

(32) *ilpon kisen-un cilwuhan hanghay han kkuth-ey*
Japanese ship-TOP boring(PART) navigation do(PART:PST) end-LOC
hangkwu-ey tach-ul naylyessta.
port-LOC anchor-ACC lower(PST:DECL)
'After the boring sailing, the Japanese ship dropped anchor at the port.'
(Lee and Maisak 2007: 650)

Remarkably many languages have or seem to have had special verbs for SAILING proper, that is, motion under sail. Sometimes—as in English (and also in Indonesian,

[11] This may be a consequence of the fact that this verb is derived of a verb with the meaning 'kick', which cannot be used with many swimming animals.

where the basic SAILING verb *berlayar* is derived from the noun *layar* 'sail')—these verbs have already obtained more or less neutral semantics. In other cases, however, they have retained their original semantic restrictions. Thus, Portuguese *velejar* and Dutch *zeilen* can express motion under sail only:

Dutch

(33) *Het maakt daarbij niet uit of ze zeilen*
it make(PRS:3SG) in.addition not out or they AM(PRS:3PL)
of op de motor varen.
or on ART engine AM(PRS:3PL)
'It does not matter whether they are sailing under sail or sailing on engine.'
(Divjak and Lemmens 2007: 163)

An important distinction found within the DRIFTING domain is that between directed motion and non-directed motion: while the parameter of directedness is found in other domains as well, it is here where it sometimes results in the contrast between several dedicated verbs. Again, Indonesian has already provided an example of this distinction (the contrast between the verbs *hanyut* and *terombang-ambing*), but it is by no means restricted to Indonesian. Japanese, for instance, has at least two verbs of DRIFTING: while *nagareru* denotes passive motion driven by current, *tadayou* describes passive motion in different directions (to and fro):

Japanese

(34) *Yama no yōna koori ga nagarete kuru.*
mountain GEN similar ice NOM AM:CNV come
'Ice floes similar to mountains drift here (with the stream).'

(35) *Kobune ga taikai o tadayou.*
boat NOM ocean ACC drift
'The boat drifts in the ocean.'
(Panina 2007: 622, 630)

Within the FLOATING domain, a clear cut-off line is found between 'simple floating' and 'being in a confined space'. The latter sometimes requires different expressions, which almost always involve existential or locative verbs. Thus, consider the following Arabic example:

Standard Arabic

(36) *tu:ǧadu qitʿatu khubzin fi: al-ħasaʾi.*
be.located(3F:SG) piece(NOM) bread(GEN) in ART-soup
'There is a piece of bread in the soup.'
(Letuchiy 2007: 491)

According to Letuchiy (2007), Arabic also possesses two dedicated FLOATING verbs *ʿa:ma* (denoting directed DRIFTING) and *Tafa:* (referring to floating up and being on the surface), so the appearance of a locative verb in (36) may at first look surprising. Note, however, that it is not obvious whether the 'subject' serves as Figure here, since quite often such utterances characterize the container in respect of its contents. Moreover, expressions like (36) are normally thetic. Clearly, it is this that relates the subdomain of 'being in a confined space' to existential expressions, which are also thetic (Sasse 1987) and frequently characterize the location. Presumably, the semantic properties of this subdomain show too much deviation from any aquamotion prototype, which can (albeit need not) be reflected by the choice of a non-aquamotion verb.

4.6 Conclusion and open ends

This chapter proposed a typology of aquamotion lexical (sub)systems which is based on the differentiation between the SWIMMING, SAILING, DRIFTING, and FLOATING domains. It should be emphasized once more that this distinction is not purely descriptive, since it is based on similarities between unrelated languages. The widespread occurrence of its manifestations points to the fact that it is not arbitrary and perhaps mirrors universal tendencies in conceptualization of aquamotion.

We find it important, however, to briefly outline here the difficulties to be faced while describing aquamotion in terms of SWIMMING, SAILING, DRIFTING, and FLOATING, which require specific attention.

First, despite the fact that we have presented the four domains as easily determinable, they seem to be non-homogeneous and presumably have more and less prototypical contexts. Certain less prototypical contexts may sometimes be expressed by a verb belonging to a different domain, which makes the borders between the domains somewhat fuzzy. For example, while individual species of fish are usually thought to swim, the motion of groups and schools of fish may be expressed by general verbs of motion, as is observed in Persian (Kuznetsova 2007: 243). Similarly, the motion of birds in water is sometimes considered less agentive than that of the prototypical SWIMMING Figure and is covered by FLOATING verbs—this is the case, for instance, in Standard Arabic (Letuchiy 2007: 486).

Second, such extensions of some domains at the expense of others may lead to the semantic reanalysis of aquamotion verbs, which may acquire semantics not based on the distinction between SWIMMING, SAILING, DRIFTING, and FLOATING. Thus in Hebrew, the root *šat*, which originally belonged to the FLOATING domain, is now used for the SAILING domain as well and instead is associated with a more abstract idea of aquamotion without visible effort, a sort of 'gliding' on a surface (Arad 2007). An even more dramatic shift evidently occurred with the Russian verb pair *plyt'/plavat'* mentioned in the previous section (see Makeeva and Rakhilina 2004 for details). In Old Russian, these verbs were seemingly used almost exclusively for DRIFTING/FLOATING, yet currently they cover the whole range of aquamotion contexts. A similar change happened in some Malay dialects of East Indonesia, where the verb *hanyut*, qualified as belonging to the DRIFTING domain in section 4.4, appears in contexts which apparently presuppose control (Mark Donohue, pers.com.). In quite a few languages we also observe the use of the SWIMMING verbs for the description of FLOATING, as in the following Indonesian example:

(37) *Sayur* *kol* *berenang.*
vegetable cabbage AM
'There is cabbage (in the soup, but it is a little and there does not seem to be anything else in the soup).'

Of course, this kind of shift requires an explanation and it is not always clear whether it should be based on the distinctions between various domains or some other semantic features.

Finally, the parameters that distinguish between the four domains are numerous and worthy of further investigation: presumably at least some of them may explain further diversity observed in rich aquamotion systems. It should be noted that a possible clue to the organization of the semantic field examined here may be found in different degrees of semantic markedness of various verbs (Lander 2008), but we are aware that this is only one of the possible perspectives.

Despite these complexities, the very principle of the cross-linguistic comparison of lexical systems based on distinguishing between various domains seems to be promising and may become a useful tool for discovering the laws that govern the lexical structures of languages.

5

Spatial directionals for robot navigation

ANDI WINTERBOER, THORA TENBRINK,
REINHARD MORATZ

5.1 Introduction

Previous research on spatial projective terms such as *to the left (of)* and *in front (of)* typically focuses on static (locative) usages. In these approaches it is often assumed that dynamic (directional) usages, i.e. those expressing motion in a direction specified by an expression such as *to the left* or *forward*, can be (more or less) directly derived from insights gained on the interpretation of the locative expressions (e.g. Herskovits 1986; Levinson 2003; Eschenbach 2005). This assumption goes back to a proposal by Miller and Johnson-Laird (1976) who state that dynamic usages are closely interrelated to static ones, as reflected by the fact that the same basic expressions can often be used in both kinds of contexts.

Without doubt, there is a high degree of overlap between these two kinds of usages of spatial terms. In fact, the interpretation of dynamic utterances potentially involves similar complexities to those identified in the literature for static usage. For example, in the sentence *Put the cup behind the plate*, an underlying relative reference system (cf. Levinson 2003) can be identified: since the plate does not have any intrinsic sides, the term *behind* needs to be interpreted relative to an observer's perspective. In *Put the rucksack behind you*, in contrast, the reference system is intrinsic because the addressee's intrinsic back is used for reference. These distinctions are well known from the investigation of static usage of projective terms.

However, directionals[1] also involve aspects that do not directly mirror static usage. For instance, static usage always involves an explicit referent (such as *the*

[1] In this chapter, following Eschenbach (2005), we use the term 'directional' for dynamic usage of projective terms only. This term stands in contrast to the term 'locative' for static usage.

cup in *the cup is to the right of the plate*) as well as an (implicit or explicit) relatum (here *the plate*). In contrast, in a very common usage of directionals it is not necessary to refer to an explicit reference object or a relatum, as in *turn left* (Tenbrink 2011). Moreover, this utterance may be interpreted either as a rotation or as a movement instruction. In both cases, the quantity of the movement needs to be determined; this cannot be derived directly from knowledge about the static usage of projective terms. Furthermore, as Tutton (this volume) shows, dynamic spatial relationships can be conceptualized in markedly different ways from static ones. Thus, the analysis of the acceptability features and the interpretational scope of directional terms is an important research field in its own right. In this chapter, we focus on a restricted scenario in which a particular subset of directionals is used regularly and spontaneously by speakers, namely, linguistic movement instructions to a robot. This kind of usage does not involve an entity other than the addressee (the mover), who is not expressed linguistically in instructions taking the imperative form. Accordingly, there is no conflict of reference frames.

One of the aims of the research project SFB/TR 8 on Spatial Cognition (Bremen/ Freiburg; funded by the German Science Foundation DFG) is to enable fluent and intuitive communication between humans and robots about spatial issues. Our basic scenario involves asking users who are not informed about the robot's capabilities to instruct the robot to move towards one of several similar objects present in a configuration. This scenario is essential for a broad range of service robot application contexts (Moratz et al. 2001). While it could be expected that users spontaneously refer directly to the goal object by using static locative terms, as in 'go to the box on the left', users unfamiliar with a system relatively quickly switch to low-level strategies such as 'go left' when advising a robot, especially if the goal-based strategy fails for some reason (Moratz and Tenbrink 2006). Thus, speakers frequently use projective terms dynamically, indicating directions in which a robot might move, avoiding the mention of objects. Therefore, we decided to complement our previous research on static projective terms by an investigation of a selected subset of directionals, leading to excellent performance results for instructions given spontaneously by users without the need for listing possible commands. Our robotic system starts from the interpretation of directional terms in specific ways that are motivated on theoretical grounds; its iterative development and evaluation complement these findings by showing whether the decisions are pragmatically adequate in the given human–robot interaction context.

5.2 The interpretation of projective terms in static vs. dynamic situations

Using a projective term involves indicating a spatial direction within a certain region of acceptability and with respect to an underlying reference system (Levinson 2003). Static projective terms denote spatial relations between two objects. One object serves as **relatum**, and the other (the referent or **locatum**) is positioned within a region surrounding a half axis (top, bottom, left, right, front, and back) with respect to the relatum (Vorwerg 2001). The underlying reference system (**intrinsic**, i.e. feature-based, or **relative**, i.e. viewpoint-based) determines how the directions are allocated. The size of the region depends on contextual factors (Carlson and Logan 2001), but is at all times limited to a half plane (Herskovits 1986: 181f.; Retz-Schmidt 1988). With unmodified projective terms the most likely position is on the half axis itself; with increasing distance from the axis, acceptability decreases. These effects have been treated formally in terms of 'spatial templates' (Logan and Sadler 1999); they are reflected linguistically by increased use of modifiers or combinations of projective terms (Zimmer et al. 1998). However, they also depend crucially on the discourse task (Klippel et al., this volume). Tenbrink (2007) shows that, in a situation in which an object needs to be identified, speakers adhere to a number of principles (see also Herrmann and Deutsch 1976) such as minimal effort, maximum contrast, and partner adaptation (with an imaginary partner). Thus, in contrastive reference, spatial terms are preferred that are discriminative without linguistic modifiers if possible under consideration of the other reference candidates present. In other discourse tasks where an object's location needs to be described with respect to another one, graded acceptability plays a much greater role (Vorwerg and Tenbrink 2007).

Directional expressions are often viewed as similar (and secondary) to the corresponding locative terms. Eschenbach (2005) proposes the following description:

> The directional use of a preposition refers to a path that leads into a region as characterized by the locative use of the same preposition. Combinations of *nach* ('to') or *von* ('from') with one of the locative adverbs form directional adverbial expressions. (...) [T]he spatial condition expressed by the adverb (e.g., *oben*) specifies the goal region (*nach oben*) or the origin (*von oben*) of the path the composite expression refers to.

Thus, goal (or source) regions are defined in a similar way to regions in static situations. For instance, it is possible to define a goal (or source) region on the grounds of different reference systems, using an explicit relatum. Furthermore, directionals are often used without an explicit relatum, as when an entity is moving autonomously in a direction specified by a directional, as in *turn left*. Such utterances are non-relational in the sense that no spatial relation between different entities is involved. They can be interpreted either as a rotation on the spot (see below), or they can be interpreted as a change of movement into the specified direction. Example (1) below would typically be interpreted using the external regions as defined by the addressee's internal sides (although different interpretations are possible if a different relatum is assumed). The movement *to the right* is then a movement into the goal region on the right-hand side of the addressee, as described by Eschenbach.

(1) *Move to the right!*

It can be assumed that the region of acceptability in such a situation is similar to the regions encountered in static usage, i.e. the most likely direction is a movement on (or *to*) the half axis itself. Similarly, a *forward* motion may in the standard case describe a motion at a zero-degree angle with respect to the moving entity's orientation. However, there are other options. In a context containing a path (such as a street with curves), it may need to be interpreted to mean something like *follow the path in a more-or-less forward direction* (e.g. Gryl et al. 2002). And if somebody who is already in a forward motion is addressed by *now to the right*, depending on context this might involve a motion towards, say, a 45-degree angle rather than 90-degree, since the forward motion is merged with the rightward motion. In a route instruction context, again, *turn left* induces a search for a path on the left-hand side of the moving entity; in particular, the future direction is determined by the first intersection of the current path with another path situated on the left of the mover (Gryl et al. 2002). Thus, depending on the discourse situation it may or may not be feasible to apply the notion of 'spatial template' in a similar way as for static usage. In fact, with respect to some contexts this notion seems to be rather irrelevant, since the interpretation of the spatial term depends on other factors rather than abstract spatial areas around a focal axis: for example, street networks can take on peculiar shapes and are referred to in various ways depending on context (cf. Klippel et al., this volume). Also, since directional usages often only give the goal direction without a clear end position, the exact distance that should be covered is unclear.

As already indicated, movements into a newly specified region need to be differentiated from rotational movements, in which an expression like *left* does not specify a future direction to move into, but only a reorientation towards the left side. This may not always be obvious: depending on context, a brief utterance like *to the right* or *rechts* may be intended to mean either or both. How rotational descriptions should be interpreted is addressed in, for instance, Habel (1999). Here too the expressions are underspecified with respect to the quantity of the movement; this may concern the distance to be covered in a specific direction as well as the angle of rotation. Both of these may be influenced by contextual factors which require further empirical investigation.

Terms such as *vorwärts/geradeaus* ('forward'/'straight ahead') carry a dynamic element already in their semantics, in contrast to the projective terms *to the left/front*, etc. While it could be assumed that, in dynamic contexts, these are approximately synonymous to *nach vorne* ('to the front'), there are in fact systematic differences in usage, as illustrated by the following:

(2) *Ich gehe nach vorne.* ('I am going to the front.')
(3) *Ich gehe vorwärts/geradeaus.* ('I am going forward/straight ahead.')

If uttered on a train, (2) would probably be interpreted to mean that the speaker intends to go towards the front section of the train, regardless of whether the speaker is currently oriented towards the train's front or happens to be looking in a different direction. But (3) can only mean a forward motion on the part of the speaker (defined by the speaker's orientation), which may or may not coincide with the forward direction of the train. With respect to the latter type of expression, Eschenbach (2005) notes:

> The adverbs *vorwärts, rückwärts,* and *seitwärts* ('forward', 'backward', 'sideways') specify the alignment of a path relative to the intrinsic reference system of the figure. *Vorwärts* ('forward') expresses that the direction of motion is in accordance with the intrinsic orientation of the body. Thus, the reference system is bound to be intrinsic to the figure and cannot be specified differently by contextual influences. The geometric condition can be described as the alignment of the object order of the path with the intrinsic access order of the figure. The lexeme *rückwärts* is morphologically related to the noun *Rücken* (the body-part 'back') and *seitwärts* to the noun *Seite* ('side'). *Rückwärts* ('backward') expresses that the backside of the moving figure (...) is leading, i.e., precedes the center. Correspondingly, *seitwärts* ('sideways') can be used to say that a lateral side of the moving figure is leading.

The lateral axis does not offer such a distinction between only-intrinsic and more flexible expressions in German, except for *seitwärts*, which is unspecified for direction on the axis. In English, *leftward(s)* and *rightward(s)* seem to be available though used infrequently.

(4) *Ich gehe nach rechts.* ('I am going to the right.')

The interpretation of (4), uttered on a train, would probably depend on the speaker's orientation, as in (3), in spite of the fact that the surface form corresponds to that in (2). But this intuition may be due to the fact that the internal front and back regions of trains are much more prominent than their right and left sides. A different situation is provided, for example, in reference to the regions within an opera house, which are often even explicitly marked as 'left' and 'right'. Furthermore, it is likely that the interpretation of *nach vorn* ('to the front') is influenced by the availability and relevance of background entities with internal regions, such as the train in (2). Without such a mutually agreed-on background entity, a forward motion of the speaker may be more relevant, rendering the utterance synonymous to (3). In English a forward motion can only be expressed by *forwards, straight (ahead)*, and perhaps *ahead*, but not *to the front*; for the German *nach vorne*, the case is less obvious. Clearly, targeted empirical investigations are necessary to shed further light on these phenomena. Our experimental study described in the next section contributes to this issue by showing to what extent speakers in a human–robot movement instruction context spontaneously use *nach vorne*.

5.3 Human–robot interaction and directionals

In this section, we examine and point out potential difficulties in a real-world application, adopting a computational perspective. While we do not attempt to account for the full range of interpretational options sketched in this chapter so far, we have implemented the most fundamental subset, namely the usage of a directional to provide a future direction for a moving entity (a robot) without reference to an external relatum. Our aim was to achieve pragmatic adequacy with respect to the envisioned human–robot interaction scenario. In our research programme within the project SFB/TR 8 Spatial Cognition, we aim to enable efficient and intuitive communication between human users and robots. In our current target setting, a robot is instructed to move to a particular place; the users achieve this by relying on their own intuitions rather than a list of commands. Nowadays, direct control devices (e.g. joysticks or graphical user interfaces) can achieve near optimal results without linguistic modules (Tsuji and Tanaka 2005). Such a direct control system can benefit from multimodal interaction methods combining gestures and verbal commands from a predefined list (Trouvain et al. 2001). However, such systems are less suitable than language-based control systems for more advanced generic (for example conditional) tasks and interaction scenarios in which humans and robots are not co-present. For the first steps towards speech-based human–robot interaction, it makes sense to start by enabling direct natural language control in individual tasks in face-to-face scenarios, even if from an engineering point of view these scenarios could be solved by non-linguistic means more easily. Any comprehensive robotic system capable of interpreting generic natural language instructions would certainly be equipped to deal with direct speech-based commands as well. Generally, it is advantageous to enable simple control in face-to-face scenarios before moving on to more challenging generic instructions: for example, in order to familiarize new users with the speech interface (Moratz and Tenbrink 2008). Although linguistic motion control may not be a technological novelty, we do not know of accounts in the literature where naive users interact with a robot by using directionals. The latter is our particular focus.

In a human–robot interaction scenario in which a human controls a physically embodied agent like a mobile robot, not only static objects but the entire (dynamic) physical environment can be referred to. Bos et al. (2003), for instance, present a system capable of interpreting goal based (place-related) instructions such as *go to the kitchen.* Kruijff et al. (2007) and Spexard et al. (2006) describe robotic systems able to learn relationships and locations in the environment with the help of a human tutor using natural language. However, one major finding of our own previous empirical work (Moratz and Tenbrink 2008) is that participants spontaneously produce incremental (step-by-step) rather than object-based descriptions. Thus, in a scenario where users are not informed about the robot's capabilities and are asked to instruct a robot to move to one of several similar objects indicated by the experimenter, they tend to use directionals such as *move forward and then to the right* rather than goal-based static spatial instructions such as *move to the object on your right.* Since this was an unexpected result, previous versions of our system did not account for the former kind of instruction. In Winterboer (2004), an implementation of directionals for the same kind of task was successfully accomplished. In the following, we describe the main aspects of this system, which was developed in several iterations on the basis of the results of experimentation. We discuss problem areas encountered during the development process and present the solutions found in the current implementation.

5.3.1 *The robot system architecture*

Our aim in the present work was to develop a speech interface for allowing intuitive control of a mobile robot in navigation tasks. The deployed system consisted of an AIBO robot (Figure 5.1), a speech recognition and natural language understanding module using Nuance Communications tools, and a robot motion control module. Among other possible behaviours, AIBO robots can move in several directions as well as rotate on the spot. Nuance Communication's speech recognizer allows specification of a speech recognition package on the basis of their grammar specification language (GSL), which is used for both language modelling and parsing, and requires a careful design process taking into account the linguistic knowledge of the domain. The recognized utterances trigger predefined actions which are sent to the robot by the robot motion control module, AIBOControl, via WLAN. To carry out the predefined actions, a navigation component based on AIBOControl, acting as a compact version of the powerful SimGT2003 (Burkhard et al. 2002), was implemented. In our implementation, the robot could not detect or recognize objects.

For the experiments, we enabled the AIBO robot to perform forward and backward motions, to stop a current movement, to turn on the spot, and to skew, i.e. to move in a direction of approximately 45 degrees to the left or right for a distance of one metre (see Figure 5.2 below). The skewed movement was implemented in order to combine simple forward movements with turns, as could be intended, for example, by an utterance like *go to the right.* The decision to use a 45-degree angle was largely arbitrary, but motivated by the idea that a default forward direction is

FIGURE 5.1 Sony AIBO ERS-210

combined with a partial reorientation to the left or right. Though one may argue that a 90-degree angle for such instructions might be more intuitive, we hypothesized that restricting the angle of such a skewed movement would support the user in approximating the goal in small steps. This decision was additionally motivated by the results of pre-tests highlighting that 90-degree angles were rarely, if at all, beneficial (or in fact used) for solving the predefined navigation tasks. Moreover, in our system, all lateral directionals such as *(turn) left/right* were interpreted to indicate only reorientation no matter whether the term *turn* was actually used or not; thus, only instructions explicitly containing path-of-motion verbs such as *go* were considered to indicate movement in addition to reorientation.

For every movement type, different linguistic variations could be uttered. To define the content of our lexicon, containing approximately ninety words, we took into account the theoretical considerations described above as well as the variability of users' linguistic choices that we observed in earlier experiments (e.g. Moratz and Tenbrink 2006). The user study described in this chapter addresses our experience with a system that was specifically designed to deal exclusively with incremental (i.e. not goal object based) utterances.

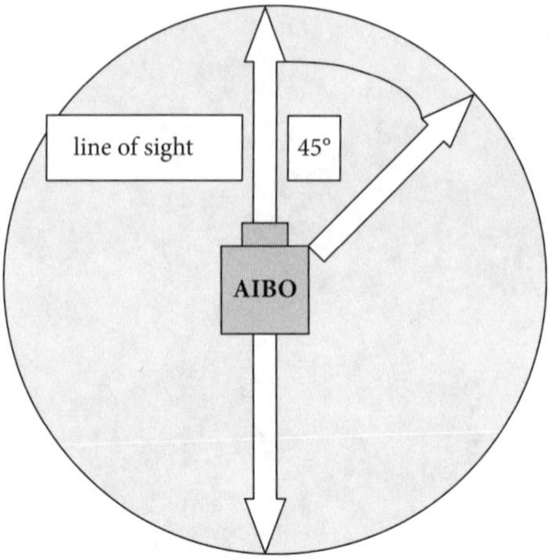

FIGURE 5.2 Possible AIBO robot motions

The system interpreted utterances such as *geradeaus (gehen)* ('(go) straight on'), *vor/vorwärts* ('forwards'), and *geh/lauf/fahre* ('go/walk/drive') as a *forward movement. Backward movements* could be expressed by *zurück/rückwärts (gehen)* ('(go) backward') and the like. *Left* and *right rotational movements/turns* could be triggered by *dreh links/rechts* ('turn left/right'), *links* ('left'), *nach links* ('to the left'), and similar terms; *left* and *right skewed movements* by *geh links/rechts* ('go left/right'), etc. Finally, a *stop* could be expressed by *stop/halt* ('stop'). The full lexicon can be found in the Appendix.

Thus, a range of semantically similar expressions was treated as if they were synonyms. For example, apart from directionals indicating a forward movement, the forward direction was treated as a default for underspecified indications of movement (*go*). In general, although the interpretation decisions do not necessarily account for subtle differences in the expressions' semantics (as, for example, addressed by Nikanne and van der Zee, this volume), the experimental results will show whether the deployed procedure is pragmatically adequate for the purpose at hand. This is a sensible approach, especially in light of the fact that a number of issues are still unresolved in the literature, including the preferred angle for a skewed movement or a turn. This question is only relevant in scenarios where no additional information can be derived from the scenario itself, as, for example, information provided by a street network (Klippel et al., this volume). In accord with the findings reported above, the expressions *nach vorne* ('to the front') and *nach hinten* ('to the back') were not implemented; it was assumed that these expressions would not occur in the given context, since internal reference systems were less likely to be employed (cf. section 5.2 above).

5.3.2 *Experimental study*

We asked participants to instruct the AIBO robot to move from a given start position to a goal position by using natural language instructions. Based on our previous work we expected that naive users, who were not informed about the robot's capabilities or its inability to detect objects, would spontaneously choose an incremental instruction strategy by using directionals to control the robot. To test this hypothesis, we did not tell the users what kind of instruction they should use, in order to find out about their intuitive strategies. Furthermore, there were a number of open questions that needed to be addressed in order to allow for effective and intuitive instructions using directionals. For example, prior to the study we could not know whether the participants would prefer continuous robot movements until a definite verbal 'stop' command was used, or whether limited movements until a specific distance was covered would be preferable. In addition, the pragmatic adequacy of the above interpretation decisions needed to be examined.

After an evaluation phase, we performed a revision of the existing system. To achieve a functional speech interface, several further experiments were conducted with the revised system. Using this iterative approach of alternating model building and empirical phases, a direct feedback between simulation and experiment was achieved. Altogether, the experiment was carried out in five stages (experiment parts) involving varying numbers of participants.

5.3.3 *Procedure*

The experiment was conducted in rooms of the University of Bremen. Twenty-one participants (fifteen male; six female) were asked to navigate the AIBO robot to particular objects or locations pointed at by the experimenter, using German language instructions. Two participants took part twice (at the beginning and at the end of the experimental study). The mean age of the participants was twenty-nine (range: 19–44). Thirteen of the twenty-one participants had a computer science background. The experiment took approximately fifteen to twenty minutes per participant. Altogether, ninety-three navigation tasks using various configurations were completed.

The participants sat in front of a desk and were equipped with a headset for instructing the robot. They were requested to deal with several scenes (four configurations out of eight), which consisted of a start position and a goal position, plus up to four objects (identical rectangular white cardboard boxes of the same size and material, measuring approx. 35 × 25 × 30cm) arranged in a configuration (see figure 5.3). The marked area of the room used for the experiments measured roughly five metres by four, including the area where the participants sat. The experimental setting was carefully designed to minimize the high variety of factors that may influence the performance of a speech-based navigation task. For example, markings on the floor guaranteed that the positions of the robot and the obstacles, as

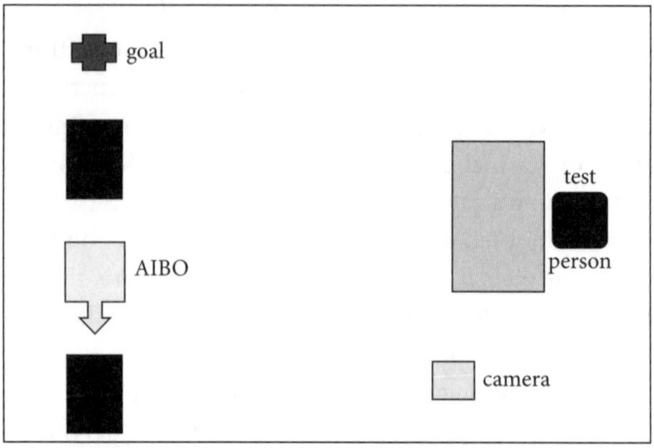

FIGURE 5.3 A bird's-eye view of the layout of one of the configurations used

well as the goal could be precisely replicated for each participant. In addition, to avoid order effects, the order of the particular navigation tasks was randomized.

Each time the robot arrived at the intended goal position (marked by a 30 × 30cm paper cross on the floor), the configuration of the objects was changed. The participants did not get a response if their instruction was not understood by the speech recognition; in fact, the robot did not talk at all. If the user's instruction could be interpreted by the robot, the robot started to move; otherwise, nothing happened. Thus, in accordance with the methodology proposed by Fischer (2003), the test participants did not receive any hints concerning the implemented computational model or the linguistic abilities of the robot. If the participants' instructions were not successfully recognized, they had no indication regarding the reasons, and therefore developed their own intuitive strategies for achieving successful communication.

5.3.4 *Results*

Altogether, we collected 1,536 instructions, 1,181 of which were successfully recognized and carried out by the robot, yielding a recognition rate of 76.9 per cent. The following general results pertain to all experiment parts.

Our hypothesis that participants would primarily use incremental instructions (i.e. directionals and motion verbs such as *go*) to instruct the robot was confirmed. In fact, only one participant directly referred to the goal position in four instructions before turning to incremental instructions. Note that in our previous experiments, described in Moratz and Tenbrink (2006), those participants whose initial incremental instructions were not successful typically did not spontaneously switch to the goal-based strategy. If they started out using a goal-based strategy and their instruction failed for some reason, they usually directly switched to the (non-implemented) incremental strategy. In the present experiment, the users did not attempt to use a different level of instruction, such as goal-based instructions, after unsuccessful attempts. Instead, a typical reaction was a modification of the utterances concerning lexical or syntactical choice. This result corresponds to earlier findings according to which users tend to switch to lower-, but not higher-level strategies in case of failure (Fischer and Moratz 2001).

The range of expressions we expected from previous experiments as well as theoretical considerations corresponded fairly exactly to the instructions actually used by the participants. Only forty-seven instructions contained an expression that was not contained in the lexicon; therefore, 96.9 per cent of all utterances were theoretically interpretable (the remaining failures were due to speech recognition rather than system coverage). This is an impressively high proportion, especially in light of the fact that the participants were not previously informed about the robot's capabilities.

As expected, the specific directional terms *nach vorne* ('forwards') and *nach hinten* ('backwards') were almost never used, confirming our expectation that they were not typical in the given context. However, the fact that one participant did use *nach vorne* four times (before switching to *geradeaus* ('(go) straight') shows that this usage is not entirely ruled out.

The participants did not exhibit fundamental problems with the interpretations of their instructions. They seemed to be surprised about the skewed movement (the robot's reaction to the—rarely used—instructions containing path-of-motion verbs plus lateral directionals, e.g. *go left*); the simple turning behaviour (which was the result of all verb-less instructions plus those containing the verb *turn*) appeared to be easier to handle and was used almost exclusively. This seems to be related to the fact that this was the only compound movement, consisting of a turn on the spot and a movement in a new direction. In addition, it was not a useful kind of movement in most of the configurations, as the size of the room and the location of obstacles and goal positions in the room usually required fine-grained rather than extensive robot movements. In general, however, the robot appeared to behave in an expected way, apart from a number of problems described below.

These results show that the initially implemented lexicon was suitable to a very high degree. The few—and only—modifications to the lexicon we carried out in the course of the iterative process concerned adding a 180-degree turn and removing the term *weiter* ('continue'); which was interpreted as a forward motion to begin with, but, due to the deployed keyword spotting method, turned out to be problematic in connection with instructions indicating other directions of movement. Since there was no clash between the users' intentions and the robot's reactions, there was no need for further modifications at this point. The other terms that were uttered by the participants and that were not contained in the lexicon were only used once or twice. In order to keep grammar and lexicon as concise as possible so as to obtain the best possible recognition results, we did not add such exceptional expressions to the

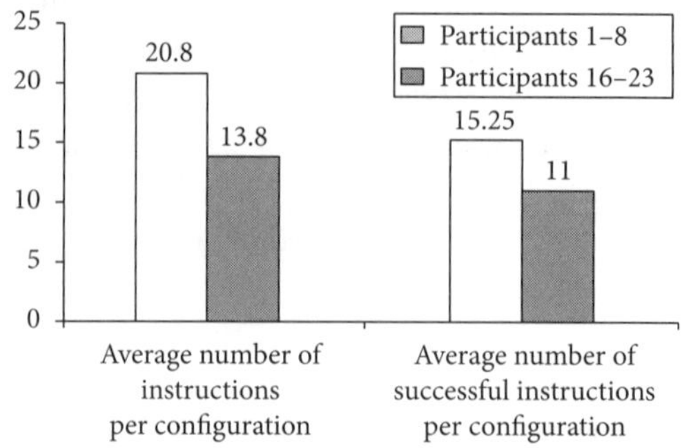

FIGURE 5.4 Average number of instructions/successful instructions required per navigation task

lexicon. However, we implemented a range of other modifications, as will be outlined shortly.

A high influence of individual differences could be observed. For instance, some participants easily lost their temper when the robot did not react as quickly as expected. Sometimes there were delays between an instruction and the corresponding robot movement, caused by the high demands of working memory required by the speech recognizer. Then, the participants repeated their instruction instead of waiting for the processing of the last utterance. Furthermore, some utterances were not correctly recognized because the instructions were uttered too quietly. An appropriate adjustment of the headset and a clear articulation supported the recognition. Finally, there were relatively big differences between the individual performances of participants. When the first instructions were not successful—i.e. the robot did not move in the intended direction or did not move at all—some participants blamed themselves for the bad experiment progression instead of putting the blame on the speech recognizer or other technical modules. Therefore, their problems only increased when they noticed that the AIBO robot did not act as expected. In general, the participants who were most successful were those who acted self-confidently and pronounced their utterances with a clear articulation.

There was an overall increase of success throughout the study, as could be expected due to the gradual improvement of the system. To illustrate this improvement we compare the first and the last experiment part. While it took the first eight participants on average about eighty-three verbal instructions per person to solve their navigation tasks, the last eight needed only about fifty-eight for theirs. Figure 5.4 illustrates this result, showing the average number of instructions needed per configuration along with the average of successful instructions (where the AIBO robot acted as expected). The relation between uttered and successfully executed instructions improved only slightly during the experiments with the first and the last eight participants (76.1 to 80.0 per cent); thus, the main difference concerns the precise way in which the instructions were interpreted. Note that instructions may be successful (causing the robot to perform the intended movement) without leading directly to the goal position, which is why, in more efficient trials, speakers used fewer successful instructions to reach their goals. In addition, not only did the last eight participants require fewer instructions on average to arrive at the goal position, they also solved their tasks in less time. The average duration per configuration until the goal position was reached decreased from roughly eighty-eight seconds (participants 1–8) to approximately sixty-five seconds (participants 16–23). Therefore, the revisions clearly enabled more effective robot navigation.

To investigate whether these results could be attributed solely to the learning experience of those two participants who were tested twice (at the beginning and at the end of the study), we carried out t-tests, which reveal that, in both cases, first, significantly fewer instructions were used no matter whether the data of these two participants was included, and second, significantly more instructions per configuration were successful after the modifications ($p < .05$). In the following, we give a more detailed account of the system's iterative development process.

5.3.5 *Iterative development process*

One of the open questions prior to the experiment had been whether the robot should carry out a continuous movement when it was instructed to move in a certain direction or to turn, or whether it should stop after a certain distance or angle. We started from the former variant, assuming that a continuous movement would feel natural to users, since they would not need to repeat instructions. Therefore, whenever a directional was recognized, the AIBO robot performed the corresponding movements in a continuous way and only stopped when the user uttered an explicit instruction, such as *Stop*.

However, it turned out that the delays between the uttered instructions and the robot reactions caused problems. Participants did not anticipate the continuous robot movements and therefore the robot frequently overshot the mark. To deal with this problem, we first reduced the speed of the robot motions when a turn instruction was recognized, in order to decrease the covered distance or angle. When it turned out that this was not sufficient, the movements were also given a restricted value. For instance, the turning movement was restricted to 45 degrees, mirroring the implemented skewed movement. The forward and backward movements were restricted to one metre each. After these modifications to the robot's motion control module, the users' interactions with the speech interface were more efficient, which clearly improved the results. Crucially, the participants seemed to get used to the restricted quantity of the movement (distance or angle) rather quickly and could focus on the next movement to be accomplished, because they did not need to stop the current movement via a new instruction. After some further experimental iterations, we settled on turning angles of 30 degrees, which seemed to be pragmatically optimal in our scenario (see Winterboer 2004 for details). This was mainly due to the properties of the predetermined spatial configurations serving as the experiment's environment. Overall, it turned out during the experiments that to successfully navigate the robot in the room allocated for the experiments, measuring just over twenty square metres, participants required fine-grained rather than extensive movements to manoeuvre through narrow passages (between two obstacles) or around obstacles, for example.

Since there were still some problems with delayed responses, we furthermore updated the prioritization of the *stop* instruction within the GSL recognition grammar in order to let the speech recognizer always choose this instruction in the case of an ambiguous utterance. Further improvement could be obtained by decreasing the WLAN traffic volume by optimally reducing the AIBO sensor data (e.g. camera data) that were automatically transferred via WLAN from the robot to the AIBO-Control robot motion control module. This effect was further supported by carrying out the experiments in a WLAN traffic-free testing environment in which no other WLAN traffic could affect the connection, and where one router was exclusively allocated to transfer the data between the AIBO robot and the computer operating the robot motion control module.

Another modification affected the lexicon as well as the motion behaviour of the AIBO robot. In some of the experiments the participants tried to about-face the robot with the two phrases:

(5) *Drehe dich um 180 Grad* ('turn (yourself) 180 degrees')
(6) *Umdrehen* ('turn around')

Therefore, we added both phrases to the lexicon and included the corresponding movement in the robot motion control module.

5.3.6 *Summary of the human–robot experiment*

We have presented the iterative development of a speech interface for an AIBO robot, aiming at solving navigation tasks by intuitive natural language instructions. By evaluating the behaviour of the users in connection with the robot's reactions and by carrying out several modifications, an empirical validation of the speech interface was obtained. Our results show that the initial interpretation decisions with respect to a range of linguistic expressions (less than ninety words in the lexicon) turned out to be pragmatically adequate. The users could, with a high degree of success, use the kind of language they intuitively expected to be successful. Users did not, with one exception, attempt to use goal-based instructions even though they were never told about the robot's capabilities and incapabilities. Thus, our expectations originating in theoretical (literature-based) considerations as well as previous experiments with a different system were confirmed. The remaining problems that were detected and addressed throughout the study primarily concerned other kinds of factor. Here, the most important revisions were the decrease of the turning angles as well as the speed, the prioritization of the *stop* command within the GSL grammar, and the reduction of the data flow between the robot and the robot motion control module. These modifications resulted in a reliable and, even for uninformed users, easily-controllable speech interface.

One question that calls for further experimentation concerns the ways in which turning behaviour and movements in a non-straight direction (skewed movements) could be expressed linguistically and interpreted optimally by the robot. In the present solution, it turned out to be easiest to have the robot turn on the spot and then, with a separate instruction, let it move forward. But other solutions are conceivable, since the semantics of directionals like *rechts* and *links* are both ambiguous (because they can denote a rotation as well as a movement in a non-straight direction) and underspecified (because angles and distances are not predefined). The participants' slight surprise with respect to the skewed moving behaviour of the robot highlight this observation. Further experimentation could shed more light on this issue.

5.4 Conclusions and outlook

The use and interpretation of (spatial) projective terms in natural discourse are influenced by a considerable variety of factors, both in static and in dynamic kinds of context. While in some dynamic contexts various underlying reference systems come into play, similar to those used in static scenarios, other usage contexts do not involve entities as relata and are therefore conceived of as non-relational. The motion instructions used in the presented human–robot interaction setting are cases in point. Such terms involve few problems; since the robot's intrinsic movements are the sole target of reference, the variability of interpretation is greatly reduced. This leads to a high pragmatic adequacy of a relatively simple system that interprets a range of different expressions in a predefined way, mapping them to suitable robot reactions. As our experiments have shown, incremental motion descriptions based on dynamic projective terms are an essential part of any efficient and robust motion command strategy for navigating mobile robots intuitively. Nevertheless, the ambiguity and underspecification of directional terms leaves room for different ways of interpreting the instructions. This needs to be carefully balanced with respect to the requirements of an actual scenario. For such a goal, an iterative system development starting from theoretical assumptions is particularly useful, as our example demonstrates. The step-by-step method can meet some of the challenges posed by the formalization and implementation of linguistic encoding of spatial complexity, illustrated by Weisgerber (2008).

Eventually, in order to cover a greater range of interaction settings, a number of system modifications will be necessary to account for the complexities involved in employing directionals for purposes that go beyond simple robot movements. Furthermore, a number of aspects concerning the use and interpretation of directionals still require empirical research, not only in a human–robot interaction situation but also with respect to psycholinguistic issues. Thus, while our robotic system starts from a simple scenario, the present research has outlined some of the problems and ambiguities involved in more complex kinds of situations that need to be dealt with in the future.

Acknowledgements

The experiments were conducted when the first author was at the Transregional Collaborative Research Center 'Spatial Cognition', Faculty of Mathematics and Informatics, University of Bremen. Funding by the Deutsche Forschungsgemeinschaft (DFG) is gratefully acknowledged. We also appreciate support and many fruitful discussions with researchers in the SFB/TR 8 and the University of Edinburgh.

Appendix: contents of the lexicon

Forward movement:
geradeaus ('straight'); *geradeaus gehen* ('go straight')
vor / vorwärts ('forwards')
geh / gehe / lauf / laufe / fahr / fahre ('go/walk / drive'); *los / fahr los* ('start (moving)')
weiter ('continue')

Backward movement:
zurück / rückwärts ('backward'); *zurück gehen / zurück laufen / rückwärts gehen / rückwärts laufen* ('go/walk/drive backward')

Left turn (right turn is treated equivalently):
dreh links / drehe links / drehe dich nach links / drehe nach links ('turn left')
links ('left')
nach links ('to the left')
etwas nach links / ein bißchen links ('a little to the left')
Drehung links / links herum / links umdrehen ('left rotation')

Left skewed movement (right skewed movement is treated equivalently):
geh links / gehe links / fahr links / fahre links / links gehen ('go/drive left')
lauf nach links / fahr nach links ('walk/drive to the left')

Stop
stop / halt ('stop')

180-degree turn
drehe dich um 180 Grad ('turn (yourself) 180 degrees'); *umdrehen* ('turn around')

6

The role of structure and function in the conceptualization of direction

ALEXANDER KLIPPEL, THORA TENBRINK, DANIEL R. MONTELLO

6.1 Introduction

The specification of mental conceptualizations of spatial information is a lively topic in several disciplines (e.g. Coventry and Garrod 2004; Mark et al. 1995; Regier and Carlson 2001). In linguistics, for example, the specification of spatial relations as indicated by projective terms (e.g. *left*, *right*, *above*, *in front*) has led to research on how the conceptualization of a particular spatial relation is influenced by contextual parameters (e.g. Coventry and Garrod 2004; Herskovits 1986; Regier 1996) and how a resulting conceptualization is mapped onto a linguistic expression. One crucial aspect reflected, for example, in the notion of a spatial template (Carlson-Radvansky and Logan 1997), is the finding that projective terms can be applied best when referring to a position directly on a focal axis: they are typically combined with linguistic modifiers when they deviate from that axis (Zimmer et al. 1998). Besides the de facto geometric relation between two objects (called referent and relatum by Levinson 2003), several factors influence the choice of a specific reference system and the assignment of a linguistic category (and a corresponding linguistic expression) that specifies the spatial relation between them. Van der Zee and Eshuis (2003) list the following factors: (a) the function of the objects as, for example, detailed in the extra-geometric functional framework by Coventry and Garrod (2004); (b) force dynamic properties (e.g. Talmy 1988); (c) the part structure; and (d) orientation and movement. Most of these are also relevant for other spatial term categories, such as topological expressions (e.g. *in* and *on*). Van der Zee and Eshuis (2003) additionally specify features of the referent as such that influence the reference axis categorization: axis length, contour expansion, and curvature of the main plane of symmetry.

They combine these factors in their spatial feature categorization model to generate predictions on reference axis categorization derived from the spatial features of a referent for the purpose of intrinsic directional reference on both the horizontal and the vertical plane.

While Coventry and Garrod (2004), in their extra-geometric functional framework, focus on functional aspects that are external to the geometric features of a spatial relation, the model by van der Zee and Eshuis (2003) emphasizes the influence of the geometric features of the referent as such. In the area of route directions, the structure in which route-following actions take place is specifically crucial, as it influences the conceptualization of the movement. This idea will be addressed and elaborated in this chapter. We will develop a framework that allows for characterizing conceptualizations of actions (movement) at intersections by taking into account the angle of direction change but also the configuration of the intersection as such. Further aspects, such as the availability of additional environmental features (e.g. landmarks) are also decisive (e.g. Daniel and Denis 1998). Therefore, route directions may differ from other spatial localization tasks for which it is sufficient to choose a reference axis to guide the mapping of a linguistic expression, the direction in question, and deviations thereof, as presented and discussed in Chapter 5 in this book.

Route directions are widely studied, as they allow for investigating cognitive processes at the interface of language and space, language and graphics, and the conceptualization of motion events (Allen 1997; Daniel and Denis 1998; Habel 1988; Ligozat 2000; Tappe 1999; Tversky and Lee 1999). Due to their spatially restricted domain—routes are intrinsically linear and not multidimensional—route directions have the potential to reveal cognitive processes that otherwise are difficult to access. For example, the linearization problem in language (Levelt 1989) is alleviated by the fact that the order of a linear structure is regularly expressed verbally in route directions (Denis et al 1999).

Zwaan and Radvansky (1998) proposed to view language not primarily as information that is analysed syntactically and semantically and then stored in memory, but rather as a set of instructions on how to create a mental representation of a given situation. In this spirit, we aim to investigate how an appropriate situation model is instantiated that contains just the right amount of information at a decision point in a route instruction, yielding a set of cognitively ergonomic route directions (e.g. Daniel and Denis 1998; Lovelace et al. 1999). In the present chapter, we therefore focus on the question of what aspects of a spatial situation are verbalized at decision points in order to convey the information necessary to identify the intended direction to take, and how this influences the verbalization of the spatial relation itself. More precisely, how do people conceptualize and verbalize the actions to be performed at decision points in city street networks, depending on the general structure of a decision point (e.g. an intersection), the action itself (the change of direction, which is the functional aspect), and additional salient features (landmarks)?

6.2 Structure and function

A core element of wayfinding theory is the distinction between structure and function, which is essential for characterizing the conceptual level of route information (Klippel, Tappe et al. 2005). As the conceptual level is the basis for the externalization of knowledge in several modalities (e.g. Jackendoff 1997; Tversky and Lee 1999), the distinction between structure and function gains additional importance to account for the constraints induced by different representational media such as language or graphics. This approach has been inspired by work in spatial cognition (Montello 2005) in which a distinction is drawn between a behavioural pattern – a route – and the environment – a path. In contrast to laboratory studies on spatial relations that do not take place in a natural spatial context, our approach builds on the distinction between routes and paths, which we view as pertinent for conceptualization processes in interaction with spatial environments (see Figure 6.1).

In our approach, structure denotes the layout of elements physically present in the spatial environment that are relevant for route directions and wayfinding. This

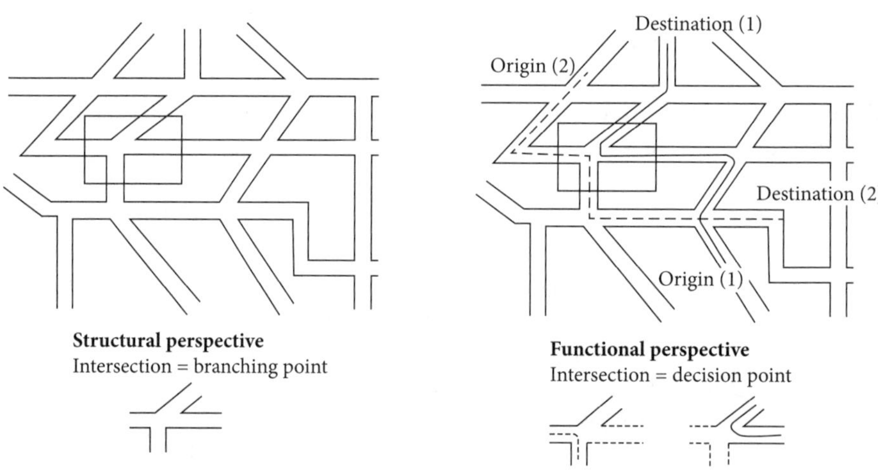

FIGURE 6.1 Distinguishing between structural and functional aspects of route information. Without any action taking place, an intersection is referred to as a branching point, i.e. the structural aspect (left part). In the course of route following, an intersection becomes a decision point and the action to take place demarcates functionally relevant parts (right part) (Klippel 2003). With kind permission from Springer Science & Business Media: Klippel, A. (2003). Wayfinding choremes. In W. Kuhn et al. (eds.): COSIT 2003, LNCS 2825.

comprises, for example, the number of branches at a street intersection and the angles between those branches. Function is related to the actions that take place in spatial environments. The functional characterization is contained within the structural characterization; that is, routes exist within those parts of path networks that are necessary for specifying the action to be performed.

6.3 Direction concepts at intersections

The general structure of a branching point is its spatial layout (the physical structure); that is, the size and number of branches, and angles between the branches. Examples for different general structures are T-intersections, circles, forks, different numbers of branches, highway exits, and so forth. The actions performed at an intersection can be roughly classified according to different direction models, for example, as left, right, and straight. Additionally, superimposed rule structures may come into play (which are not addressed in detail in this chapter), such as turning restrictions or the Australian hook turn. These rules are especially important for the design of navigation systems that provide the navigator with information to establish a suitable situation model.

The performed action itself, i.e. a turn with a specific angle of direction change, can be conceptualized with respect to the spatial structure in which it is embedded. For example, a half right turn may be conceptualized differently at a four-way intersection as compared to a fork in the road (see Figure 6.2). From our experiences

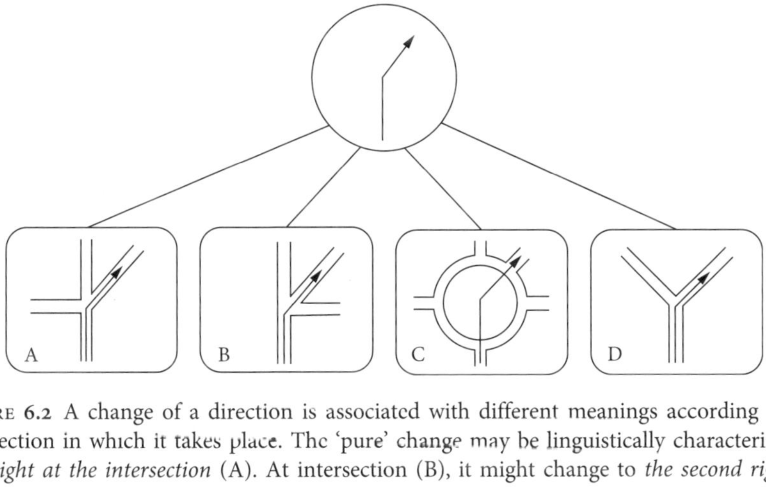

FIGURE 6.2 A change of a direction is associated with different meanings according to the intersection in which it takes place. The 'pure' change may be linguistically characterized as *veer right at the intersection* (A). At intersection (B), it might change to *the second right*; at roundabout (C), it changes to *the second exit*, and at (D), it becomes *fork right* (Klippel, Hansen et al. 2005).

with route direction corpora, we derived some first ideas on strategies speakers adopt to assign verbal labels to actions occurring in different structures. There are standard intersections, like a four-way intersection, and standard actions, like *left*, *right*, and *straight*. If standard actions occur at standard intersections, unmodified projective terms are used, for example, *turn right* (at the intersection). Additionally, people tend to adopt a direction model that comprises axes and sectors, expressed, for instance, by modifications of the projective terms if the angle of the intended direction departs from the prototypical axis. For example, *turn right* may change to *turn sharp right* and may be modified to *turn very sharp right*. While these directions allow some flexibility, i.e. they can be modelled as sectors, the concept for *straight* seems to be an axis and is applied only to this axis as far as simple intersections are concerned (Klippel et al. 2004). Otherwise, *straight* can also be interpreted in the sense of *follow the course of the street*, even if there are curves (Gryl et al. 2002).

The strategies participants adopt change if the action to be instructed takes place (a) at a complex intersection or (b) if competing branches require a disambiguation of the situation. For the identification of objects in a spatial configuration, Tenbrink (2005) provides results on how the contrast of competing objects can be enhanced by choosing a suitable reference system and spatial axis that allow for unambiguous reference, without necessitating a high level of precision. The exact spatial location is usually not specified if there are no competing objects close by, and projective terms are modified only if necessitated by the presence of competing objects on or near the same spatial axis within a reference system. An exception is the case of a position directly between two axes, in which case both projective terms are combined, in accord with the principle of redundant verbalization formulated by Herrmann and Deutsch (1976).

Klippel and Montello (2004) present some ideas on how contrastive reference can be achieved in route directions. Besides rendering the direction concept precise, for example, by providing detailed descriptions according to the direction model, and possibly relying on clock directions or an absolute reference system, speakers seem to adopt the following strategies: naming the structure in which the actions take place plus a coarse direction concept (e.g. *fork right*), a comparison of possibilities to take (e.g. *furthest right*), a conceptual change to ordering information plus a coarse direction concept (e.g. *the third to your left*), the description of competing directions not to take, or any combination of these strategies. The situation changes again if landmarks are present, as they can be used to anchor movement at an intersection and to identify the direction to take.

Although we use natural language expressions here to refer to mental concepts of route directions, it is important to note that the two are not identical. Verbalization is one possible way to externalize mental concepts (alternatives are graphics or gestures), and different verbalizations may be based on the same conceptualization. In our approach, we focus on the identification of systematic patterns in speakers' verbal descriptions that we believe point to underlying concepts.

To develop a systematic characterization of route directions and their underlying conceptualization, we present an analysis of a route direction corpus qualitatively at first, with respect to the underlying conceptualizations of direction change at intersections. We support the analysis by presenting quantitative data on strategies participants used to generate directional terms. In this way, we provide a framework for the characterization of motion and associated direction concepts in constrained spatial structures, and specifically add to research on defining criteria for good route directions and formalizing direction concepts (Dale et al. 2005; Klippel, Hansen et al. 2005; Ligozat 2000; Lovelace et al. 1999).

6.4 The route direction task

On the basis of the ideas and findings just discussed, we reanalysed the data collected in a route direction task (Klippel et al. 2003). This task was set up for participants as a simulated one-way dialogue. The scenario was to instruct, from a central office, an imagined bike messenger how to go through a town. Thus, the dialogue situation was 'on-line', but no feedback was provided by the bike messenger, i.e. it was a one-way dialogue. The stimulus map (see Figure 6.3) was built on topographical data of a street network of a medium-sized town in Germany; the landmarks were added afterwards to specific intersections. The route to describe was indicated by a solid black line; a green flag marked the starting point. The map was presented on a computer screen; the verbalizations were recorded with a tape recorder and afterwards transcribed. Twenty-two students of the University of California, Santa Barbara, participated in the experiment and received course credit for their participation. One participant had to be excluded due to technical problems. As the presentation of the map was timed to two minutes, the action at the last intersection was verbalized by nineteen instead of twenty-one participants, as two of the participants did not complete the task in time (for more details see Klippel et al. 2003).

6.4.1 Methods and analysis

The analysed corpus consists of twenty-one verbal route directions, in English, given for the route indicated in Figure 6.3. As discussed above, three aspects can characterize the conceptualization of a wayfinding action at an intersection: (a) the structure of the intersection; (b) the action itself (related to the functional aspect, or purpose, of route following); and (c) the availability of disambiguating features.

To capture these aspects systematically, we analysed verbalization data for five selected decision points, which differ with respect to the salience of their spatial

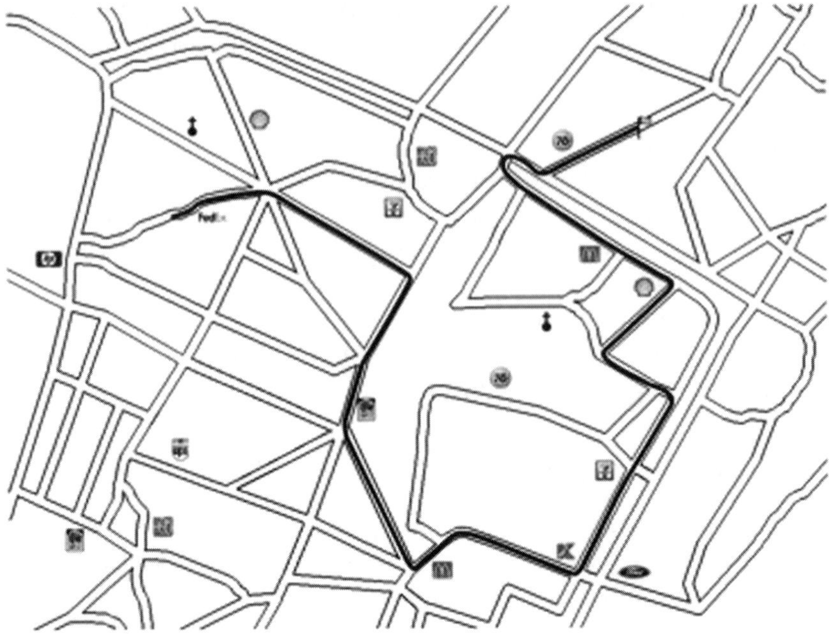

Figure 6.3 Map marked with route, shown to English-speaking participants (Klippel et al. 2003). With kind permission from Springer Science & Business Media: Klippel, A., Tappe, H., and Habel, C. (2003). Pictorial representation of routes: chunking route segments during comprehension. In C. Freska et al. (eds.): Spatial Cognition 2002, LNAI 2685.

structures, the presence of competing directions, and their deviation from a prototypical direction. The data were coded with respect to seven relevant conceptual categories. Two of the authors discussed the annotations until complete agreement was reached. Based on previous experience annotating natural language data for investigating concepts in spatial settings (Tenbrink 2009), a schema was developed that comprises the following categories, in order to provide deeper insight into the influence of the structural complexity of decision points on the conceptualization process:

I. Main direction concept. The main direction concept is the primary direction change indicated in an utterance. We viewed projective terms such as *left*, *right*, and *straight on* as the primary means to indicate a change of direction in a route instruction; these indicate direction via a location-based spatial axis. There are, however, alternatives, such as *make a U-turn*. We also distinguished unmodified projective terms from modified projective terms (such as *sharp right*) to identify the level of detail in the verbalization of the main direction concept, and checked for occurrences of more than one modification.

II. Use of verbs. In addition to spatial terms expressing the main direction concepts, verbs may also be used to characterize the change of direction in a meaningful way. Only one utterance in our data does not contain a verb at all. The variability in the verbs used points to the cognitive salience of expressing motion in suitable ways according to the situation. In order to capture direction changes that may be indicated by verbs rather than projective terms or other terms, we distinguish between (a) neutral verbs such as *go*, *move*, *turn*; (b) verbs that indicate that the route has a specific shape that needs to be followed, such as *follow*, *follow along*, *continue*; and (c) verbs that indicate a direction change, a 'drift', or small angle towards either right or left, such as *veer*. Such occurrences further highlight the range of options available to speakers for indicating the peculiarities of a spatial structure and making use of them to create route directions.

III. Redundancy. Although redundancy is not particularly indicative of the direction concept applied, it may offer a valuable means to draw conclusions about the complexity of an intersection and the cognitive effort that is required to conceptualize unambiguously a direction change in a spatial structure. Therefore, we took note of the presence of more than one spatial description in relation to a single decision point.

IV. Scene. Some utterances contain information about aspects of the spatial situation that is not directly relevant for the intended action—e.g. by describing the existence of competing alternative directions. Like redundancy, such information may serve as additional material indicating the conceived complexity of the situation if it is used systematically.

V. Reference to structure. In our data, the structure of the street network is referred to with varying levels of detail. On the one hand, a salient spatial structure such as an intersection may function as a landmark, as in *turn right at the second intersection*. On the other hand, the specification of a direction change may be achieved by reference to the structure in which the direction change occurs. In this case, the structure of an intersection is specified in some detail, as in *take the third to the left at the six-way intersection*. Occurrences of such a specification may be an indication of the complexity of the conceptualization necessary to verbalize the action to be performed. We distinguished between utterances in which spatial structures were mentioned at all versus those not containing reference to structure, and further identified if the spatial structure was specified in some way or simply mentioned.

VI. Ordering concepts. Participants invoke rendering concepts as a means to distinguish the intended route segment at a decision point from competing branches. This occurs by using natural numbers, as in *second to the right*, or by referring to neighbouring directions, as in *next*.

VII. Landmark use. A landmark may be mentioned together with a direction change either to influence the identification of the correct future route, as in *turn right at the statue*, or to confirm that the correct route has been identified, as in *turn right and you will see a statue*. Such choices reflect the conceptualization of the scenario as complex with respect either to the identity of the location at which the direction change takes place or with respect to the identification of the future direction itself.

6.4.2 *Results*

Table 6.1 shows the results of our analysis broken down by the corresponding decision points. If not indicated otherwise, percentages in the table are based on the total number of utterances made with respect to a decision point (twenty-one utterances for Intersections 1–4, nineteen for Intersection 5). Our main goal concerns the interplay of structure and function in route directions, aiming to systematically specify the underlying conceptualizations of directions. We analyse our results in

TABLE 6.1. Frequency of occurrences of conceptual categories according to decision points

Intersection number	1	2	3	4	5

I. Main direction concept	95.2	95.2	95.2	85.7	89.5
a. unmodified projective terms	95.2	95.2	95.2	66.7	84.2
b. modified projective terms	0.0	0.0	0.0	19.0	5.3
II. Use of verbs	100.0	95.2	100.0	100.0	100.0
a. neutral verb	95.2	95.2	100.0	61.9	68.4
b. course of route	0.0	0.0	0.0	28.6	10.5
c. drift	4.8	0.0	0.0	9.5	21.1
III. Redundancy	9.5	4.8	4.8	4.8	31.6
IV. Scene	0.0	0.0	4.8	0.0	36.8
V. Reference to structure	19.0	52.4	14.3	66.7	68.4
a. specified structure	9.5	42.9	0.0	42.9	57.9
b. unspecified structure	9.5	9.5	14.3	23.8	10.5
VI. Ordering concepts	9.5	42.9	0.0	0.0	47.7
a. by numbers	9.5	28.6	0.0	0.0	47.7
b. by 'next'	0.0	14.3	0.0	0.0	0.0
VII. Landmark use	47.6	4.8	95.2	95.2	94.7
a. decision influencing landmarks	47.6	4.8	95.2	85.7	15.8
b. decision confirming landmarks	0.0	0.0	0.0	9.5	78.9

terms of the frequency patterns of our seven conceptual categories, separately for each spatial situation.

6.4.2.1 The main direction concept People apply several means to render direction concepts in route directions more precise. As shown in Table 6.1, most utterances contain projective terms (category I), which indicates that direction concepts are principally encoded by projective terms or at least entail them. As an alternative, a small number of utterances employ compass directions. Other exceptions, occurring at Intersections 4 and 5, were utterances like *go up*, *all the way past Taco Bell*, *keep going on the main road*, and *through an intersection*, all of which indicate their main direction concept by contextual information without using projective terms.

Our data contain no utterances with more than one modifier of a projective term, i.e. no occurrences of expressions like *very sharp right*. This means that our participants considered only one hedge term (cf. Lakoff 1973; Vorwerg 2003) sufficient to indicate a gradual membership in a specific direction category, such as *slightly right*. Additionally, as the results for categories Ia and Ib (Table 6.1) show, modifications generally occurred only very infrequently. It is especially striking that no modifications at all were given at Intersection 1; in spite of the fact that the direction change is between two major axes. Even in the case of the most complex intersections (4 and 5), the percentage of modifications is low. This is in contrast to the specification of spatial relations between objects in object localization tasks, as for example found by Vorwerg (2003), and results by Klippel and Montello (2004), where participants often expressed gradation effects by using combinations of hedge terms, such as *take a slight right*, for a direction change similar to the ones in our present analysis (e.g. Intersection 4). In a referential identification task where spatial reference primarily serves to achieve contrast, precise descriptions are also rare, although people do tend to combine two projective terms in the case of a position between two axes (Tenbrink 2005, 2009), and they do account for increased complexity in the scenario. Vorwerg and Tenbrink (2007) directly compared referential identification tasks and localization tasks, finding clearly that speakers' spatial descriptions are more detailed if the position between objects needs to be described, rather than just identifying an object's identity in answer to a 'which' question. In both cases, however, the presence of competing objects led to an increased use of modified projective terms. We do not observe this in our present data, where an increase in spatial complexity does not necessarily lead to increased description complexity, at least not as far as the usage and modification of projective terms is concerned. This is a striking result, since route description tasks are similar to 'which' questions in that the future direction needs to be identified out of a set of competing directions. Clearly, speakers systematically choose different methods of identifying the intended direction, other than modifying the projective term used for conveying the main direction concept.

How are direction concepts conveyed instead? One option, as indicated in section 6.4.1, is to encode directional information in the verb. While neutral verbs in combination with a projective term occur most frequently at standard intersections (such as Intersection 3 in Table 6.1) and when direction changes are close to the main lateral axis, i.e. approximately 90 degrees left or right (as at Intersections 2 and 3), verbs that inherently indicate a change of direction reflect direction concepts other than orthogonal left and right turns. Our analysis shows that verbs referring to the course of the route, such as *follow*, occur nearly exclusively at Intersection 4, which indicates that they require a special spatial configuration. Some possible candidates—all of them present in Intersection 4—are the absence of competing branches in a similar direction, no more than a moderate change in direction, and possibly the availability of a landmark immediately after the intersection in an unambiguous location. The use of such 'course of the route' verbs is often accompanied by a characterization of structure. Drift verbs such as *veer*, in contrast, most frequently occur at Intersection 5. Here, it seems specifically to be the presence of competing branches in a similar direction that induces speakers to use the verb to indicate that the direction deviates from the prototypical axis. However, since drift verbs also occur in other situations, they can be said to serve as a general alternative means to indicate such deviations, similar to modifications of the projective term. In the following subsections, we discuss other alternative means of conveying direction concepts.

6.4.2.2 Ordering concepts Ordering concepts may be applied in situations where more than one alternative for a specific direction change is available. Instead of relying on rendering the gradedness of a direction change more precise, it might be more reliable to coarsen the direction concept and combine it with ordering information as provided by the spatial structure. In specific spatial situations, the change of direction may be completely specified by ordering information, primarily by counting streets (category VIa, Table 6.1), e.g. *take your second left*. In the real world, such an expression may be used to identify an exit on a roundabout or highway exit.

Although ordering information is generally assumed to be robust (Schlieder 1995), ambiguity can be involved in its linguistic representation. Ordering can occur within or between intersections, which can typically be disambiguated by referring to the spatial situation itself. For example, at Intersections 1 and 2, all ordering concepts referred to the streets between intersections, while at Intersection 5, counting was done within the intersection itself. However, in the latter case there were further complications: an utterance like *take the third road on your left* can be interpreted in two ways, as counting may start either with the branch closest to the straight direction or with the one closest to the back direction. However, it is probably reasonable to assume that speakers typically count the branches as they encounter them along the route, that is, from the perspective of the mover. Since there is only one occurrence in our data in which this assumption does not match the spatial situation, we conclude that in spite of potential complications, ordering is a strong method to disambiguate directions at complex intersections.

6.4.2.3 Landmark use In our scenario, landmarks are very prominent, as they are the only environmental features we provided in the map (besides the street network and the route). This fact in itself explains the high frequency with which landmarks are mentioned (cf. category VII, Table 6.1) in situations where a landmark is available for reference, especially since mentioning landmarks is generally recognized to be a cognitively ergonomic means of providing route directions (e.g. Tom and Denis 2003). Mentioning landmarks simplifies the description of the action to be taken, because further explanations are often unnecessary if a landmark sufficiently distinguishes the intended action from alternative choices.

Some interesting conclusions can be drawn from analysing the frequency with which landmarks are mentioned together with the positions of the landmarks, as different landmark positions have different saliencies with respect to the action performed at an intersection (Klippel and Winter 2005). At Intersection 1, only about half of the participants combined their instruction to change direction at the decision point with the mention of a landmark. Others tended to conceptualize the landmark as belonging to the route segment before the intersection. This is illustrated by the following utterance (emphasis in intonation being transcribed here in capitals): *from the green flag walk straight... you'll pass a 76 gas station on the RIGHT... immediately after that, hang a right.* Here, the participant explicitly states that the relevant intersection occurs only after the landmark, thus using the landmark as an indicator in spite of its slightly remote position. Other participants mentioned the landmark but did not (grammatically) integrate this information with the decision point, as exemplified by: *past the 76 gas station... and then you turn RIGHT.* The distinction is subtle but nevertheless informative, since it reflects different conceptualizations of the situation. In the first example, the portion of the route is conceptualized as one part where the action to take is anchored by a landmark; in the second example, the action is split up into the two distinct parts of passing a landmark and making a right turn. Landmarks in the latter case are also referred to as *Wegemarken* (route marks) by Herrmann et al. (1998).

Intersections 3 and 4 differ from Intersection 1 in that the landmarks are positioned directly at the decision points. Here, the landmark was regularly used to anchor the action, as indicated by utterances like *turn right at the K-Mart*, where the direction change is directly associated with the landmark. At Intersection 5, on the other hand, the landmark is positioned only after the decision point. Not surprisingly, the function of the landmark shifted towards confirming the decision rather than anchoring it (category VIIb, Table 6.1). Since this intersection is particularly complex, most participants made use of this strategy. The following utterance illustrates the difficulty: *there is gonna be.. a.. c..centre, a corner where there is a convergence look like THREE streets.. and you're gonna gooo.. whoa.. that's gonna be a TOUGH one.. you're gonna have to.. take.. the THIRD street.. on your LEFT.. aaand.. if you take it, it's gonna be SOMEwhat of a LEFT bend.. and you SHOULD PASS a FEDEX.. if you don't pass the FedEx, then you've taken the wrong street and you're going the wrong way, ah…*

Additionally, intersections without any salient properties can function as landmarks due to their ordered occurrence within a specific part of the route. An example is found at Intersection 2, which is preceded by another intersection. Using the first intersection as a landmark results in utterances like *turn right after the first intersection*. Apart from these cases, the intersections themselves can be conceptualized as landmarks. The following section deals with this point.

6.4.2.4 Structure Our data reflect the fact that reference to spatial structure can fulfil several functions. An intersection can be used as a landmark (cf. Klippel, Richter, and Hansen, 2005), especially if it is distinguishable from the background information (Lynch 1960; Presson and Montello 1988). In the case of route directions, the background (i.e. the context) is set up by the route as such and the structural characteristics of the preceding intersections. In these cases, spatial structures in our data were simply mentioned as such, i.e. referred to as *corner*, *intersection*, *curve*, etc. (category Vb, Table 6.1). Typically, such references appear as basic-level terms that are generally assumed to be the most general and most cognitively efficient expressions (Mervis and Rosch 1981).

Alternatively, the naming of structural aspects can be part of establishing a proper situation model, to prepare for conceptualizing the action to be carried out at an intersection. As the example in the previous section shows, some intersections are viewed as extremely difficult, which is reflected in the complexity of the utterances. The labelling of an intersection by an informative term such as *six-way intersection* can be helpful in this case. Our data show that the intersection's structure is increasingly mentioned as the complexity of the intersection grows (category Va, Table 6.1), and also that the intersection's structure is specified more frequently in cases where the structure provides substantial additional information and is simple to refer to. For example, in Intersection 2 the decision point occurs at a *dead end*, which is easily recognized. Intersection 3, in contrast, is rather prototypical (Evans 1980; Moar and Bower 1983; Tversky and Lee 1999); the mental situation model initiated by referring to this intersection simply as *intersection* matches the encountered configuration sufficiently closely.

Interestingly, at Intersection 3, all references to intersection structure serve to describe the location of the landmark instead of the future direction of movement, as in *at the corner where the K-Mart is located*. This reflects the fact that, in this case, describing the (prototypical) intersection structure is insufficient, because there is another similar intersection and another corner nearby. The decision point needs to be identified unambiguously, which is achieved by mentioning the landmark.

Finally, another potential structural aspect which is not covered by our scenario but which is obviously salient to speakers is the distinction between main and minor roads. Our data contain several references to the *main road*. As all streets in our map have the same width, participants seemed to infer this information from some cue such as the course of the streets.

6.4.3 *Discussion*

Our analysis shows that speakers make use of a broad variety of strategies to instantiate a situation model that is suitable for identifying the intended future direction of movement at a decision point (i.e. an intersection). Apart from using hedge terms to render direction changes—specified by projective terms—more precise, as is done when describing spatial relationships between two objects, a number of further options is available in the domain of route directions. Clearly, spatial direction is only one of several salient aspects of the spatial situation that speakers make use of in order to convey the intended movement. Another prominent aspect, which has been dealt with frequently in the research literature, is reference to landmarks. Since landmarks serve different functions, their exact position with respect to decision points is pertinent for characterizing the action to be performed. The following general tendencies with respect to landmarks can be inferred from our analysis:

1. A landmark conceptualized at a position before a decision point may sometimes be used to identify the intended intersection, but it can also be mentioned separately in order to identify or confirm the route segment before the decision point.
2. A landmark conceptualized at a position at a decision point will (a) frequently be used to identify the intended intersection, especially if other intersections are nearby; and (b) frequently be used to anchor the direction change that has to be performed at the intersection in lieu of mentioning the intersection as such. Linguistically the anchoring is encoded as *turn* (*right*, *left*) (*before*, *after*, *at*) {landmark X}.
3. A landmark at a position after a decision point can be used to confirm that the correct direction has been identified. This will be done most frequently with particularly complex intersections.

Furthermore, speakers resort to other strategies that allow them to indicate future directions. To characterize these systematically, we propose the following general categories that reflect the conceptualization of turns at decision points and thereby correspond to different kinds of spatial knowledge. These categories reflect results of the data analyses we report in this chapter, as well as our general experience studying route directions.

1. Qualitative direction concepts expressed by projective terms, references to absolute directions, and direction-indicating verbs, e.g. *turn right, go west, veer right.*
2. Qualitative modifications (hedges) specifying direction, as in *slightly right.*
3. Quantitative measures of directions in degrees, e.g. *turn exactly 90 degrees.*
4. Clock directions, e.g. *turn to three o'clock.*
5. Reference to structure, e.g. *dead-end, fork.*
6. Ordering concepts, e.g. *the first exit.*
7. Reliance on landmarks to indicate direction, as in *where the statue is.*

These categories can typically be combined with each other, as in *veer slightly right 45 degrees at the first street on your right, where the statue is.* In our data, they occurred with different frequencies; some did not occur at all (e.g. reference to a clock direction), in spite of the fact that they do (infrequently) occur in other spatial contexts, as our own research has shown (e.g. Tenbrink 2006). Qualitative concepts occur almost throughout; but in contrast to other discourse tasks, they are seldom modified, indicating that speakers prefer other means of rendering their descriptions sufficiently precise. Our analysis of the results has, apart from a number of interesting details with regard to the distribution of options, shown that the complexity of a decision point—in terms of the combination of both structural and functional aspects—generally plays a major role in the choice of concepts. Thus, complex decision points lead to a number of systematic changes in speakers' utterances. Specifically, the more complex the intersection:

(a) the more verbose is the description, employing several of the above-mentioned options;
(b) the more varied are the verbalizations (e.g. strategies other than using projective terms are applied);
(c) the more references are made to intersection structure;
(d) the more alternative instructions are offered (redundant information) (see category III, Table 6.1); and
(e) the more references are made to competing directions (see category IV, Table 6.1).

The notion of complexity has, in the course of our analysis, proved to be crucial and yet difficult to specify. It concerns neither the structure alone (e.g. the number of branches) nor the change of direction as such; rather, it concerns a complex interplay among several factors. For example, although Intersections 2 and 3 are structurally very similar, the concepts expressed with respect to these locations during the course of the route description differed considerably (see Table 6.1). This is clearly motivated by the specific kind of direction change to be made at each of the intersections, and the ensuing range of competing or interfering directions that become relevant in each case. Intuitively, it should be possible to simply say *keep going straight at the intersection* even if the intersection in question is structurally complex. With a main direction concept such as 'straight', such a decision point does not imply a high degree of functional complexity. This observation is consistent with our results, although the data we report here do not explicitly include such a case. However, the remainder of this corpus of directions (see also Klippel et al. 2003) shows that, for instance, the intersection following Intersection 4 (see Figure 6.3 and Table 1) is hardly mentioned at all by participants. Typically, speakers combine their descriptions by spatially chunking subsequent individual decision points into higher-order route direction elements (HORDE), as in *when you get to the second intersection, you're going to make a left*. Similarly, the turn-off preceding Intersection 2 in our current data is typically only referred to by way of an ordering concept such as *your second right*, if at all.

Our analysis suggests that it is possible to derive cognitive measures of complexity, and that participants' strategies change along with the complexity of the intersections. The results therefore add to approaches at the interface of architecture and psychology that aim to derive measures for the legibility of buildings and built structures (e.g. Weisman 1987; O'Neill 1992). Generally, our results fit with earlier work in the area of route directions (e.g. Denis et al. 1999), spelling out the effects of route and path complexity in more detail than has been done before. In the context of a different setting, Bethell-Fox and Shepard (1988) suggested that dealing with complexity might be something that requires training but does not pose difficulties to a speaker. In the case of route directions, as personal experience attests, it is likely that complexity may specifically pose one major reason why spontaneous route directions given on the street are often unsuccessful (Habel 1988). It may also be the case that North Americans handle complexity less efficiently than Europeans due to the often more regular street grid structure (as conjectured by Davies and Pederson 2001). On the other hand, some studies indicate that there are no general differences in how route information is organized in the two continents; for example, landmarks are used in both languages to chunk route parts (Klippel et al. 2003).

Our analysis of route verbalizations shows how strategies change depending on the complexity of the interplay of structure and function. The tendencies we identify can provide a basis for a more systematic model of route directions, which is desirable for a number of reasons. For example, aspects of complexity and the ensuing changes in verbalization are not systematically implemented in current web-based navigation services (with the exception of ordering concepts at circles). Furthermore, the interaction of structural and functional aspects is not sufficiently accounted for in formal characterizations of spatial relations (as in many qualitative spatial reasoning models, e.g. Frank 1996).

6.5 Conclusion and outlook

In this chapter, we have systematically addressed verbalization data in a route description task by relating features of the descriptions to features of the decision points. We have identified patterns of speakers' choices that point to conceptualizations of complexity in relation to the given task (i.e. the functional rather than the structural aspect), and identified the range of means by which direction-givers identify future directions at complex decision points. Crucially, modifications of projective terms are not a primary means of describing direction change; rather, speakers use direction-indicating verbs, refer to landmarks and spatial structures, and offer additional information about the spatial situation.

Our research points to a number of desirable future research directions. Although the analysis in this chapter only concerned English-language data, the system we developed for the analysis (see section 6.4.1 and Table 6.1) allows comparison of route directions given in different languages. Our discussion of the complexity of decision points and the interplay of structure and function (with its impact on the conceptualization of actions) suggests avenues for exploring culturally influenced aspects of route directions. Therefore, a detailed analysis of the structuring of route knowledge in different languages and cultures—even a comparison between North American and European speakers—may shed light on differences based on language or on the environments to which speakers are accustomed. An interesting future endeavour would be to identify linguistically and culturally shared structuring principles for the organization of route knowledge, and to pinpoint systematic differences. Such research becomes especially important as companies offer navigation services that operate globally.

This leads us to the question of optimal or cognitively ergonomic route directions, especially with respect to automatic systems. It has been known for some time that a typical strategy of web-based route direction systems is cognitively inadequate, namely, to rely completely on street names as indications of direction change (cf. Tom and Denis 2003). Our approach is therefore to extract general principles for disambiguating direction changes at intersections, in order to specify how appropriate situation models can be instantiated with the use of verbal descriptions covering the conceptualization of the action to be performed with a minimum of information and a maximum of specificity (e.g. Grice 1989).

Our analysis of the verbalizations showed that the concept of 'at', at a decision point, is used in a spatially constrained sense. For anchoring an action at an intersection by a landmark, the landmark's position has to be directly at the meeting point of the branches. Further research is needed to detail the influences on conceptualizing landmark positions in cases where further objects are present. Additionally, there seem to be contextual factors as, for instance, introduced by the modality—such as *on foot*, *by bike*, or *by car*—of travel (Wahlster et al. 1998) that influence whether an object is used as an anchor for an action at a decision point or used to identify the route segment before the decision point. A detailed analysis of nearness concepts of landmarks and decision points is therefore one of our future goals, in accordance with approaches to the formal characterization of commonsense knowledge (Yao and Thill 2005). Generally, an important future aspect of our work will be to identify a method to formally characterize the interplay of structure and function on the conceptualization of motion in networks as part of route knowledge and directions.

Acknowledgements

This work was supported by the Cooperative Research Centre for Spatial Information, funded by the Australian Commonwealth's Cooperative Research Centres Programme, and by the SFB/TR 8 Spatial Cognition, funded by the Deutsche Forschungsgemeinschaft (DFG). We would like to thank Heike Tappe for invaluable comments on earlier aspects of this work, and Nadine Jochims, Heidi Schmolck, and Hartmut Obendorf for assistance in the original data processing. The data were collected for collaborative research between the DFG-funded projects Conceptualization Processes in Language Production (HA 1237–10) and Aspect Maps (FR 806–8) during a research stay by the first author at UC Santa Barbara.

Part 2

Granularity

7

Granularity in taxonomy, time, and space

JEFFREY M. ZACKS, BARBARA TVERSKY

7.1 Establishing grain

One thing people do with language is establish spatial scale or grain, allowing speakers and hearers to share understanding of the sizes of objects and distances of places under discussion. One might suppose this is done with spatial predicates, terms like *near*, *far*, *big*, and *small*. This reasonable hypothesis turns out to be wrong; in fact, spatial predicates for the most part take their scale from their referents. If one of us were to tell you that you can get a great sandwich near the Saint Louis Arch you might reasonably take the spatial predicate *near* to refer to a radius of several blocks. However, if we were to say that 'the sandwich is on the counter near the fridge', a two-block walk would be quite a shock. Near is certainly nearer than far, but the distance metric used—the spatial grain—is set by the things involved. A far atom is a shorter distance away than a near galaxy; a large shrew is shorter in length than a small rhinoceros.

Sometimes spatial predication is combined with its scale-setting referents by morphological rules. For example, there is a ferry in Ontario, Canada called the 'Chi-cheemaun', because the Ojibwa root word for *canoe* is 'cheemaun', and in Ojibwa repeating the initial syllable indicates large size (Bloomfield 1957). In Italian, it is the suffix that indicates that tortelloni are larger than tortellini. These morphological transformations serve to set relative scale within the more general scale set by the names of the things.

Talmy (1983) pointed out that this fact—that spatial scale in language depends primarily on the objects being talked about rather than on structural linguistic properties—is by no means a necessary condition. 'It would be very easy to imagine that objects capable of fitting in one's hand and broad geographic terrains, say, might have very different spatial characteristics of relevance to humans and that language forms would reflect such differences' (p. 263). Talmy argued that the schemas that underlie spatial language abstract away information about scale (and shape) in order to provide generativity, allowing a small number of spatial terms to be combined with open-class words to cover a large semantic space.

That the referents of spatial expressions establish spatial scale has been demonstrated in studies in which participants estimated the distances described in sentences like *A secretary is just approaching the flower stand* (Morrow and Clark 1988). The estimated distance between the secretary and the building increased when *flower stand* was changed to *department store*. Spatial predicates also affect distance estimates: a secretary described as in front of the department store is estimated to be closer to the store than one described as behind the store (Carlson and Covey 2005).

Similarly, language can set temporal scale. As for space, scale is set by the interaction of a predicate and a referent. If a waiter says that a soufflé is nearly ready, one can expect it in a few minutes; however, if a builder describes a new house as nearly ready, this implies at least several days (if not weeks or months) delay. Consider the Beatles singing about the passage of time: 'Please, mister postman, I've been waiting *a long, long time* (oh yeah) since I heard from that gal of mine' (Holland et al. 1964). We can imagine that the forlorn singer has been anticipating a letter for days or even weeks. Now consider the same predicate in a different context: 'Lets all get up and dance to a song that was a hit before your mother was born, though she was born *a long, long time* ago...' (McCartney 1967). Now the same spatial term indicates decades, because the referent of time is in this context quite different. Of course, spatial and temporal scale setting can be combined, as in *A long time ago in a galaxy far, far away...*

Things and events not only set spatial and temporal scale, they structure the very way we think about space and time. Unlike surveyors or physicists who structure space and time in terms of global physical measurements, people structure space and time around the objects in space and the events in time; objects and events are perceptible, often manipulable, in ways the surrounding space and time are not (e.g. Tversky et al. 1999; Zakay and Block 1997). That objects structure space and events time is revealed in distortions of space and time that depend on the relative number of objects or events. Conceptions of space and time are embodied in the sense that the meaningful distinctions of scale are those differentiated by classes of human interaction with the scale. For space, the space of the body, the space around the body, and the space of navigation differ both in the way they are perceived and the behaviours they subserve, and consequently, in the ways they are conceived (Tversky et al. 1999). The space of the body captures sensations and movements of the body. The space around the body is the space of reach by hands or eyes. The space of navigation, too large to be seen at a glance, is the space bodies potentially explore and traverse. Other spatial scales can be distinguished based on natural correlations of perception and action (Freundschuh and Egenhofer 1997; Montello 1993). For time, too, scales that are of significance to human activity are naturally distinguished, marked nicely by language: *minutes, hours, days, weeks, years, centuries, millennia* (e.g. Conway and Rubin 1993).

Temporal and spatial scale, as analysed above, can be regarded as a hierarchy of parts, or a **partonomy** (Miller and Johnson-Laird 1976). That is, minutes are parts of hours, hours parts of days, days parts of weeks, and so on. Scale can also be established conceptually, as a hierarchy of breadth. Breadth forms another kind of hierarchy, one based on kinds rather than parts, termed a **taxonomy**. Taxonomies of common objects serve as a paradigm case: rocking chairs are kinds of chairs, which are kinds of furniture; pippins are kinds of apples, which are kinds of fruit. As Rosch and her colleagues demonstrated, one level of that hierarchy, the basic level, the level of CHAIR and APPLE and SHIRT rather than the level of FURNITURE, FRUIT, or CLOTHING or the level of ROCKING CHAIR, PIPPIN APPLE, or DRESS SHIRT, has a privileged status across a broad range of cognitive operations (Rosch and Lloyd 1978). Notably, it turns out to be the level at which the amount of information per category cut is maximized. It is also the level most frequently used by adults, first used by children and first to enter language; it is the highest level at which a generalized image can be constructed and the highest level for which a behavioural routine is appropriate. People adopt the basic level as a default taxonomic scale. Referring to an object at a different taxonomic level conveys that this is the level at which relevant distinctions are made. Relevant distinctions are those that separate the named object from the contrasting categories at the same level of specificity. For example, if one begins a sentence by referring to an object at the basic level, as in *I usually take our car to work*, an ending such as *but sometimes I ride my bike* would be appropriate. However, if one were to begin with a subordinate category such as *I usually take our sedan to work*, a listener would expect the end of the sentence to make a contrast at the same level, as in *but I sometimes drive our station wagon*. Choice of a referent implicitly selects a range of possible contrasting alternative referents. The contrasting referents differ from the chosen one on a salient feature or features, which form a level in a hierarchy, in this case, a hierarchy of kinds. Car and bike contrast as kinds of vehicles whereas sedan and station wagon contrast as kinds of cars.

The mechanisms by which we establish spatial, temporal, and taxonomic scale in language have much in common. Cognitive linguists and psycholinguistics have argued this is no accident (Clark 1973; Lakoff and Johnson 1980). The argument holds that time and taxonomy are abstract domains, and as such are related to the physical spatial domain by metaphor. That is, we think of each of them concretely, frequently in terms of space. This leads to expressions for time such as *I can't believe fall semester is already just ahead*, and *We have entered a new era*. Similarly, people talk about *breaking down a high-level taxonomic class into low-level subclasses.* As for taxonomies, choice of a referent also selects implicit possible contrasting referents on a spatial or temporal level, objects about the same size or events about the same duration. A refrigerator selects a body-sized spatial scale and the Empire State Building selects a larger one, a building-sized scale. Likewise, preparing a meal selects a temporal scale of hours and minutes, and constructing a house one of months and days.

Selecting a level of reference, then, establishes spatial, temporal, and taxonomic expectations. Once a spatial, temporal, or taxonomic grain is established, information is processed against the background of that grain. This means that setting a scale through language can affect the processing of subsequent information. The empirical results of Morrow and Clark (1988) and Carlson (2005) show this clearly to be the case. However, in these examples the form of the processing is preserved across changes in scale. Whether predicated of atoms or galaxies, *near* always means a smaller distance than *far*. The examples discussed so far show scale invariance—relative relations are preserved with changes in scale. We take it as self-evident that people think about things at different spatial, temporal, and taxonomic scales. As the foregoing examples indicate, it is uncontroversial that language can indicate the scale relevant at a particular time. Here we argue for a stronger claim, that scale invariance often fails in cognitive representations. In other words, changes in scale often change the form of the computations involved. We will describe three very different examples of this process in action, beginning with the most abstract case, taxonomy, followed by an example from the temporal domain, and concluding with a spatial example.

7.2 Objects and scenes

In naming an object or a scene one sets a taxonomic scale. Subordinate-level terms establish a fine-grained taxonomic scale, basic-level terms establish an intermediate scale, and superordinate-level terms establish a coarse-grained scale. The same object might be referred to as a *recliner* (fine-grained), as a *chair* (intermediate), or as a *piece of furniture* (coarse-grained). The same scene might be referred to as a *hardware store* (fine-grained), a *store* (intermediate), or *indoors* (coarse-grained) (Tversky and Hemenway 1983). Referring to an object at different taxonomic scales has a profound effect on the conceptual and perceptual representation that is created. For objects this can be seen in the features that people list. When objects are labelled at a coarse-grained taxonomic scale, few attributes are listed and most are functions. Furniture, for example, is described as *things you take with you when you move* or *the things that make you comfortable in the house.* When an intermediate taxonomic scale is used, many more features are listed and most of these are parts (e.g. legs, back, seat). When a fine-grained taxonomic scale is used, people list a small number of additional features that distinguish amongst members of a basic-level category. These features tend to be colours and materials rather than parts (Tversky and Hemenway 1984). The mechanism of these effects appears to be that referring to an object at different taxonomic scales evokes different sets of contrasting objects. People form representations in which the features that distinguish the members of the evoked contrast class are salient, so this leads to a failure of scale invariance.

Because parts are the salient distinguishing attributes at intermediate taxonomic scales, parts drive search processes when people identify objects. Parts are a special sort of feature, because they are the critical features of behaviour or action selection as well of perception. For example, the arms of a chair support selected actions—picking up the chair and resting one's own arms—and have a distinctive elongated shape. The seats of bicycles and chairs support (literally!) selected actions—sitting—and have a distinctive flat and rounded shape. Thus, parts form a bridge between appearance and function.

Scenes, too, have a preferred level of reference, the level of RESTAURANT, SCHOOL, or FOREST rather than the level of INDOORS or OUTDOORS or the level of FAST FOOD RESTAURANT, ELEMENTARY SCHOOL, OR PINE FOREST (Tversky and Hemenway 1983). As for objects, superordinate scene terms elicit few features, basic-level terms elicit many more, and subordinate terms only a modest increase. The attributes that characterize basic-level scenes are the objects and activities frequent in the settings. Objects can be regarded as parts of scenes, and activities their functions, as most of the activities listed entail interactions with scene parts such as objects.

The fact that labelling at an intermediate taxonomic scale facilitates distinct forms of processing links objects and scenes. Effects of taxonomic scale on thinking about objects and scenes likely interact with perception and cognition about events. Events are parts of scenes, and objects are parts of both scenes and events. In the following section we will shift from considering effects of taxonomic scale to temporal scale, and show how the objects that are parts of events play different roles at different scales.

7.3 Events

Just as objects and scenes form hierarchies of kinds and parts, so do events. Here, by 'event' we mean a sequence of actions that is perceived to have a beginning, middle, and end. The temporal scale of events defined this way may range from events measured in nanoseconds (the decay of a subatomic particle) or seconds (blowing out candles) or minutes (fixing a flat tyre) to hours (coronation of a king) or years (the French Revolution) or millennia (the evolution of the solar system). However, studying events in the laboratory from on-line perception to cognition restricts the range to events lasting seconds or minutes. The kinds of events studied in the laboratory are perceived and conceived as consisting of discrete parts (Zacks and Tversky 2001). For example, the parts of 'serving good wine' rated most important are 'select a bottle', 'fill the glasses', and 'pour a sample' (Galambos 1983). Establishing a level in an event part hierarchy sets a temporal grain.

To explore the cognitive effects of attending to events at different granularities, we filmed an individual performing one of four everyday activities: making a bed, doing the dishes, fertilizing a houseplant, or assembling a saxophone (Zacks, Tversky, and Iyer 2001). We showed these films to observers who were asked to tap a button whenever in their judgment one meaningful unit of activity ended and another began, a variant of procedures introduced by Newtson (1973). Observers segmented twice, once at the coarsest level that made sense, and once at the finest level that made sense. Half the observers described the action in each segment as they segmented. Both within and across observers, the boundaries of coarse units corresponded to the boundaries of the nearest fine unit more than expected by chance. That is, fine-grained units were hierarchically embedded in coarse-grained units.

The segment-by-segment descriptions observers provided gave insight into the criteria for segmentation at coarse and fine levels, especially to their differences. Over 90 per cent of the descriptions were actions on objects: *put on the top sheet, rinse the glass*. Thus, the data of interest are the actions on objects, which can be referred to by a rich variety of syntactic and semantic devices. Several of these linguistic devices allow abbreviated, more economical, utterances because the missing information can be presupposed, for example, using pronouns instead of nouns, eliding or dropping terms, repeating terms, and grouping. Viewers' utterances reflected the way they perceive event organization, indirectly setting a temporal grain. Descriptions of events at a coarse grain focused on entire objects or object parts, as in the components of a bed or a saxophone, which were nouns, whereas descriptions of events at a fine scale focused on actions on those objects, which were verbs. This result was not a consequence of the organization of the particular events. A set of experiments compared events grouped at the coarse level by objects or by actions. The degree of hierarchical organization was higher when event segments were separated by objects at the coarse level and actions at the fine level, indicating that event organization is more apparent when coarse unit boundaries correspond to changes of object (Dowell et al. 2004). A consequence of the way the mind organizes the events of life is the establishment of a temporal grain: at the coarse level, the time entailed to act on an entire object, and at the fine level, the time entailed by articulated actions on the same object.

Thus, changing the conceptual grain of description changed not only the aspects of those events that were highlighted but also the temporal grain of the events described. This finding joins other findings of differences between coarse- and fine-grained segmentation. Fine-grained units appear to be identified to a substantial degree on the basis of physical movement patterns (Newtson et al. 1977; Zacks 2004), whereas coarse-grained event boundaries may be more dependent on inferences about actors' goals. People better recognize visual details from activities after segmenting them at a fine grain (Hanson and Hirst 1989, 1991; Lassiter and Slaw 1991; Lassiter et al. 1988). Several areas of the cerebral cortex are more active at coarse-grained boundaries than at fine-grained boundaries (Zacks et al. 2001). It is unlikely that all of these effects reflect true failures of scale invariance, but together they make a strong case that the form of processing is qualitatively different when observers focus on fine or coarse temporal grains.

7.4 Mental spatial transformations

Mental representations are useful as a repository of knowledge, but they are a static repository. We often need to imagine circumstances different from those we remember, notably for anticipating what will happen next, and that requires mental transformations. For the comprehension of events, spatial mental transformations are central. Disparate research traditions converge to indicate that two types of spatial mental transformations are fundamental, each based on fundamental changes in the spatial–temporal world (Zacks and Michelon 2005). One is object-based transformations, including mental rotation (Shepard and Metzler 1971), which allow imagining objects at different orientations or positions. A second is perspective transformations, which allow imagining the body at different orientations, hence different viewpoints on the surrounding world (Parsons 1987). Both the perspectives and the mental transformations get extended to other domains, notably temporal and social. One perspective is from outside, looking onto an object or environment. For objects, this is the usual perspective of interaction. For environments the dominant perspective is from within, as in when one stands inside a room. This is the usual perspective of navigation. The outside perspective is more unusual; it occurs occasionally when people overlook a landscape or peer into a space such as a glass-walled squash court. Yet people seem easily able to adopt such an outside perspective at will, because creating maps of various kinds is widespread across cultures (e.g. Tversky 2005). People's facility in adopting these two perspectives is reflected in language as well. In describing environments, people adopt one of two perspectives, or a mixture of both: survey perspective for the view from without and route for the view from within (e.g. Taylor and Tversky 1992a, 1992b, 1996). Similarly, in representing the space immediately surrounding the body, people typically adopt the perspective of an observer embedded in a surrounding environment (Bryant et al. 1992; Franklin and Tversky 1990).

Overall, the scale of a space influences the perspective that people take, and the consequent mental transformations they use for reasoning. For large-scale spaces people tend to reason by adopting an 'inside' perspective on an array of objects. They imagine themselves in the midst of the array, and imagine moving relative to the objects. For small-scale spaces people tend to adopt an 'outside' perspective. They imagine themselves positioned so all the objects are in front of them, and imagine the objects moving. These habitual tendencies can lead to qualitative differences in reasoning that depends on scale. Two formally identical spatial reasoning problems may by default be solved differently depending on whether the spatial scale is large or small. However, the human mind is flexible, so explicit reasoning strategies can overcome these habits to adopt one kind of transformation or the other (Bryant and Tversky 1999; Bryant et al. 1992; Franklin and Tversky 1990; Franklin et al. 1992).

Both the natural tendencies to adopt internal and external spatial perspectives and the flexibility under special circumstances are evident in mental transformation tasks. In one series of experiments, participants were asked to make spatial judgments about pictures presented on paper or on a computer screen (Zacks and Tversky 2005). There were two kinds of pictures. One set of pictures depicted small manipulable objects such as telephones and hand drills. Because they are manipulated by hand it was expected that people would tend to reason about them by imagining the objects moving or being moved. The other set of pictures depicted human bodies. Bodies were chosen because they are larger in scale and because we move about in our own bodies, as well as observe other bodies moving. For these reasons, it was expected that people would reason flexibly about them, either imagining the bodies moving or imagining themselves moving relative to the bodies.

For each type of object, participants made two sorts of judgments. In left–right judgments, participants viewed pictures of the object or a body and indicated whether a particular part of the object or body was on the right or left side relative to the intrinsic spatial reference frame of the object or body. In same–different judgments, participants viewed two pictures of the object or the body and indicated whether the two were identical or mirror images. For both tasks the orientation of the stimuli varied randomly from trial to trial.

In one experiment, each participant first made either a right/left or a same/different judgment about either an object (cell phone) or a body, and then introspected how they had solved the problem. Because people experience objects only from the outside but experience bodies both from inside and outside, it was predicted that for objects, participants would consistently report imagining the object moving, but for bodies they would reason flexibly, either imagining the object or themselves moving depending on the judgment required. In particular, it was expected that left–right problems would primarily be solved by performing a perspective transformation to align the participant's perspective with the perspective of the depicted body, because these judgments must be made relative to the body's intrinsic reference frame. Same/different problems should be solved by imagining the bodies moving into alignment, an object-based transformation. The results were exactly as predicted: when making judgments about pictures of telephones, 100 per cent of participants spontaneously reported imagining the picture moving when solving the problem—independent of the judgment required. When making judgments about pictures of bodies, however, the transformation reported depended on the spatial judgment: for left–right judgments, 71 per cent of participants reported imagining themselves moving, but for same–different judgments, 100 per cent reported imagining the picture moving.

Introspective reports of performance are supportive, but people's introspections do not always correspond to patterns of data from performance. Converging evidence comes from an experiment in which participants performed multiple trials of each combination of task and stimulus type. The critical data are the relationship between orientation and response time. Previous research has shown that when people solve problems by imagining an object rotating, response times increase with the degree of rotation (e.g. Shepard and Metzler 1971). However, when participants imagine themselves moving, for the stimulus configuration we used response times are largely orientation independent (Parsons 1987). Putting these paradigms together leads to the prediction that corresponds to participants' introspections, namely, that response times should increase with orientation for both left–right and same–different judgments about objects, but only for same–different judgments about bodies. This is exactly what obtained.

Other experiments (Shelton and Zacks, in press) extended this paradigm to larger spaces. These experiments presented pictures of bodies and pictures of rooms for same–different and left–right tasks judgments. Because the natural way of experiencing rooms is from the inside, it was expected that people would imagine themselves reorienting in rooms rather than imagining the rooms transforming. In previous work using described rather than experienced rooms, participants had rapidly reoriented when they were described as moving in the room, but took twice as long to reorient when rooms were described as moving (Tversky, Kim and Cohen 1999). Therefore, for rooms, it was expected that people would tend to favour perspective transformations for both same–different and left–right judgments. For bodies, it was expected that preferred transformations would be flexible and task-dependent as in the previous studies. In two experiments, response-time patterns for bodies replicated the pattern described previously: sharp increases in response time with increasing stimulus orientation for the left–right task but not for the same–different task. In both experiments, response times for rooms were overall less orientation-dependent and less influenced by task, consistent with using perspective transformations to solve the problems.

Although the two spatial reasoning problems are formally identical, they are spontaneously adopted in different situations. People are more likely to imagine themselves as moving and changing orientation when the situation corresponds to the natural situations in which people move and change orientation, those in which an environment surrounds a person. Likewise, people are more likely to imagine objects changing orientations when the situation corresponds to the natural situation in which people watch objects move and change orientation, those in which objects are viewed or manipulated. Importantly, the preferred transformation correlates with scale.

Despite natural proclivities, people can be induced to use both transformations in both situations. This flexibility has allowed generations of humans to create maps and models of environments they experience from within, or in the world. Those maps and models in turn allow further spatial transformations, some mental, some physical, using the external map or model: for example, finding efficient paths and routes in the service of navigation, or determining the locations of entrances and windows in the service of architecture and design. Changing scale goes hand in hand with changing spatial mental transformations.

7.5 Conclusions

The world as we perceive it consists of objects arrayed in environments; we ourselves are some of those objects. The world isn't static; objects change and move, we among them, and often the changes and movements are coherent and organized, packaged by the human mind into events. The flexibility of the mind allows objects and events to be regarded broadly or narrowly, at different scales; rooms have things or furniture or Eames chairs, and days have preparing dinner or chopping onions and getting to work or turning off the freeway. Actions observed or performed vary on scale as well, notably transformations on objects or transformations within environments. Ordinary interactions and discourse impose natural levels and transformations, as the studies reviewed have shown. But the research has also shown that other scales and transformations can be and are applied, when they are appropriate to the situation or the task or implied by language. However, applying scales and transformations that are not naturally elicited may have costs. Establishing a grain or level can in turn bias processing: many reasoning operations change their form with the scale at which they are operating.

The possibility that scale invariance may fail places limits on the generality of cognitive theories. A single cognitive theory is necessarily limited in scope. For example, theories of conceptual structure have dealt mostly with objects of intermediate size—say, a few inches to tens of feet in length. Adapting such theories to reasoning about microscopic or macroscopic entities requires checking that scale invariance holds. Theories of mental imagery need to distinguish between operations on small manipulable objects, on human-sized objects, and on geographic-scale environments. Theories of memory for temporal duration need to distinguish between events that are seconds or weeks in length. These limitations are sometimes noted informally but seldom addressed programmatically. The examples presented here can serve as reminders of these important boundary conditions.

Acknowledgments

We are grateful for support to ONR Grants NOOO14-PP-1-O649, N000140110717, and N000140210534, and NSF REC-0440103 to B. T., and grants NIH RO1-MH70674 and NSF BCS-0236651 to J. Z.

8

Granularity in the cross-linguistic encoding of motion and location*

MIRIAM VAN STADEN, BHUVANA NARASIMHAN

8.1 Introduction

In this chapter we look at similarities and differences in how people linguistically encode events of motion and location. More specifically, in order to explore how languages differ with respect to the segmentation and classification of events, we examine habitual, colloquial descriptions of caused motion into containment (as in sentences such as *He put the book into the bag*). We suggest that, while the ability to segment the continuum of experience and perception into event units and talk about them in more or less fine-grained ways is universal, there are differences between speakers of different languages in the level of granularity at which events are typically referred to in linguistic descriptions (see Bohnemeyer 1999, 2003). Based on the summary of theoretical and empirical research on event structure provided in Zacks and Tversky (2001a) and Zacks and Tversky (this volume), we identify three interpretations of granularity, which appear particularly relevant. First, there are cross-linguistic differences with regard to the partonomic level of event description: **where** event boundaries are placed in linguistic descriptions. Second, within the boundaries of an event, there are systematic differences in event classification: **which** elements are given expression. Third, languages may differ in **the level of detail** of the encoding of particular elements of the event. We begin by characterizing in

* This study is partly funded by a grant to the first author from the Netherlands Organization for Scientific Research (NWO). Many thanks to Penny Brown and Gunter Senft for their generosity in sharing their knowledge of respectively Tzeltal and Kilivila and providing us with examples. Also, we are grateful to the members of the Acquisition and Language & Cognition groups at the Max Planck Institute in Nijmegen for their input on the issues discussed in this chapter. The views expressed here are our own, as well as any errors.

further detail each of the notions we have just introduced, relying heavily on the excellent overview provided in Zacks and Tversky (2001a).

Starting with the second interpretation of granularity, any description of a motion event can be characterized in terms of a core set of elements. These include **Figure**, **Ground**, **motion**, **path**, **manner**, **cause** (Talmy 1985, 1991). In sentence (1) the noun phrase *the book* is the Figure and *the bag* is the Ground, the preposition *into* describes the path, and the verb *slide* encodes cause and manner of motion.

(1) *He slid the book into the bag.*

In addition, in caused motion events, there is a **causer** (*he* in the sentence above). Languages encode these **constituent elements** of a motion event in a variety of ways depending on the lexical and constructional resources in the language, and Talmy (1985, 1991) suggests that languages differ systematically in how they incorporate components such as manner and path in the encoding of motion events. He observes that some languages typically encode the path information in the verb, e.g. Spanish, while other languages like English typically encode manner information in the verb.

In theorizing about how events might be perceived and conceptualized, Zacks and Tversky (2001a) suggest that components such as Figure, motion, path, Ground, etc. in linguistic descriptions point to an underlying structured representation of events on which people rely in talking about events (pp. 10–11). In terms of our first interpretation of granularity, the basic building blocks of (motion) events 'should be temporal units in which the Figure, motion, path, and Ground are constant' and a change in the motion, path, or Ground relative to the Figure would mark the boundary where a new (atomic) event begins (pp. 9–10). Thus, a general motion event such as *going skiing* can be partitioned into segments such as *riding the ski lift*, *getting off the lift* and *continuing skiing*, turning at the base of the ski jump, and so on (p. 10). A change in the Figure, however, typically starts a new series of atomic events that together form an 'intentional action'. A series of intentional actions together yield a 'script'. In this manner, the smaller event units can be grouped into larger units to form a **partonomic** hierarchy. For instance, the activity of *going skiing* might itself constitute a subpart of an event such as *taking a winter sports course*, which might then be part of an event at a broader timescale such as becoming a ski instructor. At the other end of the hierarchy, the event of *getting off the lift* can have further subparts such as *stepping off the lift* (Barker and Wright 1954). In this partonomic hierarchy, Zacks and Tversky furthermore identify a 'privileged partonomic level', which includes **behaviour episodes** such as *a boy going home from school*, or *a girl exchanging remarks with her mother* (cf. Barker and Wright 1954), or, in another approach, **scenes** in a **script**: for example scenes in a 'restaurant script' include *entering*, *ordering*, *eating*, etc. (cf. Schank and Abelson 1977). When presented with actions at a subordinate level, people make inferences up to the scene level, but they are unlikely to make downward inferences to the subordinate level when presented with information at the scene level (Abbott et al. 1985). Zacks and Tversky suggest that at such a level in the partonomic hierarchy, 'cognition is particularly fluent' (p. 10).

Our second interpretation of granularity has to do with event classification. Events can also be characterized by a **taxonomic** hierarchy that is based on kind-of rather than part-of relationships. Thus, *frisbee golf* is a kind of *golf*, which in turn is a kind of *sport* (Zacks and Tversky, 2001a:5). Some evidence for a preferred basic level on a taxonomic hierarchy exists as well. For instance, Morris and Murphy (1990) found that participants responded fastest to basic-level labels when given an excerpt from event descriptions (e.g. *scream during the scary parts*) and asked to verify a category label at the subordinate level (*horror movie*), basic level (*movie*), or superordinate level (*entertainment*). Similarly, *going skiing* could be sub-classified further as *going downhill skiing* vs. *going cross-country skiing*. And *going downhill skiing* might be differentiated further into *bunny-slope skiing* versus *mountain-slope skiing*. Interestingly, it also appears that languages differ in the degree of specificity with which events are sub-classified. When talking about motion events English speakers specify the manner of motion, e.g. whether it is a running motion or a hobbling type of motion (using verb-particle combinations such as *run in* or *hobble out*) strikingly more often than do speakers of Spanish, who may omit such details even though their language allows such notions to be expressed (e.g. with a gerundial phrase as in *entrar corriendo* 'enter running') (Slobin 1996b).

Depending on the context, people can talk about events at different temporal levels and different degrees of specificity. Which level of temporal resolution and specificity is chosen depends to a large extent on the particular setting in which the event is described. When asked a question such as *What did you do today?*, it is likely that people will give an answer that is at a higher temporal resolution (*I went to the theatre*) than that of an answer to a question such as *What did you do last year?* (*I took a trip to Guatemala*). But if the conversation takes place during a dinner party the answer will also have a higher temporal resolution than if it takes place during an expensive trans-Atlantic collect-call. This choice for a particular temporal resolution is part of a set of more general maxims governing discourse, which relate to the expected truthfulness, informativeness, and relevance of utterances in verbal interaction (Grice 1975). For instance, if you are looking for somebody in a large building and you ask someone *Where is Sally?*, you expect the answer to be as precise as is necessary for you to find Sally, but no more precise than this. An answer like *She is in the building* when the speaker actually knows she is in the library on the eleventh floor is too poor, while an answer like *She is in the newly renovated library on the eleventh floor near the window at the second desk from the left sitting in a red chair, reading a book on conversational implicatures* may be unnecessary prolix. Again, what we judge to be adequate depends very much on the situation in which the utterance is made; for instance, if the library is large and many of the desks are hidden from view it may actually be very helpful to know that Sally is near the window.

In this chapter we suggest that the lexical and grammatical resources of a language, and the typical patterns of discourse in a culture, also constitute important variables influencing what is considered the appropriate level of informativeness for a given situation. Thus, in addition to a privileged level of granularity in the sense used by Zacks and Tversky, we also identify a 'basic level' when we refer to what is *typically* encoded in descriptions of comparable everyday situations like those above, where we assume that the informational needs are similar ('*Where is Sally?*', '*Where is my cup?*'). The basic maxims governing verbal interactions are assumed to be similar, but how they are employed by speakers of different languages varies. These differences result in different communicative strategies, including, as we shall argue, systematic differences across languages in the granularity of description at the 'basic level' in all three senses of the term that we describe in this chapter: what constitutes an event; which elements in the event deserve mention at all; and with what richness of detail these elements are expressed.

Summarizing, there is evidence from the literature that events can be characterized in terms of hierarchies, either partonomic (involving partitioning events into **constituent elements**, as in Talmy's work, or into temporally arranged **parts** as described by Zacks and Tversky) or taxonomic (classifying events into larger or smaller subtypes based on which components of an event are included in the event description and the specificity with which they are described). In describing events, people are likely to zoom in at a particular grain level of event segmentation and classification, depending on the context. In the remainder of this chapter, we survey cross-linguistic data that suggest that the level on the hierarchy (either partonomic or taxonomic) at which a speaker chooses to describe an event also varies, within semantic domains, according to the specific language in which the event is encoded. We present data from a number of different languages: English, Dutch, Hindi (Indo-European, spoken in Northern India), Tidore (Papuan, spoken in Eastern Indonesia), Tzeltal (Mayan, spoken in Mexico), Kalam (Papuan, spoken in mainland Papua New Guinea) and Kilivila (Austronesian, spoken in insular Papua New Guinea), focusing on descriptions of caused motion into containment such as *he put the ball into the box.*

8.2 The unit of analysis

Our unit of analysis is the independent clause, and in the following sections we examine how languages differ in the placement of event boundaries that are delineated at the clausal level. We also examine how fine-grained event descriptions are encoded within the clause, as expressed in the **predicative unit**, which we define as a complex of one or more relational entities in a single clause with a predicative function (including simple verbs, verb + particle constructions, verb + light verb constructions, etc., but excluding modifying elements such as adverbials, or the secondary predicate in depictive constructions). Thus, the verb *hobble* in *she hobbled slowly* constitutes a predicative unit, whereas *hobble out* is the predicative unit in *she hobbled out*. Note that we do not consider the direct object of the verb (*the box* in the phrase *kicked the box*) to be part of what we define as the predicative unit. Further, we focus in our discussion on those predicative units that occur in 'basic level' descriptions, defined earlier as unmarked, habitual descriptions of situations that are frequent in natural discourse. In the context of caused motion into containment these would be the typical answers to questions such as: 'What happened to Figure X?', 'Where is X?', or 'What is the causer A doing to Figure X?' For these expressions we can then ask: which part of the continuum of experience and perception is selected for expression, and how abstractly or richly is it described?

8.3 Partitioning events in language

The first interpretation of granularity hinges on the question of **where** humans place event boundaries in their linguistic descriptions at the level of the clause. We have some evidence from psychology that within cultural groups (predominantly North Americans) there is strong agreement on what constitute natural event boundaries (Newtson 1973; Zacks and Tversky 2001a; Zacks and Tversky, this volume). Further, as discussed in the introduction, sequences of smaller or more elementary events can be built into larger structures to form a hierarchical organization (Byrne 2002; Zacks, Braver, et al. 2001; Zacks and Tversky 2001b). Three levels of granularity are distinguished (Zacks and Tversky 2001a). At the lowest level, events are perceived as physical changes in the environment. These are the smallest segments in the continuum of perception and experience that are conceived of as single units. Intentional actions form the intermediate level and concern goal-directed actions and causal relations between physical changes. These intentional actions can be grouped to give scripts, the highest level. Scripts are recursive in the sense that they can be parts of other scripts, and this distinguishes them from intentional actions. If the perception of goal-directed actions and causal relations are universals of human cognition and central in our conception of changes in the environment, it may be expected that all languages will have expressions of this type of event.

It is not necessarily the case, however, that humans in all cultures will choose the same segments of an event in describing it at a particular level of granularity. For instance, von Stutterheim et al. (2002) showed that speakers of German are more likely to express an endpoint of a motion event than are speakers of English or Spanish. Where the latter would typically describe a scene such as a boat sinking as *the boat was sinking*, the Germans would say (the equivalent of) *the boat sank to the bottom of the ocean*, even when the endpoint of the event was not visible. The explanation for this difference in preferences is given as the absence of a productive progressive aspect marker in German that allows for a focus on the event as ongoing, which both English and Spanish do have.

Languages may also differ in how many physical changes are grouped together as one intentional action at the clausal level. Where a unitary event starts and what constitutes the endpoint may be different for different languages and cultures. For instance, speakers of Tidore (Papuan, spoken in Eastern Indonesia) typically include inceptions of events, or precursor events. When shown a video-clip of a man chopping wood, they are likely to describe this as follows:

(2) *Nau=ge* *oro* *peda* *tola* *luto*
boy=there fetch machete chop fire.wood
'The boy fetches a machete (and) chops fire wood.'

Note that this is regardless of whether the actual picking up of the machete is shown. English speakers clearly do not regularly do this. Pawley (1987: 346) shows that for Kalam, a Papuan language of Melanesia, intentional actions are systematically reported as: 1. movement to scene of first action; 2. action; 3. movement from scene of 2 to present or final scene; 4. action(s) at present or final scene. Hence, an event which in English would be encoded as *I gather firewood*, would, in Kalam, be expressed as '*I go* (1.) *wood strike* (2.) *get come* (3) *put* (4)'. This type of event report is in fact very common in the Papuan languages of Melanesia, as well as some Austronesian ones that perhaps adopted this strategy through language contact (cf. van Staden and Senft 2001; Senft, forthcoming; van Staden and Reesink 2008). This is possibly related to the general avoidance of having more than one full noun phrase or more than two overt (pronominal) arguments per predicate-argument structure so that all ditransitive actions and all actions involving manipulation of multiple objects are distributed over more than one predicate (de Vries 2005; Du Bois 1985, 1987; Heeschen 1998), but clearly these languages also articulate atomic events that in a language like English are simply not mentioned. In this interpretation of granularity, speakers of different languages can be shown to be different as to where they habitually place the boundaries for event reporting.

In events of caused motion into containment we find similar language-specific differences in how events are partitioned. An English speaker will encode in a verb + preposition/particle construction, the causer manipulating the object, the path of the caused motion, and the result state in which the Figure is contained by the Ground: *he put the ball into the box*. A speaker of Kilivila (Austronesian, spoken in insular Papua New Guinea) will first express the event where the causer takes up the (Figure) object and then goes on to describe caused motion, and the topological relation between the Figure and Ground objects at the endpoint (3), or additionally, the inception of the action and path of motion (4), all in a single clause, within a single intonation contour (Senft, p.c.):

(3) *E-kau boli e-sela olopola bokesi*
s/he-take ball s/he-put inside box
'S/he takes a ball she puts it into the box.'

(4) *ba-ito'uila ba-kau ba-lova bi-suvi o vado-la*
I.FUT-start I.FUT-take I.FUT-put.through I.FUT-enter LOC mouth-its
'I will start I will take (it) I will put (it) through it will enter its mouth.'

These are typical descriptions of caused motion in natural discourse. The prosodic contour shows them to be single units, and indeed, in repair, the entire sequence will be repeated and never just part of it, showing that they function in every respect as single clauses. When a single verb clause is deemed grammatical at all, native speakers of Kilivila will consider it 'foreigner talk' in those contexts (Senft, p.c.).

Tidore similarly has serial verb constructions that express 'causer picks up Figure' and 'Figure is placed inside Ground'. Consider the following descriptions of caused change of location into containment events in which a single subject first 'fetches' an object and then 'puts' it in a container:

(5) *Una oro fanai kam gure toma oti ngge ma-doya*
he fetch bait 'contents' put LOC perahu there its-inside
'He fetched the bait put (poured) them inside (into) the perahu.'

(6) *Ngona musti no-oro goroho ngge gure toma tempayang nde ma-doya koliho*
you must you-fetch oil there put LOC container here its-inside back
'You must fetch the oil and put it back inside this container.'

Descriptions of similar scenes in a language such as Hindi (Indo-European, spoken in Northern India) place narrower event boundaries and do not express the event leading up to the 'putting' event within the independent clause. Consider the following equivalents of the Tidore examples in (5) and (6) above. In Hindi, such complex events (fetching/bringing + putting) are encoded using an adverbial clause containing a participial verb together with the main clause (examples taken from elicited descriptions of video stimuli showing placement events: Narasimhan, in prep.):

(7) *ek aadmii=ne Tebl=se pleT uThaa kar kap=par rakh-ii*
a man=ERG table=ABL plate lift CONJ cup=LOC put-Sg.Fem.Prf.
'Having lifted (the) plate off the table a man put it on (the) cup.'

(8) *ek mahilaa=ne kuch pustakE Tebl=par aa kar rakh-II.*
a woman=ERG some books table=LOC come CONJ put-Pl.Fem.Prf.
'Having come (to the table) a woman put some books on (the) table.'

Such descriptions are natural and 'unmarked' descriptions of placement events. The availability of a serial-verb structure as part of the grammatical toolkit of the language can only be part of the reason why there are systematic differences in event report between Kilivila and Tidore on the one hand, and Hindi on the other. For instance, Hindi does have a verb + verb structural template. But the second position of the V-V compound is limited to a (fairly) restricted set of 'light verbs' (e.g. *de* 'give', *le* 'take', *jaa* 'come', cf. Hook 1991) and does not allow the insertion of semantically 'full' verbs as in Tidore. Further, compared to participial verbs in adverbials, the light verb is more tightly integrated with the main verb. For instance, the relative order of the constituent verbs of a V-V compound is fixed and phrasal constituents such as direct objects cannot intervene between them, **rakh Tebl=par do* 'put table=LOC give'). In Hindi, V + V templates (e.g. *Daal de* 'put give') are used with high frequency primarily to express aspectual distinctions (e.g. completion, inception) related to either one of the two events expressed in Tidore or Kilivila (e.g. the fetching event or the putting event). The second verb 'give' is not a fully lexical verb; the lexical verbs for 'bring' and 'put' cannot be composed in the same predicative unit to describe two consecutive events:

(9) **tel botal=mE laa Daal-o*
*oil bottle=LOC bring put-IMP
*'Bring–put the oil in the bottle.'

Thus, at the clausal level of encoding events, Tidore event reports systematically select larger portions out of the continuum of experience and perception as single-event units, labelling those aspects of the scene that are left to inference in Hindi descriptions of similar scenarios.

We emphasize that the grammatical and lexical resources of a language are not the only sources of cross-linguistic differences in the 'width' of the event segment encoded in the predicative unit of the independent clause. We must also take into account the **typical discourse preferences** of speakers of a language from among grammatical options within a language, which allow the same event to be described at different levels of granularity. For instance, it is not the case that event descriptions are obligatorily in the form of a serial verb construction in Tidore. The following description from Tidore shows an alternative way of packaging events in a clause: the 'fetching' event can be encoded in a separate clause from the 'putting' event, separated by the conjunction *la* 'so (that)':

(10) *Oro* *una* *toma* *Cobo* *gosa* *ino* *la* *gure* *una* *toma* *kurunga*
fetch he LOC C. carry this.way so put he LOC cage
ma-doya *ma*
its-inside just
'(They) fetched him from Cobo carried here so that they just put him in a cage.'

In summary, we suggest that the ability to partition events for the purpose of talking about them is a cognitive ability that all humans share, and that when pushed, speakers of a given language will be able to play with these event boundaries and verbalize events at a coarser or finer grain level. But the basic level of granularity that speakers typically use is not fixed across languages. And we find that the grammatical and lexical resources of the language to some extent reflect the default level of granularity. For instance, serial verb constructions allow for the encoding of 'wider' event boundaries in a single chunk. While this suggests a structuring of events for the purposes of speaking (cf. Slobin 1985, 1987, 1991), whether the linguistic encoding of events influences the partitioning of events for *non-linguistic* purposes is a matter for further research.

8.4 Levels of generality in event classification

Once the boundaries of an event are determined, the events can be classified **taxonomically** on the basis of the number of elements that are encoded by the predicate at the clausal level, and the refinement in the expression of these elements. In this section we discuss each in turn. Consider again the event of caused change of location into containment. It has been shown, that for such types of events, languages lexicalize similar components or **elements** in motion event descriptions (e.g. the sentence *The boy rolled the ball into the box*) (Talmy 1985, 1991):

- Figure: **ball**
- Ground (Source/Goal/Midpoints): **the box**
- path: **into**
- (caused) motion: **roll**
- manner: **roll**

Thus, the expression of a caused motion into containment potentially encodes at least a motion or translocation, a manner in which the motion occurs, a directionality of the motion, a Figure object that is inserted, a Ground object that is the container, and a causer. We refer to these as the **elements** in the event, to avoid confusion with the **parts** of the event that are related through connection in time.[1]

[1] Note that the elements in event report that are distinguished in Talmy's approach apply to each level in the partonomic hierarchy. Figures, Grounds, manners, etc. may be identified for intentional actions, but also for script-level expressions and for physical changes.

These elements in motion descriptions are not always all expressed. For instance in *the boy left the house* **manner** is not expressed, and in *she ran out* there is no **Ground** expression. Again, languages are shown to be different in the resources they have to express elements of the motion description, in particular in the predicative unit, as well as in how they typically make use of these resources to express the various elements in a motion description. A description can be said to be more fine-grained if the predicative unit describes relatively fine-grained distinctions in the type of event. More fine-grained descriptions show a more precise taxonomic classification of events. We mentioned earlier how the game *frisbee golf* is characterized as a subtype of *golf* based on the specification of one of the elements of golf, namely, the type of object it is played with (cf. Zacks and Tversky 2001a). Similarly, *run* and *walk* are more specific than *move* because they express aspects of the manner of motion, and *descend* or *move up* are more specific than *move* because they express the directionality of the motion. The English verb for caused motion into containment *put* is highly general since it expresses aspects neither of the Figure or the Ground, nor of the kind of topological relation that is brought about. In English these features are expressed with more specific verbs such as *insert* (11) or *cram* (13), as well as in the prepositional phrase introduced by a basic preposition, by a relational noun, or by a particle (11–13):

(11) *He* ***inserted*** *the books* ***into*** *the bag.*

(12) *He put the books* ***inside*** *the bag.*

(13) *He crammed the books* ***in.***

Hindi, too, uses a single verb in conjunction with a Ground-denoting phrase. Two different construction types are found, one in which a spatial nominal forms a possessive construction with the Ground object ('box's inside') as in (14), and one in which a locative case enclitic marks the containment relation directly on the Ground object ('box–in'), as in (15):

(14) *us=ne is=ko thaele=ke andar ghus-aa-yaa.*
He=ERG it=ACC bag=GEN inside enter-CAUS-Sg.Msc.Perf.
'He inserted it inside the bag.'

(15) *us=ne is=ko thaele=mE ghus-aa-yaa.*
He=ERG it=ACC bag=LOC enter-CAUS-Sg.Msc.Perf.
'He inserted it in the bag.'

Tidore shows a refinement in the predicate not often taken into account in motion descriptions. Tidore speakers will almost invariably indicate the **direction** in which an entity is moving or is located, even when to the English ear this may appear entirely redundant. If in a small room there is only one table and someone asks where her mug is, the answer is likely to be something along the following lines:

(16) *ngona na-mok=ge katina toma meja ntina=ge*
you your-mug=there be.landwards LOC table landward.one=there
'Your mug is in a landward location on the landward table'

Not only is the information that the hearer must turn 'landward' to find the mug mentioned twice, it also appears rather redundant given the fact that there is only one table, and this table is clearly visible to both speaker and hearer. For an English speaker, this may sound unnecessarily prolix, but for a speaker of Tidore anything less is too imprecise. While the sentence without the directional and locational may be grammatical, speakers will observe that 'we just don't say it that way', or that 'it is not really clear where the mug is now'.

We find that in descriptions of events of caused motion into containment as well, Tidore expresses the directionality or orientation of the motion with respect to speaker/hearer position. This element is not obligatory, but it is extremely frequent: in Tidore the directional verbs are among the ten most frequent verbs in the language, along with verbs for 'say', 'put', 'move/go', and 'make'.[2] The constructions used in Tidore are like the Hindi constructions described above. They use relational nouns in possessive constructions in combination with a general (locative) preposition as in examples (17) and (18). However, these constructions are normally augmented with a specification of the direction of the motion, for example 'seawards' or 'landwards':

(17) *Una wo-gure ena* ***hoo*** *toma gardus ma-doya*
he he-put it **seawards** LOC box its-inside
'He put it seawards in the box.'

(18) *Dadi rofu ena gure* ***isa*** *toma hono*
so weed it put **landwards** LOC bowl
'So (you) put the weed landwards in a bowl.'

While directional notions, e.g. deictic notions encoded in *go* and *come*, or vertical direction in *ascend* and *descend*, can also be stacked in expressions in Hindi (*wo hamaarii taraf andar aayaa* 'he came inside, towards us') and English (*he put the book in the northward direction on the shelf* or *she inserted the pencil in the hole in the upward direction*), these are neither natural nor habitual expressions of caused motion into containment as in Tidore. Tidore does encode simple motion to a goal resulting in a containment relation (e.g. *insert in the cup*) just as in Hindi and English. However, owing to the possibility of incorporating a directional verb with a main verb in a single predicative unit, it typically sub-classifies the class of caused motion-into-containment events more finely than in Hindi or English.

[2] Directional verbs in Tidore implicate but do not entail motion. 'Fact of motion' may be expressed separately by the verb *tagi* 'move, go', but this element, too, is not obligatory in a motion event.

We have shown how languages differ in where event boundaries are placed in describing an event, and in which elements pertaining to the motion event are encoded in the predicative unit of the event description (e.g. directionality in Tidore). Another way in which languages can differ has to do with how finely events are classified based on how much information is provided about the elements which *do* receive mention. For instance, descriptions of events of caused motion into containment typically imply a Figure and a Ground: for example the English verb *put* entails that something (the Figure) is placed somewhere (the Ground). However, the degree to which properties of elements such as the Figure and/or Ground objects are specified can vary across languages. This is then our third and final interpretation of 'granularity' in motion descriptions. Predicates in different languages have interestingly different characteristics in this respect. In a language such as Hindi, the mono-morphemic verbs of caused motion into containment include *bhar* 'fill (liquid/aggregates)', *ghusaa* 'insert, fill (non-liquid masses) stuff', *ghuseD*| 'cram', and *ThUUs* 'force down, cram in'. While the latter three verbs imply force-dynamic interactions between the participants involved in the action, there is no semantic specification of the spatial characteristics of the Ground object, other than that it is a (3D) container. Dutch, apparently like English, also has a generic verb *stoppen* 'put, insert'. But this verb can be used only for containment relations being impartial to the kind of Figure that is located. However, in addition it has a choice of predicates depending on the classification of the Figure as canonically 'sitting', 'standing', or 'lying' (Lemmens 2002; van Staden et al. 2006; cf. also Levinson and Wilkins 2006, and Ameka and Levinson 2007, for further detailed studies in the cross-linguistic encoding of positional information). In static descriptions, the use of these verbs depends on inherent properties of the Figure, such as the presence of a long axis or whether it has a natural, functional 'base' on which it may be placed and on the configuration into which it is placed. Thus, objects with a long axis that are vertically oriented will be 'standing', but so too will objects that are 'standing' on their functional base. This then includes both bottles and plates 'standing' on a table or in a cupboard. Objects that have their long axis oriented horizontally will usually be 'lying', and objects in a containment relation are typically 'sitting', although depending on the focus they may sometimes be described as 'lying'. In dynamic descriptions, the verb used for objects that end up being in a 'standing' position is *zetten* 'to put standing'; for a 'lying' position, *leggen* 'to put lying' is used; and for containment relations the verb is *stoppen* 'put sitting', but also *leggen* 'to put lying':

(19) *Hij legt / stopt / *zet de bal in de doos*
he lies / puts / stands the ball in the box
'He puts the ball in the box.'

(20) *Hij legt / *stopt / *zet de bal op tafel*
he lies / puts / stands the ball on table
'He puts the ball (lying) on the table.'

(21)	*Hij*	*zet* / **legt* / **stopt*	*het*	*kopje*	*in*	*de*	*kast*
	he	stands / lies / puts	the	cup	in	the	cupboard

'He puts the cup standing in the cupboard.'

Motion and locative descriptions in a language such as Tzeltal (Mayan) contain much detail on the precise orientation and properties such as the shape, size, etc. of the Figure or Ground object involved. While a derived verb of caused motion into containment such as *otz-es* places little restriction on the Ground object (other than that it has an 'inside region'; Brown 1994: 769), other verbs are more particular. For instance, *tik'* requires a Ground object which is a 3D bounded space with a narrow opening (e.g. bowl, narrow-mouthed gourd, cage), *lap* requires a flexible Ground object (cloth, mat), and *t'um-an* a liquid in a container (ibid.).[3] Other predicates encode various properties of the Ground objects, along with the action of positioning such an object, or the predication that it is positioned (e.g. sitting). Examples include *chejp*, (set down) a bag-like container (e.g. netbag), *pajch*, set down a wide-mouthed container (e.g. bowl), and *wajx*, set down a tall oblong-shaped object (e.g. bottle) (Brown 1994: 760–9).

English speakers may wonder whether it is at all relevant in non-contrastive situations to specify that the apple is not just in a box, but in a box with a narrow opening or in a vertically standing oblong box. Yet Tzeltal apparently does care for these sorts of distinctions as evidenced by the large number of verbs that convey this type of information. Even if a more generic description is possible, speakers' choice of the more specific one is relatively frequent.[4] The fine-grained specification of Figure and Ground argument properties in Tzeltal verbs contrasts with the verbs typically used in the caused motion description in Tidore, which are highly unspecific and include *gure* 'put' and *ten* 'put, place'. In fact, apart from a derived causative verb *somasusu* 'cause to be entered', there is not a single dedicated mono-morphemic verb in Tidore that means 'to cause a relation in which one object is in or inside another object' (i.e. a word that could be glossed as 'insert'). Only a few caused locative verbs give semantic detail with respect to the kind of Figure or the kind of Ground that is involved. For instance, *sose* is a causative locative verb used only for spreading out tablecloths on tabletops.

In English, we find relatively general verbs of caused motion into a container. For instance, monomorphemic verbs such as *cram*, *fill*, *stuff*, *insert*, *dip*, *dunk*, *pierce*, etc. imply something about the manner and potential end result of the action; but they are not very informative about the properties of Figure and Ground objects, with the

[3] Tzeltal locative descriptions may also specify properties of the Figure (Brown 1994; see also Talmy 1985 for related observations with respect to Atsugewi).

[4] Such preferences for more general versus more specific descriptions varies, even in related languages. For instance, the Mayan languages Yukatek and Tzeltal have similar resources for encoding spatial information but differ in their preferences (Bohnemeyer and Brown 2007).

exception of *dip* and *dunk* which imply that the Ground is a liquid or mass. However, English has a set of denominal verbs which provide highly specific information about the typical shape, size, and even material (e.g. bottles are usually made of glass, tins of metal) of the entities which might function as the Ground object in events of caused motion into containment: *bag, bin, bottle, box, can, tin, crate, garage, house, jail, kennel, pocket*, etc. (Levin 1993). We can classify verbs of caused motion into containment from the languages we have discussed along a continuum of specificity based on whether they:[5]

- specify only caused motion, with containment specified by a relational noun such as *inside* in English, or left to pragmatic inference (e.g. the Tidore verb *gure* 'put' used with a general locative as in 'put LOC bag'),
- specify that the Ground is a container (e.g. verbs such as Hindi *bhar* 'fill'),
- imply characteristics of the container including shape, width of the opening, rigidity, physical state (solid vs. liquid) (e.g. the Tzeltal verb *lut* 'insert tightly between two objects (usually lips or teeth)'; Brown 1994),
- name a class of containers (e.g. *bottle, can* in English).

In this section, we have described the sub-classification of motion-event descriptions in terms of distinctions made on the basis of features such as **directionality** and the properties of the **Ground object**. At the level of the predicative unit, languages pack information about events of caused motion into containment to different degrees, and there is both cross-linguistic and intra-linguistic variation in this respect. It remains to be seen how we can characterize the scope and limits of this variation in a systematic way.

8.5 Conclusions

In this chapter we have shown that there is considerable variation in terms of where event boundaries are placed at the clause level in order to talk about events of caused motion into containment, and how richly the event is characterized in terms of its constituent elements. Much further research is required to determine whether there is a small number of granularity levels in the way languages encode information lexically and combine them in specific construction types, or whether there is continuous variation in this respect. Thus, while taxonomic and partonomic hierarchies might underlie the representation of events for speakers of all languages, a number of factors underlie the selection of the particular levels which speakers select for the segmenting and categorizing of the continuum of experience and perception.

[5] Recall that we are talking only about information expressed by **predicative units** (e.g. verbs, particles, directionals, and their combinations); if we include information encoded in the noun phrases (e.g. *the bag, the cupboard*, etc.), then English and Hindi also specify detailed information about the properties of the Ground.

We suggest that one of these factors is the particular preferences that speakers of different languages have for encoding events at a particular granularity for unmarked, basic-level descriptions of the event. Such preferences may vary intralinguistically as well. Further cross-linguistic research is required to investigate the issues we have raised, as well as some interesting implications of this variation, including the extent to which language-specific preferences might impinge upon non-linguistic cognition and vice versa.

9

Granularity, space, and motion-framed location

MARK TUTTON

9.1 Introduction

This chapter examines what will be termed here 'motion-framed location'. Motion-framed location refers to the use of motion to encode a sequential locative relationship. Such framing of location within a motion event context is commonly encoded by the spatial–temporal prepositions *before* and *after*. The sequential locative relationships investigated in this chapter predominantly concern stationary objects being located in relation to other stationary objects: for example, *the bus stop is **before** the pedestrian crossing*. In cases such as these, the respective locations of the Figure and Ground[1] entities are determined as a function of their distance from a (typically unlexicalized) observer. This distance is measured in terms of time, considered as a function of the motion necessary to reach the Figure and the Ground. The entity which is *before* is closer to the observer, who is conceptualized as an agent in motion. Motion is the concept which underpins the 'Sequential Sense' (Tyler and Evans 2003) of such prepositions—at least as far as they encode the physical, locative relationships investigated in this chapter. The ways in which motion-framed location operates is addressed in the present work through an analysis of the spatial–temporal prepositions *before* and *after*, as opposed to the spatial locative prepositions *in front of* and *behind*. Two interpretations of granularity are at the core of this investigation: following one interpretation the prepositions are examined in terms of the amount of locative information they encode (cf. Narasimhan and Cablitz 2002), and following the other they are examined in relation to the scales of

[1] I use Talmy's (2000) distinction of *Figure* and *Ground* in this chapter. The Figure is 'a moving... entity whose path, site or orientation is conceived as a variable' (Talmy 2000a:311), while the Ground is 'a reference entity, one that has a stationary setting relative to a reference frame with respect to which the Figure's path, site or orientation is categorized' (ibid.:313).

space (Freundschuch and Egenhofer 1997; Montello 1993) at which they encode locative relationships. Spatial–temporal and locative prepositions are shown to differ in terms of locative semantic granularity (specificity), as well as in terms of the scales of space at which they may be used. Nevertheless, in certain cases both types of preposition may be available to encode the same locative relationship. When this occurs, speakers have the choice between anchoring the locative relationship in a static scene, or one in which the role of motion is stressed.

Previous research sheds little light on how the concept of motion can be used to encode locative relationships, although Vandeloise (1986) provides a notable exception in his analysis of the French prepositions *avant* and *après* ('before' and 'after'). The analysis presented here works towards a closer consideration of the question. Such consideration is necessary if we are to fully understand how speakers conceptualize locative relationships when they prepare to talk about them (cf. 'thinking for speaking', Slobin 1996a).

9.2 What is granularity?

As a preliminary observation, many interpretations of granularity are predicated upon the notion of detail: this gives rise to terms like fine-grained or its polar opposite coarse-grained (Gullberg 2011), both of which are commonly used as modifiers to define relative levels of focus or detail. Zacks and Tversky (this volume) explore variations in granular representation by showing how taxonomies represent objects and scenes at different degrees of detail: to reuse their example, an object might be encoded by a superordinate level (coarse-grained) term—for example, 'piece of furniture', a basic-level term, 'chair', or a subordinate-level (fine-grained) term, 'recliner'. Narasimhan and Cablitz (2002), working in the spatial domain, suggest that 'one way of viewing granularity is in terms of how much detail about events is provided in typical descriptions of events' (p. 18). The key words to retain here are *detail* and *events*: granularity is a concept which relates to the investigation of different levels of precision (detail) in different relationships (events). Even the basic task of defining granularity is coloured by the concept it targets: a definition may be fine-grained, coarse-grained, or somewhere in between, depending on how detailed a definition is sought (cf. Schegloff 2000: 719). Any level of detail is, in fact, a function of the criteria (semantic or otherwise) used to measure granular level; these criteria will differ, depending on the particular event under consideration. For example, motion verbs may be analysed to determine to what extent (if any) the semantic feature of manner of motion is encoded (cf. Vulchanova et al., this volume). The criterion used to determine granular level in such an instance might be a two-step process, outlined as follows: a. does the verb encode any details about the manner in which the motion event is executed, and b. if so, just how specific is the manner of motion encoded? Level of precision or specificity is a relative concept, with what is precise being determined, in part at least, by what is less precise, or coarser-grained. For example, lexical verbs like *walk* and *saunter* both meet the first requirement of encoding manner of motion in the verb stem. There is divergence, however, when the second criterion is applied: while *walk* (when applied to a human agent) encodes a motion event in which one uses one's legs to move, *saunter* refines this idea by making parallel reference to the leisurely pace at which this motion event is executed. The inclusion of this second semantic detail entails that the lexical verb is more precise, and may be said to be of a finer grain than *walk*. The encoding of manner as a refining element in motion event predicates is also noted by van Staden and Narasimhan (this volume), who furthermore point out that the encoding of other semantic information, such as direction of movement, can play a similar refining role.

Narasimhan and Cablitz (2002) consider several interpretations of granularity and apply two of these to their research. The first of these is a perception of granularity as 'the specificity with which languages carve up a semantic domain at the lexical and constructional levels' (p. 1). Gullberg (2011) applies this interpretation of granularity when she points out that commonly used placement verbs in Dutch and French differ in the degree to which they lexicalize the spatial properties of the Figure. In other work on Dutch placement verbs, Lemmens (2002, 2006) argues that one of the crucial spatial properties which influences lexical verb choice is whether the Figure has a base or not. The following example (Lemmens 2002) brings this observation to light:

(1)	*Ik*	*zet / leg*	*de boter*	*in de koelkast*
	I	set / lay	the butter	in the fridge

The use of *zetten* implies that the butter is in a butter dish and hence has a base, whereas *leggen* refers to the butter as a baseless package, most likely resting on its longer side (Lemmens, personal communication). French, in contrast, would simply use the causative verb *mettre* ('to put') in both situations, and therefore not encode this semantic difference. Following an interpretation of granularity as 'level of specificity', the placement verbs used by Dutch speakers may therefore be said to be of a finer grain than those used by French speakers. Once again, this determination of granular level is relative: here, it is achieved by the comparison of the semantic features of two different sets of placement verbs. Note, moreover, that it is only the semantics of these verbs *as understood within the context of physical placement events* which are used to determine granular level; other semantic extensions which may be evident in other contexts, for example in idiomatic expressions, are not of interest. A Dutch expression like the following,[2]

[2] I thank Emile van der Zee for this example.

(2) *zich* *neerleggen* *bij* *de* *situatie*
oneself to lay down with the situation
'to lay oneself down with the situation'
'to accept the situation'

employs a figurative use of *neerleggen*: such an extension of use moves beyond the context of physical placement events and would not therefore be considered in the determination of granular level. Granular level is a function of both *context* (physical placement events) and *specific lexical semantic* criteria (spatial properties of the Figure object).

The second approach taken by Narasimhan and Cablitz is to view granularity as referring to 'scales of space' (2002: 9). Applying this concept to their study of locative predicates in Marquesan, Narasimhan and Cablitz follow the granular differentiation of spatial areas proposed by Egenhofer and Mark (1995). Egenhofer and Marks' twin typological approach splices space into two categories: 'geographic' space, which is apprehended through physical displacement, and 'table-top' space, which contains objects open to manipulation. Other research has proposed finer-grained (more specific) breakdowns of spatial layouts (Freundschuh and Egenhofer 1997). An example is work by Freundschuh and Egenhofer (1997), who propose a typology which divides space into six categories on the basis of 'manipulability, locomotion, and size of space'. These three concepts will be pivotal in the analysis of *before* and *after* which follows. Montello (1993) also suggests a finer-grained framework, his approach being to divide space on the basis of 'the *projective* size of the space relative to the human body, not its actual or apparent absolute size' (ibid.:315). Common to both the Freundschuh/Egenhofer and Montello approaches, not to mention numerous others not mentioned here,[3] is the role played by motion in configuring scalar spatial typologies. To understand how this occurs, it is helpful to look at the different categories of space which Montello proposes:

- figural space: smaller than body, no movement required to apprehend it;
- vista space: can be viewed from the one place without 'appreciable' (ibid.:315) motion necessary (e.g. rooms, town squares, horizons);
- environmental space: larger than body and requires locomotion to apprehend it (e.g. buildings, cities);
- geographical space: larger still, and requires maps/models (e.g. countries).

Scalar typologies such as this one suggest that motion is intrinsically related to how we understand and apprehend space. It is a determining factor in how humans are physically able to perceive spaces of different size (this size being calculated relative to the human observer), thereby shaping interaction between the human

[3] For a good overview of scalar approaches to space, see Freundschuh and Egenhofer (1997).

observer/agent and their environment. In what follows, this idea of motion playing a driving role in human perception of space will be developed through an analysis of *motion-framed location*. *Motion-framed location* is a way of viewing and encoding locative relationships. It allows the speaker to set the scene differently from an expression which uses a static locative preposition[4] such as *in front of* or *behind*. Each of these two different approaches, one grounded in the static, the other in the dynamic, results in the encoding of locative relationships at different levels of lexical semantic granularity (specificity). Motion-framed location, as encoded by the prepositions *before* and *after*, shows that the way we consider space differs depending on three factors: the size of the space, the manipulability of the Figure/Ground objects in the locative relationship, and the salience of an extended path of motion to the space under consideration.[5]

Two interpretations of granularity will be used in the sections which follow. One of these will be an understanding of granularity as 'level of specificity'—that is, the amount of locative information encoded by the preposition; the other will be an understanding of granularity as the scalar division of spaces.

9.3 Motion-framed location

In this section the concept of motion-framed location will be introduced by examining the Sequential Sense of the preposition *before*. To examine how the preposition *before* encodes locative relationships within the framework of motion events, an everyday space like a room might be taken as our initial spatial backdrop. If we were to provide a basic description of a typical lounge room to a listener, a host of static locative prepositions would come into play: from the book *on* the table, to the table *in front of* the sofa, to the sofa *against* the wall. The use of *before* to locate the stationary, inanimate objects typical of such environments would, however, prove problematic:

(3) *??There's a table* ***before*** *the sofa.*

The confusion stems, in part, from the potential viability of two competing lexical senses. One is a sense which glosses as *in front of*, while the other is a sense which concerns sequentiality (Tyler and Evans 2003)—that is, the idea that two objects are found one after the other. The purely static reading of *in front of*, as lexicalized by *before*, is highly constrained in modern English and generally requires a human Ground (ibid.:167)—thereby going against its use in (3). The Sequential

[4] This is not to suggest that these so-called static locative prepositions, such as *in front of*, cannot be used in the context of a dynamic motion event. They can be. For example, 'John ran in front of the car'. However, it is the verb, not the preposition, which encodes motion here.

[5] These factors borrow from the criteria of 'manipulability, locomotion, and size of space' proposed by Freundschuh and Egenhofer (1997) in determining scales of space.

Sense[6] encodes the concept of motion and is infelicitous here for three possible reasons. The first of these reasons is that an extended path of motion is not of particular salience to the relatively small space under consideration (a lounge room). Secondly, the utterance has not been placed in a context which stresses the role of motion in conceptualizing the locative relationship, thereby working against motion-encoding *before*. Thirdly, the objects in the semantic roles of Figure and Ground are manipulable, moveable entities which are not conceptualized as fixed points along a path of motion. In (3) it would be much more acceptable to use a locative preposition[7] like *in front of* to encode the location of the table in relation to the sofa. It is conceivable, however, that if placed in a context which foregrounds path of motion (for example, giving directions), the use of *before* may be acceptable. One such example might be if the speaker were now giving directions over the phone to a friend who is coming to pick up the table. In such a context, an utterance like

(4) *??Go into the lounge room; the table's on the left,* ***before*** *the sofa.*

is nevertheless awkward, and the meaning of *before* is unclear. There is still the temptation to understand *before* in its purely static sense of 'in front of', and this seems to constrain the felicity of the sequential interpretation. In contrast, when this static versus sequential interpretative ambiguity is removed, *before* becomes acceptable. Imagine the speaker is now explaining to a guest where the bathroom is located:

(5) *Go down the hall; the bathroom's on the left,* ***before*** *the study.*

There are three major ways in which this locative expression contrasts to (4). Firstly, the strictly static interpretation of *before* as meaning *in front of* no longer holds. The physical properties of studies are such that they do not possess inherent orientations: they have no intrinsic 'front' or 'back', nor do we commonly attribute such spatial properties to them through a 'relative frame of reference'[8] (Levinson 2003). Therefore, it is more difficult for the interpretation of *before* as *in front of* to result. Secondly, an extended path of motion is more readily conceivable when navigating about a larger-size space like a house than about a smaller-size space like a lounge room. Thirdly, the Figure and Ground entities of (5) are easily conceptualized as landmarks along a path of motion: this is because they are spatial

[6] While the Sequential Sense 'can be used to denote any set of ordered entities' (Tyler and Evans 2003:166), it is only this sense as understood within the context of static locative relationships which is of interest in this chapter.

[7] Following Huddleston and Pullum (2005), many so-called 'complex prepositions' like *in front of* are in fact divisible into smaller units: *in front* can be taken as a single syntactic unit, and so classifying *in front of* as a single unit is syntactically erroneous. While I acknowledge this point, for the sake of convention and simplicity in the analysis, I will retain the use of *in front of*.

[8] For example, an utterance like **he sat up the front of the study* is implausible, as opposed to an utterance like *he sat up the front of the bus*, in which the Ground entity has an intrinsic front. There are a few exceptions: for example, if describing the plans of a house to someone, one might say *the study is behind the lounge room*, thereby conferring front/back properties onto the Ground.

areas which exist at fixed points in space. In contrast to this, the table and sofa of (4) are entities which are subject to shifts in location and are therefore less readily conceptualized as landmarks. These factors conspire to favour the use of sequential *before* in (5), as opposed to in (4).

Motion-framed location makes requirements of the physical entities which assume the Figure and Ground roles, as well as of the spatial areas which contain them. Central to motion-framed location is the agent who executes the real/virtual motion event. This agent may not be overtly lexicalized, but inferrable from context. For instance, the 'bathroom' in (5) can only be *before* the 'study' if there is a conceptualized agent in virtual motion to validate the locative sequence. In this example the agent is taken to be the addressee of the utterance, who is appealed to through the imperative form 'go'. While not a central point of investigation in the current chapter, it is interesting to consider how a crucial facet of a motion event—such as the agent in motion—may be understood in context without being directly lexicalized.

9.4 *Before* and *after* vs *in front of* and *behind*

As mentioned earlier, Freundschuh and Egenhofer (1997) identify three factors at work in scalar typologies of space: locomotion, the manipulability of objects, and the size of a space. These three factors—the first of which I will modify to 'extended path of motion' as opposed to simple 'locomotion'—are pivotal to the felicitous use of sequential *before* and *after*. The latter prepositions differ on all three counts from the locative prepositions *in front of* and *behind*.

9.4.1 Before *vs.* in front of

There are important differences in the spatial scenes evoked by the prepositions *before* and *in front of*, as the following examples suggest:

(6) **The post box is **in front of** the roundabout.*

(7) *The post box is **before** the roundabout.*

The first remark to be made is that *in front of* defines the location of the Figure in terms of the frontal surface of the Ground: this surface, depending on the object under consideration, may be attributed by an 'intrinsic' or a 'relative frame of reference' (Levinson 2003). Herskovits provides a good example of the latter reference frame when she points out that 'a front can be induced on an inanimate object by facing it' (Herskovits 1986: 160). This is exactly what is implied by (6), where the reader assumes the intervention of an oriented human observer to attribute a front to the roundabout. However, we do not typically assign spatial properties such as fronts or backs to roundabouts and this may explain the infelicitous use of *in front of* here. No such problem is encountered with *before*, which does not require any particular spatial property—such as a 'front'—of the Ground. Instead, the space in which the locative relationship is anchored must be large enough to enable the agent's extended path of motion. Thus, the static scene encoded by *in front of* foregrounds a particular surface of the Ground, whereas the dynamic scene encoded by *before* foregrounds a real or virtual path of motion. In both cases, there is foregrounding of a different spatial element. This has necessary consequences for the perceived location of the Figure. Consider the following sentences, which describe one person giving directions to another person looking for a telephone booth:

(8) *There is a telephone booth on the left,* ***in front of*** *the cinema.*

(9) *There is a telephone booth on the left,* ***before*** *the cinema.*

The location of the telephone booth differs crucially from one sentence to the next. While *in front of* in (8) references a particular surface of the Ground entity (this surface being determined by our habitual interaction with cinema buildings and our passage through a designated entrance), *before* makes no reference to any specific surface of the building. It is the cinema's overall location, determined relative to the agent's path of motion, which is central here: the telephone booth is located prior to the Ground *as a whole*, and not to a sub-part of this whole (i.e. a 'front'). This means that an object which is *before* another object is not necessarily *in front of* it. A second observation is that whereas (8) locates the telephone booth by referencing an intrinsic property of the Ground (its 'front'), the use of *before* in (9) is necessarily indexical: a Figure can only be *before* a Ground once the location—real or imagined—of an agent in real/virtual motion is taken into account. That is, the person giving directions in (9) needs to know the route their addressee (the virtual agent in motion) is going to take to reach the cinema—and hence successfully locate the telephone booth on the way. This entails that any use of sequential *before* will be indexical in nature, since paths will vary following the current location of the agent and other contextual variables (such as individual variations in route preferences). This contrasts to *in front of*, where indexical variation is not an issue when an intrinsic frame of reference is used.

A further set of examples reveals another major difference in the way the two prepositions set the spatial scene. Consider the following sentences:

(10) *There's a speed camera* ***before*** *the traffic lights.*

(11) *There's a speed camera* ***in front of*** *the traffic lights.*

Our perception of the distance between the Figure and Ground entities shifts depending on whether *before* or *in front of* is used. *Before* allows the interpretation that a larger distance holds between the locations of the two entities than does *in front of*. Such a change in the reading of proximity is likely due to the motion-encoding and temporal properties of *before*.[9] The temporal properties suggest that an event needs to take place to validate the period of time which is understood as elapsing between the locations of the two entities. The motion event encoded by *before* validates this temporal shift from the first entity to the second. Moreover, there is the possibility of inserting a verb phrase directly after the preposition:

(12) *There's a speed camera* ***before (you get to)*** *the traffic lights.*

Before licenses the verb phrase *you get*, and in doing so illuminates the fusion of temporality, motion, and location in its spatial use. In (10) and (12) the Figure is not located directly in front of the Ground: its exact position is less precisely determined. In (11), however, the interpretation is that the speed camera occupies a location within the frontal region of the lights: there is a certain degree of frontal alignment between the Figure and the Ground. Secondly, the speed camera is understood as being proximal to the traffic lights. The notion of proximity, however, is relative. Therefore, *in front of* may be used to locate a Figure at a considerable absolute distance from a Ground, as in the following example:

(13) *There's a cloud* ***in front of*** *the sun.*

The acceptable distance between two objects shifts as a function of object size (Carlson 2009). That is, there may be millions of miles separating the cloud and the sun, and *in front of* may still be used. However, if a cup were a metre away from a saucer on a kitchen counter, *in front of* may prove a difficult fit—even if the cup and saucer are frontally aligned. Conversely, a Figure may be close to a Ground but not frontally aligned with it, and *in front of* may still be employed. This is because the felicity of the preposition depends on factors such as the presence of other objects in the surrounding environment (cf. Herskovits 1986). Nevertheless, the concerns of frontal alignment and proximity are more central to *in front of* than they are to *before*. Therefore, the location of the bus stop in the following sentences is attributed a very different reading depending on the preposition used:

(14) *Get off at the bus stop* ***before*** *the cinema.*

(15) *Get off at the bus stop* ***in front of*** *the cinema.*

In (14) the bus stop may be located at a significant distance from the cinema—perhaps half a kilometre away—whereas in (15) it is (approximately) located within the horizontal region extending out from the cinema's frontal surface. Instead of focusing on spatial properties like surfaces, the sequential sense of *before* hinges on the interrelated factors of motion and time. It presents the Figure and Ground as

[9] Vandeloise (1986) noted this interconnectivity of motion and time in his analysis of the French prepositions *avant* ('before') and *après* ('after').

points along an extended path of motion, which is governed by the direction(s) taken by the agent to reach the Figure. This extended path of motion allows for the reading of distance between Figure and Ground objects, as in (14). The idea of directed motion underpins the locative relationship by validating a temporal relationship: what is *before* is also what is closer to the agent in a temporal sense (time being understood in terms of the motion required to reach the Figure entity[10]). All of this contrasts markedly to *in front of*, which encodes neither time nor motion. Consequently, there is not the focus on path of motion encoded by *before*, which means that the Figure and Ground do not have to be conceptualized as landmarks along a path. This explains why manipulable items such as sofas and tables may fulfil Figure and Ground roles when *in front of* is used, as opposed to *before*.

Given the focus on extended paths of motion, sequential *before* should logically operate when characterizing locative relationships in large-size—as opposed to small-size—spaces. I will understand 'small' here to mean spaces of room-size or smaller, following Freundschuh and Egenhofer (1997). This suggests that *before* will not be used to encode locative relationships in 'figural' spaces and in certain 'vista' spaces (following Montello's scalar typology, outlined above). These size-related selection restrictions should exist independently of whether the space is an internal or external one. Hence, if we were directing a tired hospital visitor down a long corridor to a coffee machine nearby, we might say something like the following:

(16) *The coffee machine's down the hallway, just* ***before*** *the nurses' station.*

Depending on the vantage point of the speaker, the space described may be either an example of Montello's vista space (if the Figure and Ground objects are visible in the distance) or environmental space (if they are not). When we turn to an internal vista space of smaller size—the lounge room of (3) and (4) for instance—the felicity of the preposition changes. This suggests that the size of the space which contains the Figure and Ground entities may play a role in the use of *before*. Therefore, when the size of the physical space is further reduced—so that we are now dealing with figural space—sequential *before* is similarly restricted. Imagine that the hospital guest has bought a coffee for the nurse. He couldn't describe its location by saying **the coffee's on your desk, just before the computer*. Small figural spaces like desks, along with the manipulable objects which they support, are not conducive to instances of motion-framed location. In contrast to this, *in front of* can be used at all scales of space: this includes the 'geographical' spaces of Montello's typology, provided that a 'front' may be applied to the geographical entity under consideration:

(17) *French Guinea lies* ***in front of*** *the equator.*

[10] The interconnectivity of motion and time is revealed by Evans (2003), who proposes the 'Complex Temporal Sequence' model as a way of understanding temporal sequentiality as a function of motion. His concern here, however, is with temporal events and not with locative relationships, although the latter seem to fit the mould he proposes.

Sequential *before* may also be used at this scale, provided that the locative relationship is situated within a motion event context:

(18) *Switzerland is* ***before*** *Austria when travelling east across Europe.*

In light of these observations, the following hypothesis is proposed:

> *A motion-framed locative preposition like* before *requires a larger-sized space than does a static locative preposition like* in front of. *This entails that* before *may be used at medium or large scalar levels, but not at small scale levels (i.e. in figural spaces, following Montello (1993)). This is because* before *encodes an extended path of motion, and requires stability in the location of the Figure relative to the Ground. Such locative stability is more easily achieved when the inanimate, non-manipulable objects of larger-sized spaces are used.*

9.4.2 After *vs.* behind

Whereas *before* encodes the location of the Figure as being closer to the point of view of the observer, *after* stipulates that it is further away. An everyday outdoor space like a street provides a ready example of this:

(19) *The taxi rank is on the left,* ***after*** *the crossing.*

(20) **The taxi rank is on the left,* ***behind*** *the crossing.*

The temporal properties of the preposition *after* entail an understood progression of movement in the direction of the crossing and onward to the taxi rank. The unacceptability of *behind* in (20) is explained by several reasons. The first of these is that we do not habitually attribute a 'front' or a 'back' to pedestrian crossings. Secondly, the Figure is larger than the Ground—a factor uncharacteristic of Figure objects (Talmy 2000). Interestingly however, no such size constraint applies to the use of *after* in (19). The potential for a larger Figure object is confirmed by the following sentence:

(21) *The car park is* ***after*** *the traffic lights.*

There are several reasons which explain the use of *after* with larger Figure objects. Unlike locative prepositions such as *in front of* and *behind*, *before* and *after* do not identify a salient surface of the Ground in relation to which the Figure is located. This suggests that the Ground's spatial properties—such as size and individual surfaces—are less important when *before* and *after* are used. This enables *after* to co-occur with Ground objects for which front/back distinctions are not habitually applied, and which are of considerably smaller size than the Figure:

(22) *The shopping centre is* ***after*** *the roundabout.*

After, like *before*, has a preference for Figure and Ground entities which have stable positions in space. Note the difficulty of saying

(23) *??The cat is* ***after*** *the roundabout.*

However, if the Figure is modified to incorporate a fixed, inanimate aspect of the environment—such as a footpath—the felicity of the utterance changes:

(24) *The cat is on the footpath,* ***after*** *the roundabout.*

In (24) it is no longer simply the cat's location which is at issue: it is also the location of the footpath upon which it is standing. The inclusion of the latter as a fixed, non-manipulable point of reference enables the use of *after* in the locative expression. This, however, does not mean that inanimate entities must absolutely intervene for the felicitous use of *after*. Consider a slightly tangential example which foregrounds order as opposed to physical location:

(25) *John is* ***after*** *Michael in the line.*

While John and Michael are moving, animate entities, their locations are framed within the containing structure of a line. The two men are not fixed points at space and cannot easily be conceptualized as landmarks along a path of motion. However, they do possess stability on another related level: their distance *relative to one another* is presumed to remain constant—even as both advance in the line. This entails that there is stability in their locative relationship, owing to the consistency of the distance which separates them. In contrast, 'the cat' of (23) may conceivably be walking along the footpath, meaning that its location relative to the roundabout is constantly shifting. This locative transience is neutralized to an important degree by framing the cat within the larger, fixed space of the footpath, thereby conferring the necessary quality of locative stability.

It was previously noted that the distance between the Figure and Ground, along with their alignment on the frontal axis, is more heavily constrained by *in front of* than by *before*. This observation also applies to *behind* and *after*:

(26) *There is a busy intersection* ***behind*** *the shopping centre.*

(27) *There is a busy intersection* ***after*** *the shopping centre.*

While the instinctive interpretation of (26) is that the intersection lies within the horizontal domain extending out from the back of the shopping centre, this concern of frontal alignment is much weaker in (27). Here, the intersection is readily understood as failing to align with any point of the Ground's back surface at all. While there is not necessarily much difference in the perceived distance between the Figure and Ground in these two sentences, this does not mean that *behind* and *after* make similar requirements concerning object distance. Hence, it is possible to say the following:

(28) *The gas station is two miles* ***after*** *the shopping centre.*

but more difficult when *behind* is substituted for *after*:

(29) *??The gas station is two miles* ***behind*** *the shopping centre.*

This is not because expressions of absolute distance cannot co-occur with *behind*: note the possibility of saying *he stood a metre a behind me*. Rather, it seems that *after* will tolerate a larger distance between the same two landmarks than *behind* will. In (29), *behind* cannot be used because world knowledge tells us that there are probably other landmarks closer to the gas station than the shopping centre. This foregrounding of proximity is of less salience to *after*, which privileges instead the role of the Ground as a fixed landmark along the extended path of motion.

As was the case with *before*, *after* encodes location in terms of a motion event and the time required for the agent in (real/virtual) motion to reach the Figure and the Ground. The entity which is calculated as being further in terms of this time/motion interface is attributed the role of Figure and is said to be *after* the other object, which assumes the semantic role of Ground (cf. Tyler and Evans 2003: 176). The consequence of this, however, is that the Ground is not normally conceptualized as an oriented entity, which possesses a 'back'. *Behind*, on the other hand, encodes a 'back', which is understood to be either intrinsic to the Ground or applied through a relative frame of reference. The encoding of location via a frame of motion in *after* thus comes at the cost of eliminating a basic front/back distinction.

It has already been shown that sequential *before* cannot be used in small scale space, and that it requires the Figure and Ground to be in a stable locative relationship. This leads to a preference for fixed, non-manipulable landmarks to fulfil the roles of Figure and Ground. The same conditions hold true for *after*. A simple example illustrates this point. Imagine a speaker giving directions to their flatmate, who wants to borrow a suitcase:

(30) *??When you go into my room the suitcase is on the floor,* ***after*** *the desk.*

Despite framing the locative relationship in terms of a motion event (as lexicalized by the verb *go*), the use of *after* to encode a motion-framed locative event is nevertheless unnatural. This is due to two reasons. Firstly, as was the case with *before*, small-size spaces like rooms do not provide an ideal spatial setting for extended paths of motion. Secondly, suitcases and desks are manipulable objects which are not easily conceptualized as fixed points along a path of motion. These factors conspire to set a preference for a static locative preposition to encode the locative relationship, as opposed to a spatial–temporal one like *after*.

As was the case for *before*, when the physical space increases in size and the Figure and Ground entities are more easily conceptualized as fixed points in space, *after* becomes possible.

(31) *The lecture theatre's on the left, just* ***after*** *the double doors.*

After, like *before*, may also be used in relation to the 'geographical' spaces of Montello's typology, when framed within a motion event context:

(32) *Ljubljana is **after** Salzburg when you travel by train to Slovenia.*

(33) **Ljubljana is **behind** Salzburg when you travel by train to Slovenia.*

Behind cannot be used in (33) because we do not habitually attribute fronts and backs to countries. This, however, does not preclude *behind* from being used at the 'geographical space' level: all that is required is a large enough landmark for which the properties of a 'front' and a 'behind' are salient. Therefore, the following may be said by a person on the Indian subcontinent side of the Himalayan Range:

(34) *The Tibetan Plateau is **behind** the Himalayan Range.*

The use of *behind* in this example encodes location by appealing to a static scene. In contrast, it would be harder to say '?The Tibetan Plateau is *after* the Himalayan Range', since it is more difficult to conceive of situations in which one would be crossing over the Himalayas. Such an expression would nevertheless be possible if one were travelling in an airplane and about to approach the Himalayan Range. This demonstrates the salience of extended paths of motion to the use of *after* when encoding static location.

In certain situations, speakers may be able to choose between prepositions which foreground *either* the motion event *or* the locative event. Hence it is perfectly conceivable to give directions to a space like a cinema by saying that it is *just after the Spanish restaurant, on your right*, or by describing it as *next to the Spanish restaurant, on your right*. The former locative predicate shows how the simple copula verb 'be' can play a role in the encoding of motion, simply by licensing the preposition *after*. 'The language of motion events is a system used to specify the motion of objects through space with respect to other objects' (Huang and Tanangkingsing 2005: 207). *Before* and *after* satisfy this definition by encoding the real or virtual motion of an unlexicalized agent, relative to a Figure and Ground entity. It is this motion which leads to the sequential locative configuration of the two entities. This shows how motion can come to be a primary concept in the construction of locative relationships.

9.4.3 Implications for granularity and 'thinking for speaking'

A parallel may be drawn between the contrasting locative semantic granularity of sequential *before* and *after* on the one hand, and *in front of* and *behind* on the other. The latter reveal a tighter perception of the spatial properties of the Ground by encoding a front/back distinction which anchors the locative relationship. In contrast, the Ground is viewed at a coarser level when *before* and *after* are used: no subpart of the Ground is singled out for attention, suggesting that it is considered as a whole unit. *In front of* and *behind* also require intrinsic front/back properties of the Ground, or that such properties be conferrable through a relative frame of reference. This excludes certain landmarks to which front/back distinctions are not habitually attributed, such as roundabouts (cf. (6)). Furthermore, the concern of frontal alignment is of greater salience to *in front of* and *behind* than it is to *before* and *after*, as is the distance between Figure and Ground objects. On the basis of this, *in front of* and *behind* encode a greater degree of locative information than do *before* and *after*, and may thus be said to be of a finer locative semantic grain. On the other hand, sequential *before* and *after* make more requirements as far as scales of space are concerned. They are not easily used at the level of 'figural' space—whereas *in front of* and *behind* are; they require a large spatial area to allow the foregrounding of an extended path of motion—a condition not set by *in front of* or *behind*; *before* and *after* also require locative stability in the Figure/Ground relationship, thereby favouring the inanimate objects of large-size spaces as opposed to the manipulable ones of small-size spaces. Considered in terms of such requirements, *before* and *after* are of a finer grain than are *in front of* and *behind*. This shows that the perceived granularity of these two sets of prepositions shifts considerably, depending on the interpretation of granularity applied.

It appears that the more a preposition foregrounds sequentiality and motion, the less salient the spatial properties of the Ground entity become. The analyses of *in front of*, *behind*, and sequential *before* and *after* have revealed important distinctions in the way the Ground entity is conceptualized in the lexicalized locative relationship. The encoding of motion-framed location comes at a price: as the salience of motion increases, the Ground comes to be conceptualized in terms of this motion. Its own spatial properties decrease in importance as time and motion characterize the locative relationship. This has important consequences for how English speakers need to consider space when preparing to encode locative relationships. Because speakers must consider the options their language makes available to them when they wish to speak, the ways in which they think when processing thought for speech is necessarily shaped by the language spoken: this is known as 'thinking for speaking' (Slobin 1996a:76). English makes available lexical items which simultaneously encode both location and motion (cf. *before*, *after*, and *following*) while also possessing others which foreground a static scene predicated on the spatial properties of the Ground (cf. *in front of* and *behind*). Following the 'thinking for speaking' hypothesis, speakers must factor in the concepts of time and motion when deciding whether to use a motion-framed locative preposition like *before*, or a static-framed one like *in front of*. Large-size spaces in which extended paths of motion are salient should, theoretically, favour the emergence of motion-framed locative prepositions. Prepositions like *before* and *after* should also emerge when there is difficulty in attributing a front/back orientation to a Ground entity. On the other hand, when the distance between objects is less, when motion is of little salience to the spatial context, and when the front/back orientation of the Ground is judged to be important, the use of static-framed prepositions should be favoured. Naturally, such hypotheses are speculative and require justification from empirical research.

9.5 Conclusion

This chapter began by broadly considering the concept of granularity. By identifying a central use as a means of referring to varying levels of specificity, the investigation led to a canvassing of the concept within the framework of lexical semantics. Moving beyond this approach to the topic, previous research undertaken by Narasimhan and Cablitz (2002) revealed a particularly pertinent line of enquiry, through the presentation of granularity as the scalar division of space. The models proposed by Egenhofer and Mark (1995), Montello (1993), and Freundschuh and Egenhofer (1997) highlighted the role of motion in human perception of space. This then led to an exploration of the ways in which *motion-framed location*, as lexicalized by the spatial–temporal prepositions *before* and *after*, come to encode static locative relationships within the framework of motion events.[11] The use of such prepositions underlies a perception of space which contrasts importantly with that underlying the use of static locative prepositions like *in front of* and *behind*. Whereas the latter foreground the role of the Ground in the perception of the spatial relationship, motion-framed locative prepositions determine location as a function of the real or virtual motion of an agent. When the two objects in the locative relationship are stationary and inanimate, the one located further from the agent is said to be *after* the closer entity, which, in turn, is said to be *before* the one located further away (cf. Vandeloise 1986).

The major point to emerge from the investigation is the different ways in which motion-framed locative prepositions set the spatial scene as opposed to static locative prepositions. The three factors of size of space, manipulability of objects, and extended path of motion were shown to be critical to the felicitous use of sequential *before* and *after*. These two prepositions require larger-than-room-size spaces which allow extended paths of motion, as well as stability in the Figure/Ground locative relationship (thus favouring large, non-manipulable objects). Whereas *in front of* and *behind* may be used to encode locative relationships at all scales of space, sequential *before* and *after* are more restricted: the analysis suggests that they may be used in larger 'environmental' and 'geographical' spaces, but only in certain types of 'vista' spaces and not at all in 'figural' spaces. In terms of locative semantic granularity *in front of* and *behind*, which foreground a particular spatial property of the Ground and for which the concepts of frontal alignment and

[11] There exist other such motion encoding prepositions, such as *past* and *following*, which remain a subject for future investigation.

distance are more salient, were shown to be of a finer grain than sequential *before* and *after*. Perhaps even more important than this, however, is the implication which the latter prepositions have for 'thinking for speaking'. *Before* and *after* suggest that speakers must consider the salience of motion events to individual locative relationships before using language. This shows that motion is fundamentally linked to location, and colours our very perception of it.

10

Path and place: the lexical specification of granular compatibility

HEDDA R. SCHMIDTKE

The aim of this chapter is to provide several formal tools for representing granularity-dependent notions such as **point-like** or **proximity**, so that they can be used for characterizing granularity restrictions in a unified way. It is demonstrated how the representational formalism can be used to encode restrictions of compatibility of spatial granularity in the understanding of spatial expressions for two different spatial tasks. It is shown how procedures for the localization of objects and for route following can be understood as derived from lexical specifications of the components of the spatial expression. The formal notions of focus regions and grains are introduced as tools to link the descriptive, spatially static lexical specification to the procedural, spatially dynamic interpretation for the tasks of localization and route following. The formal framework is illustrated with the examples of the German constructions *an ... vorbei* 'past' and *an ... entlang* 'along', which combine with the same preposition (*an* 'at/on/by'), and demonstrate that the dynamic, granular interpretation allows us to model different degrees of acceptability of sentences.

10.1 Introduction

Granularity can be understood as a parameter of the representation process that depends on a representing agent (an observer, speaker, or hearer), on the one hand, and a represented portion of the world that is observed or talked about, on the other. Understood in this way, spatial granularity is a parameter that influences the strategies used to conceptualize objects and landmarks in a spatial layout. Human beings can flexibly choose the representation strategy that seems most appropriate for a given task (Zacks and Tversky, this volume), and they can switch between representation strategies whenever a different strategy turns out to be necessary.

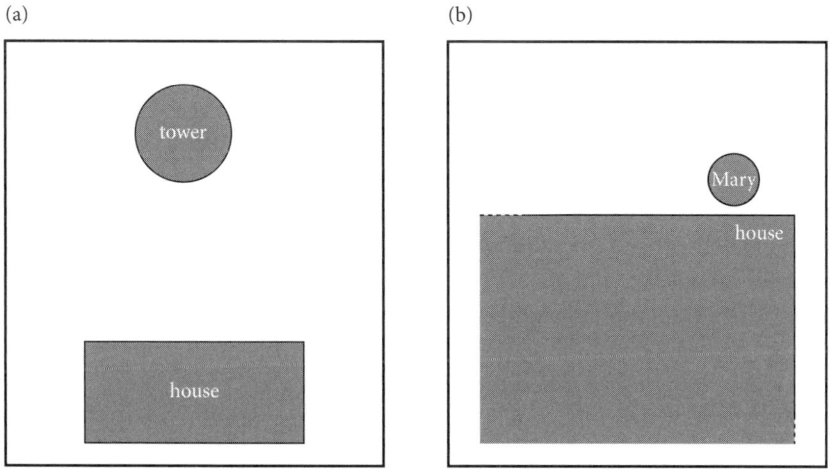

The house is to the south of the tower

Mary sneaks along the house

FIGURE 10.1 A house in two different contexts

Consider for instance Figure 10.1, showing two depictions containing the same house at different scales with corresponding descriptions. Each depiction and description contains the house and one other object. It would be intuitively plausible to say that the house is point-like or atomic in one context (*the house is to the south of the tower*, Figure 10.1a), and extended in another (*Mary sneaks along the house*, Figure 10.1b). From a more formal point of view, we can state that, in Figure 10.1a, the geographical relation *south* in the verbal description and the dominant large distance between the two objects in the depiction both serve to establish a geographical, large-scale context in which the extension of a house is negligible. The description of a slow-moving human being—small in comparison to a building—and the depiction of a small distance between the comparatively large building and the person on the other hand suggest a human-scale context with an extended representation of the building in Figure 10.1b. Applying the categorization of Montello (1993), we can assume that the sentence in Figure 10.1a and the map-like simplification indicate that the context belongs to **geographic space**, whereas the sentence in Figure 10.1b with the mention of human locomotion suggests **environmental** or **vista space**.

Two different notions of spatial granularity are involved in this example. On the one hand, **granularity**, in the sense of **grain-size**, refers to sizes and distances. However, these sizes and distances have to be understood as relative sizes and distances within a certain context or focus region. In contrast to the standard mathematical concept of distance, the cognitive concept of **proximity** is known to be context-dependent and not symmetric (Worboys 2001). On the other hand, we use the term **granularity**, in the sense of **representational granularity**, to refer to the level of detail of a representation: a point-like representation is a coarse representation of location retaining only the **position** of the object, whereas an extended representation retains information about the **shape** of an object and the main parts that constitute it.

We can illustrate this with respect to the example: both objects are point-like in Figure 10.1a, because the distance between them is much larger than the maximal extensions of each of the two buildings in the represented portion of the world. Figure 10.1b, on the other hand, contains two objects of very different size at a short distance. The house cannot be reduced to a point in this case. As mentioned before, however, human beings can flexibly change between representations as the task at hand changes: if the geographical direction between the two distant buildings is relevant, we can choose a coarse granularity, but if the relation between Mary and the house is relevant, we would **focus** on a smaller region and retrieve a fine-grained representation.

10.2 Localization of objects

Simple sentences of localization, such as *the car is in front of the building*, contain three spatially important constituents (Talmy 1983): the **Figure** or localization object (here, *the car*), the relation (*in front of*), and the **Ground**, or reference object (*the building*). This scheme can be transferred to descriptions of **paths**, such as shown in 10.1b: the **trajectory** of Mary's motion (path) bears the spatial relation ALONG to the building (ground).

Talmy gives some restrictions on the choice of FIGURE (f) and GROUND (g): he claims that the sentence (1) *the house (f) is behind the bicycle (g)* is awkward in contrast to the sentence (2) *the bicycle (f) is in front of the house (g)*, since the house in the example is a more suitable Ground object than the bicycle. He counts **size** among the criteria for suitable Ground objects: the house is much larger than the bicycle. Transferred to the observations concerning the extension of an object in a scene: if the Ground object is preferably larger than the Figure object, then the Ground is **extended** (x) with respect to a much smaller, and thus in the context **atomic** (a) Figure. Accordingly, case (1) above can for brevity be noted as fx/ga and the preferred case (2) as fa/gx. The case fa/ga is acceptable if the Ground is a salient object for reasons other than relative size.

These preferences are interesting for the lexical specification of paths, because paths can be treated similarly to linear, and thus, extended Figures: compare, for instance, *the road along the river* (type: fx/gx) with the path description *she runs along the river* (px/gx). Assuming a descriptive, spatially static survey perspective, paths can therefore be treated like extended Figure objects. The path description entails at least two levels of granularity derived from the length of the path and the size of the **bearer of motion**, i.e. the moving or moved entity. Eschenbach et al. (2000) give four subclasses of German directional prepositions: goal prepositions specify the end (GOAL) of the path, source prepositions give the start (SOURCE) of the path, and course prepositions characterize the intermediate course of the path. They either indicate an intermediate place (*durch*/'through', *über*/'over') or the shape of the path (*um*/'around', *längs*/'along').

The construction *an*... *vorbei* 'past...' according to this schema characterizes a path via an intermediate place that is close to the ground object (VIA). *An*... *entlang* 'along...' can be expected to be related to *entlang*, which is counted among the prepositions indicating restrictions on the shape of the path (SHAPE). In both cases we have to handle a linear and thus extended path. In this respect, the VIA-case is of type px/ga, whereas the SHAPE-case is of type px/gx:

sie läuft an der Statue vorbei
'she runs past the statue' (px/ga),

sie läuft am Fluss entlang
'she runs along the river' (px/gx).

The question is then, why the case fx/ga is rejected by the criterion of size, but not the case px/ga. It is argued below that the case px/ga is acceptable under a dynamic interpretation of paths as sequences of places. As a result, the VIA-case (px/ga) is read as a series of places, one of which contains a case of fa/ga, whereas the SHAPE-case (px/gx) can be specified by a series of places all of which fulfil fa/gx for the BEARER OF MOTION as FIGURE. The extended localization object (the path) can thus be matched to two more standard cases: fa/ga and fa/gx. The difference between the VIA-prepositions and the SHAPE-prepositions can then be modelled as a difference in quantification and extension of the GROUND.

Another phenomenon which fits into the scheme is that projective prepositions like *left of*, or *in front of* can be applied only in a certain area around the Ground (see also Tutton's remarks on the importance of distance for the applicability of *in front of* and *before*, in this volume). Levinson (1996) ascribes a length to the axes to mirror this. But the phenomenon can also be explained by restricting the area that is considered for describing localization. Results by Regier and Carlson (2001) indicate that the strategy for localizing the Figure changes with increasing distance. In close proximity, functional parts and the distance to the relevant side (the top for *above*, for instance) of the Ground are most important. With increasing distance, the distance between Figure and relevant axis extending from the centre of the Ground becomes the main criterion. We can conclude that the extension of the Ground seems to lose importance with growing distance: the Ground can be represented by a point.[1] This is in accordance with results of Herskovits (1997). She argues that 'representing a fixed object as a point requires seeing it from a distance' (p. 175).

[1] Which geometric point is actually chosen—be it the centre of mass or another point, e.g. the centre of mass of a functional part—should be irrelevant, if an object is **point-like** in a scene. The size of a point-like object, i.e. the maximal distance between its points, is so small relative to the other distances in the scene, that the error for choosing the wrong point can be neglected. I am indebted to C. Eschenbach for this suggestion.

Following these analyses, I will assume that the following simple algorithm can serve as a framework for discussing main concepts of granularity underlying the cognitive processes necessary for the localization of an object given a projective localization like *the fly is above the table*. In a first step, the hearer would have to localize the Ground object (in the example: the table) within a currently focused portion of the (real or imagined) world, such as for instance the immediate surroundings of the hearer or a region referred to in the most recent dialogue. With a salient Ground object the localization of the Ground within this **focus region**[2] should be a particularly easy task. A large size object in particular fills a large portion of the focus region. When the location of the Ground is known, the hearer can **focus** on the Ground object, in order to identify the relevant part of the object (the top for *above*) and the relevant axis or direction (Levinson 1996).

After the relevant side and axis have been identified, a first representation of the space within which the Figure will next be searched can be generated in the third step. Crucial questions regarding this third step are, of course, how exactly this representation is generated, whether it is actually analogous to visual images (Kosslyn 1980, 1994) as notions such as **focusing**, **defocusing**, and also the term **granularity** itself suggest, or whether the phenomena of granularity discussed can be explained also with other representational formats. In the latter case, these terms, which all have their roots in photography, have to be understood metaphorically.

From a formal point of view, it is sufficient to assume that the hearer has a choice between representations at different levels of granularity, and that a representation of a certain focus region at a fine representational granularity has more details than a representation of the same region at a coarser granularity. If we assume that more details require more memory space and that memory space is a limited resource, we can conclude that higher detail comes at the price of loss of covered area, and vice versa:[3] a highly detailed representation can only be generated if the focus region is small; a large focus region can only be searched if the representation detail is low.

We can now relate the two distance-dependent strategies identified by Regier and Carlson (2001) to the two representation types for the Ground described above, and assume that a hearer can make use of at least the following two granularity-dependent strategies for finding the Figure given the Ground object:

[2] The notion of regions should be understood as a generalized concept here and in the following; in particular, we do not restrict the dimensionality of regions.

[3] We can illustrate this point with an example using the photo metaphor. Consider we want to take a photo of a mosquito on the back of an elephant with a very limited digital camera that has a fixed maximal resolution of, say, 1000 × 1000 pixels. We cannot recognize the shape of the mosquito on a photo that shows us the shape of the elephant, as the mosquito would be reduced to a dot; and vice versa, if we can recognize the shape of the mosquito on the photo, then the elephant will be too large to fit into the picture, as only a patch of skin texture would be visible.

gx case: if the Ground is extended with respect to the current focus region, scan along the relevant side of the ground;

ga case: if the Ground is atomic with respect to the current focus region, scan along the relevant axis of the ground.

The sub-process of scanning along a line (side or axis) can be modelled as a granularity-dependent operation of inspection of certain sub-regions of the search focus region: the scan process inspects **grains** of the current focus region that overlap the line. The inspection of a grain can be explained in this model as consisting of two steps: first, the grain is focused so that it becomes the current focus region, then the salient objects within this region become accessible and, if the figure is among them, it will be found.

The key notions for this chapter are the operations of focusing and defocusing: they are used not only to shrink and enlarge the search focus region, but at the same time the grain-size is shrunk or enlarged, respectively. In this way, the flexibility of the hearer to change strategies and representations can be formally modelled with the operations of focusing and defocusing. The algorithm can be seen as a computational model of instructed searching in a granular representation of a spatial layout: defocusing coarsens representational granularity as well as grain-size and enlarges the focus region. Whether the Ground is extended or atomic depends on its size relative to the size of the focus region. If we start the algorithm from the relevant side or part of the object, that is, with the preferred gx-case, and successively defocus, the object eventually becomes point-like and we can switch to the ga-strategy. If we defocus further, the focus region might eventually contain the whole maximally relevant portion of the world, and the search would end with a negative result.

From the perspective of computational complexity, the mechanism keeps the effort needed for the search in the scanning process independent of the absolute size of the area to search. The capacity needed for storage remains constant at every step, a criterion important for computational models of attentional processes, which have to mirror the restrictions of working memory. A simple realization of the algorithm could work on a discretization of space, a raster image, whose pixels provide a simple notion of grains and whose maximal extent provides the initial focus region. However, it would be a major restriction of a theory for spatial granularity were it to be applicable only applicable to raster spaces or equally spaced grids. Instead, we follow the more general theory proposed in Schmidtke and Woo (2007), which allows for a more flexible concept of grains and grain-sizes. In the following, we therefore only consider cells that convey interesting information to be stored or to receive attentional focus. Since only an extended location, but not a point, can be a focus region, and since the ordering of extents of such regions determines the grain-sizes, Schmidtke and Woo (2007) suggest the term **extended locations**. With reference to the term **place recognition** in the examples below (section 10.5), we call the extended locations relevant for a route **places**. In particular, we talk about the **start place**, the **goal place**, and **decision places** instead of start point, end point, decision points: an extended location can be a **grain**, that is, **point-like**, with respect to a context region, but geometrically more precisey it is an extended region not a point: a point-like region can be focused, so that its shape becomes apparent, whereas a point remains a point when focused.

Places are studied in greater detail in the next section. They are presented as a granular representation of space and of object locations in space that can be used to give a procedural interpretation of the semantics of spatial expressions. The algorithmic perspective sheds light on the links between perception and language: the declarative formalizations of lexical semantics of spatial expressions are interpreted as specifications for an algorithmic evaluation. Special focus is on applicability in the context of navigation and route instructions. The procedural interpretation is advantageous in this case, since the **places** used for navigation in large-scale space are perceived one after the other, and the interpretation thus depends on local spatial relations.

10.3 Places

One of the main purposes of a prepositional description like *the book is to the left of the TV set* is to help the hearer in finding the Figure. Descriptions in route instructions take a different perspective: in the statement... *then there is a large rock at the river*, it is rather the **place** (there) that has to be located than the Figure (large rock). The area to search, in addition, may not be accessible at one time, but only as a succession of local views (route perspective). The global arrangement (survey perspective) can be constructed from these local views.

Sentences such as **go along the river, until you arrive at a bridge** can be understood as locating a path or parts of a path with respect to objects. The project of Tschander et al. (2003) addresses the question of how an artificial navigation system, the Geometric Agent, could understand an instruction given in natural language in order to successfully follow the described route in a simulated two-dimensional environment. One of the key tasks for this system is to build a representation of the places it will encounter on its route based on the linguistic instruction. Perceived extended objects like roads, lakes, and buildings have to be matched to the linguistic descriptions in the instruction.

Eschenbach et al. (2000) analyse paths as trajectories that linearly order the points that lie on it. From this ordering of points, an ordering of places encountered on the path is derived. The notion of place is not further characterized by Eschenbach et al. If we want to abstract from the concrete trajectory, a **route** can be represented as a collection of places which are to be visited according to an ordering that the instructor may have gained from the ordering of places on certain trajectories.

Thus, we can focus on local relations for finding a route, and knowledge about the global shape of the path may not be necessary for the meaning of *entlang* 'along' and *vorbei* 'past'. The notion of place can be characterized informally as follows (see Schmidtke and Woo 2007 for a formal characterization and comparison to related approaches):

- **Places** can serve as focus regions and as grains of focus regions.
- Each place is associated with a level of granularity that determines
  - **extent** and
  - **grain-size** of the place.
- Places have **sub-places** and **super-places**.
  - The operation of focusing on some part of a place p yields a **sub-place** p' ($p' \lhd p$): a sub-place has smaller extent and finer granularity, that is, smaller grain-size.
  - Defocusing a place p yields a **super-place** p'', which has larger extent and coarser granularity ($p \lhd p''$).
- The smallest sub-places accessible for focusing are called the **grains** of a place.

The sub-place/super-place relations hold only between places and are not transitive: focusing on the grain of a grain requires two steps of focusing. The relation $\lll$ is the transitive hull of the relation $\lhd$.

We use the notion of places as a geometric concept of spatially simple locations that can locate objects and make their grain-sizes and extents comparable, so that concepts of relative size can be defined (see Schmidtke 2005b, 2003, for formal definitions):

- Places determine the relative, local size of an object:
  - the **maximal extension** of an object region A is determined by the smallest places that contain A;
  - the **local minimal extension** of an object region A with respect to a focus region p_c, is determined by the largest sub-places of p_c that are contained in A.
- Places locate objects: an object o is **located at** a place p (written as $\alpha(o, p)$), if it has a grain that is contained in the region of the place. Depending on the maximal extension of the object in relation to the extent of the currently focused place, we distinguish two special cases: an object is called
  - **extended at the place** ($\alpha_X(o, p)$), if its extent is larger than that of the place, or
  - **atomic (or point-like) at the place** ($\alpha_A(o, p)$), if its extent is smaller than a grain.
- Places are the basis to define a notion of **proximity** between objects: two objects are in proximity, if they are at the same place.

The above concept of proximity is not yet sufficient to capture phenomena of asymmetry of the cognitive concept of proximity (Worboys 2001) underlying prepositions such as *an* 'at' (to be characterized in section 10.4). From the characterization of $\alpha(o, p)$ it follows that two objects can only be at the same place if they have a certain minimal size.

Figure 10.2 illustrates the special cases α_A and α_X. For reasons of legibility, we apply the following simple model of granularity in this illustration: places are depicted as circular regions and size-based granularity is modelled in such a way that the grains of a place all have a diameter of one fifth of the diameter of the place. However, the mathematical concept underlying our notion of places and granularity encompasses models with variations of shapes of places as well as concepts of granularity with varying sizes of grains (Schmidtke and Woo 2007); for instance, for a navigation task in a city, we might find a model that assumes rectangular grains on the level of size of the city blocks and street sections to be most appropriate; for a vision task, a model could be appropriate that assumes smaller grains (in terms of absolute size) at the centre of a focus region, and larger grains at the boundary. Thus, the notion of grain-size is a concept of **relative size**.

In Figure 10.2, the house is atomic at $p0$. By focusing on the **sub-places** p_1, p_2, and p_3, the extension of the house becomes relevant. α_A and α_X compared with α pose further restrictions on the granularity of an object at a place. Also, the topological criteria for α can be refined: interesting topological sub-relations of α are the following:

- p is a **place of external contact** of o ($\alpha_{\text{EXT}^c}(o, p)$) if p overlaps o only in places that have grain size (but not in larger sub-places).
- p is a place **inside** the object o ($\alpha_{\text{IN}}(o, p)$) if the region of the place is fully contained in that of the object.

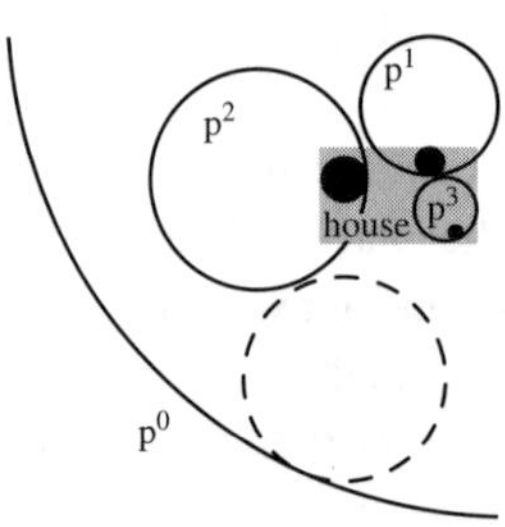

Summary of the valid relations:

place	atomic or extended	topolog. relation
p_0	$\neg\alpha(house, p_0)$	$\neg\alpha(house, p_0)$
p_1	$\alpha_X(house, p_1)$	$\alpha_{\text{EXT}^c}(house, p_1)$
p_2	$\alpha_A(house, p_2)$	$\alpha_{\text{EXT}^c}(house, p_2)$
p_3	$\alpha_X(house, p_3)$	$\alpha_{\text{IN}}(house, p_3)$

FIGURE **10.2** Relations of granularity-dependent location: the house is not located at p_0 since it is smaller than a grain. A sub-place of p_0, p_2 localizes the object as an atomic object. Both p_1 and p_3 localize the house as an extended object. The places p_1 and p_2 are places of external contact of the house; the place p_3 is a place inside the house. Examples of grains are shown with a dashed outline for p_0 and as filled circles for p_1, p_2, and p_3.

It follows that an object o containing a place p ($\alpha_{\text{IN}}(o, p)$) is always categorized as extended at p ($\alpha_X(o, p)$). In contrast, α_{EXT^c} can hold for places that locate the object as an atomic object (in the example: p_2), or as an extended object (p_1).

With places having a certain granularity, i.e. grain-size and maximal extent, the link can be made between the task of navigation and the task of localization. One strategy for giving a route instruction can be by inspection of a cognitive map. Literature on (non-instructed) artificial and biological navigation systems underlines the importance of places as primitive locations used in basic steps of navigation: recognition of places initiates a triggered response, the correct action to reach the next place on a route. Trullier et al. (1997) describe places as defined by landmark configurations. Werner et al. (2000) state that places link route segments. Mallot (1999) presents a representation of a cognitive map: he contrasts place graphs, which contain places as nodes and route segments as edges, with view graphs, which store views on places as nodes and recognition-triggered responses to views as edges. From the perspective of navigation systems, a place is defined by a number of stored views that, matched to the current view, give the system information about its current position (Mallot 1999). It can approach the place (homing) by moving so as to increase the similarity between the current and a stored view.

The strategy described in section 10.2 for locating objects using places can be extended to strategies for constructing, inspecting, and enriching a cognitive map. A route instruction can then be understood as a description of the places one encounters following the route, this description ideally being close to the way in which the places are conceptualized when encountered in the world.

Verbal route instructions are based on the following spatial representation (cf. Allen 1997; Denis 1997; Klein 1979; Wunderlich and Reinelt 1982): route descriptions contain information about landmarks, decision points, and actions a (virtual) navigator has to perform to follow the route. The instructor generates an internal representation of an area that contains the starting point and the goal. She then has to plan or remember a path between the two. The path can be verbalized by describing decision places with respect to local or distal landmarks. Decision places are those places where a decision has to be made concerning which direction or road should be chosen. In an urban environment, they lie at an intersection, junction, or fork. In an open space environment, decision places are at particularly salient constellations or at places where a turn has to be made. These locations are point-like and can be identified as places that are especially important for the route. A decision place is described by the instructor—and later recognized by the instructee—using the landmarks characterizing the place. If we categorize landmarks by the relation between the region occupied by the landmark and the region of the place, this allows us to characterize three types of landmarks:

1. **A local atomic landmark** characterizes a particular place. The landmark is completely included in the place. Example: *at the large oak tree turn left.*

2. **A local extended landmark** characterizes and links several places. The landmark is only partially included in the place. Example: *from there follow the river, until you arrive at a wooden bridge.* The river links the place at the start of the path (from there) to the place at the end (at a wooden bridge).
3. **Distal landmarks** characterize certain views and spatial relations associated with the place. The landmark is not at the place. Examples: *you can see the church steeple from there; head towards the airport.*

In the following we will mainly discuss examples involving local landmarks. However, the mechanisms carry over to the case of inspection processes on the cognitive map that yields a representation of the larger surroundings (survey knowledge).

In the next section, we will have a look at the semantics of the German preposition *an*, which being a preposition denoting proximity is especially suitable for studying granularity. We present example sentences illustrating the concept of proximity and the compatibility of sizes. In section 10.5, the concept of a route as a set of places on a path is developed. The use of *an* together with complex verbs of locomotion with *entlang* and *vorbei* is analysed. The hypothesis is that the granularity needed for encoding the meaning component of proximity of *an* is a parameter of the whole phrase and influences also the path description: *entlang* and *vorbei* both express a situation of proximity between path and Ground. They differ mainly in *entlang* being a SHAPE modifier and *vorbei* belonging to the VIA modifiers. The differences and similarities between those categories are then studied, and the concept of routes as sets of places is tested with the examples *entlang* and *vorbei.*

10.4 Size and proximity: *an*

Both *entlang* and *vorbei* can be combined with the preposition *an*, which expresses proximity or contact between Figure and Ground. *An* can be combined with extended as well as with atomic Figures and Grounds:

die Straße am Fluss
'the road by the river' (fx/gx),

die Eiche am Fluss
'the oak tree at the river' (fa/gx),

der Mann an der Ampel
'the man at the traffic lights' (fa/ga),

?die Mauer an der alten Eiche
('the wall at the old oak tree' (fx/ga).[4]

[4] Here and in the following examples, * and ? mark sentences for which the default interpretation fails or is difficult, respectively.

The last example (fx/ga) is only acceptable with the assumption that the atomic Ground (the old oak tree) is particularly salient for reasons other than size (section 10.2). Starting from the semantics of *an* given by Wunderlich and Herweg (1991), we want to investigate in this section how the notions of granularity can be incorporated into the lexical specification of a preposition with a formalization based on places. Our goal is to reach a specification which mirrors the preferences for certain constellations of Figure and Ground.

According to Wunderlich and Herweg (1991), the semantics of *an* can be specified as:

(1) *an*: $\lambda y \lambda x \textsc{loc}(x, \textsc{ext}^c(y))$

The figure x is located (LOC) in the proximal contacting external region ($\textsc{ext}^c$) of the ground y.

The relation LOC is introduced by Wunderlich and Herweg (1991) as a primitive for stating that an object (here, x) is located in a region ($\textsc{ext}^c(y)$). Accordingly, $\textsc{ext}^c$ is a function that maps an object y to a region of external contact, that is, to a proximal region around y. We can link the meaning component of proximity to the concept of representational granularity, so that context-dependency resulting from the representation process can be reflected by replacing LOC with the grain-size dependent notion α: $\alpha(x, p)$ holds if the region of x overlaps the region of the place p in at least a grain of p. There are two main differences between LOC and α: on the one hand, α is less restrictive than LOC because it does not demand inclusion; on the other hand, it restricts the minimal size of the object and therefore can be used to further restrict the compatibility of granularities. In particular, we are interested in an interpretation of the *an*-phrase that matches with the dynamic interpretations for localization phrases. In both, the situation of localization of an object and in the situation of place recognition, space is experienced as a succession of places; the goal is in both cases to find the place that matches the natural language description. By assuming a relation between three components—the Figure, the Ground, and a place—it is possible to encode differences in preference and intended meaning that result from default strategies, as well as the flexibility to choose non-standard interpretations.

In contrast to using a function $\textsc{ext}^c(y)$ that yields a unique region given a Ground object y, we can use the binary relation $\alpha_{\textsc{ext}^c}$ between a Ground y and a place p. Consequently, there can be several places p that are places of external contact with respect to y, as was illustrated in Figure 10.2. Proximity, in this specification, is a by-product of restrictions on the general property of places as granularly fixed entities.

(2) *an*: $\lambda y \lambda x \exists p[\alpha(x, p) \wedge \alpha_{\textsc{ext}^c}(y, p)]$

The general preference for an atomic figure can be expressed by using the restricted $\alpha_A(x, p)$ instead of $\alpha(x, p)$. We summarize these restrictions in the following specification: *x an y* ('*x* at/on/by *y*') holds, if *x* is atomic at a place of external contact of *y*.

(3) *an* (preferred): $\lambda y \lambda x \exists p[\alpha_A(x, p) \wedge \alpha_{\text{EXT}^c}(y, p)]$

This analysis suits cases where the PP modifies an NP, as in *der Stuhl am Tisch* 'the chair at the table'. Following Eschenbach et al. (2000), I assume that the place p is accessible in combinations with verbs of motion. The main function of the prepositions in this case is to characterize a place p:

(4) *an*: $\lambda y \lambda p(\lambda x)[\alpha_A(x, p) \wedge \alpha_{\text{EXT}^c}(y, p)]$

The two α-relations in the characterization link the Figure and the Ground both spatially and granularly, because the place p has a fixed granularity, and the α-relations demand that the place and the object be of compatible granularity: neither object may be too small by the restriction of resolution, and the distance between them may not be too large by the restriction of extent of the place. The following examples illustrate how Figure and Ground have to correspond in size and conceptualized extension in the use of *an*:

1. (a) **Der Ball rollt am Meer entlang.* 'The ball rolls along the sea.'
   (b) *Der Ball rollt am Wasser entlang.* 'The ball rolls along the water.'
2. (a) **Der Ball liegt am Meer.* 'The ball lies on/by the sea.'
   (b) **Der Ball ist am Meer.* 'The ball is by the sea.'
   (c) *Der Ball liegt am Wasser.* 'The ball lies at the water.'
3. (a) *Die Stadt liegt am Meer.* 'The town lies on/by the sea.'
   (b) *Die Stadt ist am Meer.* 'The town is on/by the sea.'
   (c) *?Die Stadt ist am Wasser.* 'The town is by the water.'
   (d) *?Die Stadt liegt am Wasser.* 'The town lies by the water.'
4. (a) *?Maria liegt am Meer.* 'Mary lies on/by the sea.'
   (b) *Maria ist am Meer.* 'Mary is by the sea.'
   (c) *Maria ist am Wasser.* 'Mary is by the water.'
   (d) *Maria liegt am Wasser.* 'Mary lies by the water.'

The examples illustrate possible sources of granular incompatibility. In all examples, the Ground is a body of seawater. Restrictions on the granularity may be encoded in the nouns and verbs:

- Ground objects *Meer* 'sea' and *Wasser* 'water': the granularity encoded in the different nouns restricts the maximal extent of the place referred to with *an* + Ground. *Ball* cannot be used with the granularity of *Meer*, since it is too small, and *Stadt* town is incompatible with the granularity of *Wasser*.
- Figure objects *Stadt* 'town', *Maria*, and *Ball* 'ball': toys and towns are restricted to certain levels of granularity (2b, 2c, 3b, 3c), in contrast to persons (4b, 4c). Human beings can occur on nearly every level of granularity. The Ground and the verb in this case are the only granularly specified entities, and consequently

the spatial and temporal extent referred to in the sentence differs: in (4b), Mary may be spending her holiday in a town by the sea, whereas she is within a few metres of the water at this moment in (4c) and (4d).

- Verbs *sein* 'to be' and *liegen* 'to lie': the verb *liegen* encoding a certain position in the case of (4a) is more restrictive than the generic *sein*. In (4b) the granularity of the sea dominates the sentence. The example (4a) has conflicting granularities: on the one hand, the grain-size of the focus region would have to be fine enough to distinguish Mary's orientation as lying, and on the other hand, its maximal extent would have to be wide enough to encompass a relevant portion of the sea. However, *liegen* can be used with towns as encoding geographic position (3a). In this case compatibility is given. The restrictions transfer to the case of verbs of locomotion (1a, 2a, 1b, 2c).

10.5 Paths and routes

Before we can analyse the meaning of *entlang* and *vorbei* in a way that includes granularity as a parameter in the next section, we need to characterize a notion of paths that allows for encoding levels of granularity. We make the assumption that a described **route** can be seen not only as a trajectory, i.e. as an oriented curve (Eschenbach et al. 2000, 1999) or ordered set of points, but also as a multi-granular sequence of places or ordered set of places. A given granularity, then, selects one of the possible conceptualizations of the path.

An example of a route that contains two different levels of granularity is shown in Figure 10.3 as one situation that could be described by the sentence *he ran through the park*. This particular instance of a route can be conceptualized on two different levels of granularity: L1 the places that correspond to the visible environment and L2 the places of each step. In the sentence *he took the same route every day*, the level L1 is intended. In the sentence *yesterday, he had to evade a bicycle and fell*, the level is L2. The example shows that both levels are easily accessible: *at the north-east intersection* (L1), *he had to evade* (L2) *a bicycle yesterday and fell*. The places of L1 provide local spatial contexts for the places of L2. The global course of the route is described not on the step level—which would be different for every instance of running—but on the level of decision places.

Defining the concept of routes as multi-granular sequences of places, we obtain a means to characterize paths on different levels of granularity, so that we can translate the concept of trajectories as oriented curves proposed by Eschenbach et al. (1999) into a granularity-dependent concept. Formally, a partially ordered set of places for a path w is described as a **route** r. The relation between a path w and a corresponding route r is given by ROUTE(w, r). Places p that belong to a route r bear one of the following relations to the route: SOURCE(r, p), GOAL(r, p), or VIA(r, p). SOURCE(r, p)

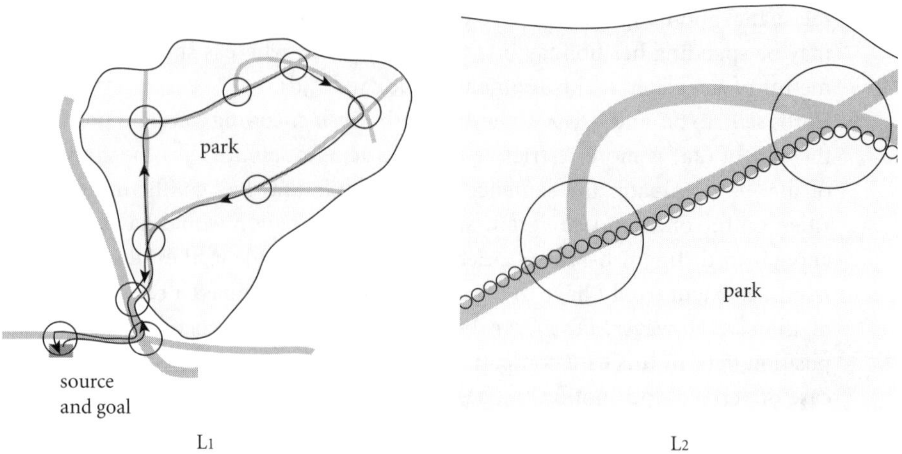

FIGURE 10.3 The sentence *he ran through the park* can be interpreted with respect to different levels of granularity. In this example, the route has two levels of granularity: L1 the level of granularity on which the route is conceptualized as a sequence of decision places, and a more fine-grained conceptualization (L2) for which the actual locations of the runner are relevant.

states that the place p is on one granularity the start of the route. If there are additional places p' for which SOURCE(r, p') holds, they have to be more detailed or less detailed places: p' is a either a sub-place of p, or p is a sub-place of p'. In the example, the house of the runner, the porch of the house, and the first step of the stairs leading to the porch constitute valid SOURCE-places at different levels of granularity. GOAL(r, p) accordingly characterizes a place at the end of r, with the same restrictions. VIA(r, p) holds for all other places on the route and, specifying the extended middle part of the route, it applies to more than one place of a route.

The path modifiers *entlang* 'along' and *vorbei* 'past' specify intermediate places of a route, i.e. places for which VIA(r, p) holds. The main question now is how the conceptualization of SHAPE-prepositions like *entlang* can fit into this scheme. With respect to the dynamic interpretations, we can argue that the restrictions on the global shape of a path can be explained as a consequence of local relations at places on the route. An instructee can *go along the river* without knowing its overall course by moving forward without losing visual contact with the river, that is by maintaining a LINK. A notion of direction (*moving forward*) is inherent in the meaning of *entlang*. It can be captured by stating that locally there are no relevant changes of direction. Globally, however, there may be several turns: if Mary walks *along the moat* (a), she will eventually have walked *around the castle* (b). The shape of the path is in (a) locally straight and in (b) on a larger scale round. The granularity levels involved are for (a) the width of the linear moat and for (b) the diameter of the castle. Schmidtke et al. (2003) propose a characterization of concepts needed to capture changes of direction. The characterization of *entlang* presented here focuses on how the common meaning component of *entlang* and *vorbei*, that is, related to the meaning of *an*, can be included in the SHAPE-preposition *entlang*, on the one hand, and the VIA-modifier *vorbei*, on the other.

10.5.1 *A case study:* entlang *and* vorbei

The German adposition *entlang* is used both

(a) as a postposition with accusative

den	*Fluss*	*entlang*
the-ACC	river-ACC	along

'along the river'

and

(b) as a preposition with dative/genitive

entlang	*dem*	*Fluss,*
along	the-DAT	river-DAT,

'along the river'

Di Meola (1998) gives a thorough account of the two main meaning components of *entlang*: he states that

> the spatial configuration underlying *entlang* is one of 'oriented parallelism' and thus necessarily contains a PATH-GOAL-schema as well as a LINK-schema. The accusative focuses on the dynamic aspect of the configuration (the spatial progression of the trajector in time), the dative on the static aspect (the spatial link between trajector and landmark) (p. 204).

In contrast to *entlang*, *vorbei* cannot be used as an adposition. However, both can be adverbs and appear as the head of a complex PP with *an*: *an der Straße entlang* 'along the street', *an der Ampel vorbei* 'past the traffic lights'. According to the findings of Kray et al. (2001), *vorbei* differs from *entlang* in two aspects: *vorbei* does not require parallelism and allows greater distance between Figure and Ground. Further necessary restrictions are that path and Ground have to be disjoint for *vorbei*, but not for *entlang*, and that *vorbei* is telic in contrast to *entlang*.[5]

In addition, *an... vorbei* prefers an atomic Ground (ga), whereas *an... entlang* needs an extended Ground (gx), as the following examples show. The path itself is in all cases globally extended, but realized locally by the point-like places.

1. *Maria geht an der Mauer entlang.* 'Mary walks along the wall.'
2. *?Maria geht an der Mauer vorbei.* 'Mary walks past the wall.'
3. *?Maria geht am Tor entlang.* 'Mary walks along the gate.'
4. *Maria geht am Tor vorbei.* 'Mary walks past the gate.'

[5] Telicity can be tested with temporal adverbs like *stundenlang* 'for hours' that show whether the situation denoted by the expression is an event or a process (cf. Egg 1994): **stundenlang an A vorbeigehen* vs *stundenlang an A entlanggehen*.

The more problematic example 2 could mean that Mary passes by the short side of the wall. Sentence 3 suggests that the gate is very large, like the gate of a factory for instance.

The differences between *vorbei* and *entlang* can be reflected in a characterization built on the basis of routes and places. We describe *vorbei*$^*(r, y, p)$ as stating that there is a place p in the middle of the route r (VIA) that is a location of external contact for y, and this place is unique in the sense that only sub-places may also have the property of locating y in this way. Uniqueness ensures telicity, i.e. that the part of the route on which the ground is passed is completed by the time the end of the route is reached. *entlang*$^*(r, y, g)$ is defined so that all places in the middle of the route that are of granularity g should be places of external contact of y or places inside y.[6] Using only places p of a granularity compatible to a certain granularity g (comp(p, g)) we can ensure that parallelism in a rough sense of equidistance is given. The idea of a link between path and ground (LINK-schema) is thus embedded directly in the concept of compatible size. The PATH-GOAL-schema is encoded in the ordering of the places on the route.

(5) $\text{VORBEI}^*\ (r, y, p) \Leftrightarrow \text{VIA}(r, p) \wedge \alpha_{\text{EXT}^c}(y, p) \wedge \forall p'[(\text{VIA}(r, p') \wedge \alpha_{\text{EXT}^c}(y, p')) \rightarrow p' \lll \text{p}]$

(6) $\text{ENTLANG}^*\ (r, y, g) \Leftrightarrow \forall p[(\text{VIA}(r, p) \wedge \text{comp}(p, g)) \rightarrow (\alpha_{\text{EXT}^c}(y, p) \vee \alpha_{\text{IN}}(y, p))]$

The semantics of the adposition *entlang* supposes that the path can be conceptualized as a route that satisfies the conditions of ENTLANG^*:

(7) *entlang* $(+\text{acc/dat})$: $\lambda y \lambda w \exists r \exists g[\text{ROUTE}(w, r) \wedge \text{ENTLANG}^*(r, y, g)]$

For the combinations with an *an*-PP the following characterizations can be used:

(8) *vorbei* $(+\,an - \text{PP})$: $\lambda Q \lambda w \exists r \exists p[\text{ROUTE}(w, r) \ \wedge\ \text{VIA}(r, p) \ \wedge\ Q(p) \wedge \forall p'[\text{VIA}(r, p') \wedge\ Q(p') \rightarrow p' \lll \text{p}]]$

(9) *entlang* $(+\,an - \text{PP})$: $\lambda Q \lambda w \exists g \exists r \forall p[(\text{ROUTE}(w, r) \wedge \text{VIA}(r, p) \wedge \text{comp}(p, g)) \rightarrow Q(p)]$

We can now explain the difficulties in interpreting examples 2 and 3 above (p. 181) and the need for a non-standard interpretation of the Ground. Example 2 interpreted as characterized above refers to a unique place on the route where Mary encounters the wall. But with this restriction, the Ground and the route have to be situated in such a way that there is no more than one place. This is most easily fulfilled by an atomic Ground. In sentence 3, only a very large gate would be suitable to provide a route with more than one place of external contact sufficient to match

[6] It is necessary to use $\alpha_{\text{EXT}^c}(y, p)$ together with $\alpha_{\text{IN}}(y, p)$, because especially the use as postposition with accusative—e.g. *den Gang entlang* 'along the hallway'—may specify places situated in the region of the ground. Cf. Di Meola (1998) for details.

the granularity $\textsc{geh}^G(Mary)$ of Mary's walking. An extended Ground is needed, because it should be present at more than one place.

10.5.2 *Combination with verbs of locomotion*

The restriction to granularly homogeneous routes is needed for *entlang* but not for *vorbei*: the limitation to places of a certain size provides a means to specify the concept of parallelism locally instead of globally: if Mary always stays within some fixed distance from the river while moving forward, she *moves along* the river. She may be closer to the river or farther at different places, and she may even cross the river, if she cannot go further on one side of the river at one point. The important criterion is that she is never too far away from the river, so contact—e.g. in the sense of visual contact, walking distance, etc.—is not lost.

There are two main uses of *entlang* as part of a complex verb of locomotion: with an accusative object (1 below) and with an *an*-PP (2). *Vorbei* can be used with an *an*-PP (3) or without an additional argument (4).

1. *Er läuft die Straße entlang.* 'He runs along the street.'
2. *Er läuft an der Straße entlang.* 'He runs along the street.'
3. *Er läuft am Tor vorbei.* 'He passes by the gate.'
4. *Er läuft vorbei.* 'He passes by.'

Following the analysis of Olsen (1996), the meaning of a particle verb can be derived from the semantics of the verb and that of the particle. The following specification for the verb of locomotion *laufen* is derived from the characterization by Eschenbach et al. (2000):

(10) *laufen*: $\lambda P\lambda x\lambda s[\textsc{lauf}'(s, x, w) \wedge P(x, w)]$

(11) *entlanglaufen* + ACC: $\lambda y\lambda x\lambda s[\textsc{lauf}'(s, x, w) \wedge \exists r[\textsc{route}(w, r)\wedge \textsc{entlang}^*(r, y, \textsc{lauf}^G(x))]]$

(12) *entlanglaufen* + *an* – PP: $\lambda Q\lambda x\lambda s[\textsc{lauf}'(s, x, w) \wedge \exists r[\textsc{route}(w, r)\wedge \forall p[(\textsc{via}(r, p) \wedge \text{comp}(\textsc{lauf}^G(x), p))Q(p)]]]$

(13) *vorbeilaufen*: $(\lambda Q)\lambda x\lambda s[\textsc{lauf}'(s, x, w) \wedge \exists v \; \exists r\exists p[\textsc{route}(w, r) \wedge \textsc{via}(r, p) \wedge \alpha_A(v, p) \wedge Q(p)\wedge \forall p'[\textsc{via}(r, p') \wedge \alpha_A(v, p') \wedge Q(p') \rightarrow p' \lll \text{p}]]$

As the examples 1 and 2 above show, *entlanglaufen* needs an external argument (y and Q), whereas *vorbeilaufen* can have an implicit argument (v), as needed to capture example 4.

$Q(p)$ takes the meaning of the prepositional phrase with *an*. The granularity of x's running ($\textsc{lauf}^G(x)$) has to be compatible with that of the place p. This granularity is adjusted between the components via the places p. The complex verb with *entlang* has a granularity that depends on the bearer of motion and the mode of motion ($\text{LAUF}^G(x)$), which reflects the fact that *entlang* is more restricted by the verb in the allowed distances than *vorbei*. In the examples below, the large distance of 10 metres is acceptable with the case of *vorbeirollen*, but a case of *entlangrollen* with this distance and bearer of motion (*Ball*, 'ball') is much harder to understand: the places p that cover a distance of 10 metres to the gate do not fulfil the requirement $\text{comp}(\text{ROLL}^G(\mathit{ball}'), p)$. Verbs that describe motion events on a larger scale like *reisen* 'travel' in contrast to *laufen* 'run' also have a coarser granularity when used with *entlang*: if *Mary travels along the coast*, she may well take several trips inland. It is only necessary that the destinations also lie in some sense close to the coast.

1. *Der Ball rollt in 10m Entfernung am Tor vorbei.* 'The ball rolls in 10m distance past the gate.'
2. *?Der Ball rollt in 10m Entfernung an der Mauer entlang.* 'The ball rolls in 10m distance along the wall.'
3. **Der Ball rollt am Meer entlang.* 'The ball rolls along the sea.'
4. *Der Ball rollt am Wasser entlang.* 'The ball rolls along the water.'

We can similarly model that *der Ball rollt am Meer entlang* is difficult to interpret: places that fulfil the requirements of *am Meer* are of a much larger granularity than the places that fulfil $\text{comp}(\text{ROLL}^G(\mathit{ball}'), p)$. For the case of *der Ball rollt am Wasser entlang*, we can thus infer that *am Wasser* is either less restrictive or that it refers to a finer granularity. The low acceptability of *die Stadt ist am Wasser* 'the town is by the water' suggests the latter. However, this would entail restriction of the meaning of *Wasser* 'water' to small portions of water, so that the possible places are selected appropriately in the *an*-phrase for this case; however, the seawater itself does not have any natural boundaries that limit its extent to finer levels of granularity.

The specification being built on the notions of place, we can use the lexical specification directly in the dynamic tasks of localizing objects, and understanding and following route instructions. The Geometric Agent of Tschander et al. (2003), for example, should understand *vorbei* as specifying an intermediate place with a unique local landmark. *Entlang* on the other hand signals a landmark that works as a link between several places. The Geometric Agent may execute an instruction with *entlang* on the lowest level by a simple wall-following mechanism. *Vorbei* splits the route into two parts: those places encountered before the ground and those encountered after it. It could serve to keep the agent from recognizing a place as the end of a route, before the intermediate place has been visited.

10.6 Summary and conclusions

It was shown that representational granularity and grain-size are two important aspects of granularity and that these aspects can be specified based on a formal concept of extended locations or **places**. A place was determined by a spatial location, an extent, and a resolution. These three components interact to yield an efficient structuring of space and objects in space. Spatial granularity is present in the notions of extent and resolution. Places as filtered geometrical conceptualizations of the complex world can be used to establish a link between a dynamically, sequentially, and locally perceived environment and the global characteristics encoded in linguistic descriptions. The meaning of the preposition *an* 'at/on/by', depending on proximity as one meaning component, was chosen as an example for a concept relying on granularity: it was analysed as identifying a place at the border of the Ground. We showed that the preposition reacts to incompatibilities between granularities encoded in the lexemes. The actual distance demanded for a particular case of an *an*-PP is constrained by the levels of granularity implicit in the different components of the sentence. The extent and grain-size of the place determine this granularity and give clues to the hearer on how to find the place described.

Building on this hypothesis, a link was made between the conceptualizations of space as received from the senses (place recognition) and as imagined from a route instruction (decision places). Paths can thus be seen as sequences of places on different levels of granularity. The formal characterization yields a flexible framework for analysing path specifications like *entlang* 'along' and *vorbei* 'past'. Both characterize the intermediate course of the path. The main difference between the two lies in scope: *entlang* is described as defining *all* intermediate places on one level of granularity of the route to be places of close proximity to the Ground, whereas *vorbei* can be analysed as indicating *one* intermediate place that is a place locating the Ground. Accordingly, *entlang* needs a Ground that is extended, and *vorbei* is preferred with a point-like Ground. This result is also in conformity with the difference in situational types associated with *entlang* and *vorbei*: *entlanggehen* describes a process, whereas *vorbeigehen* is telic and indicates an event.

The proposed specification properly reflects that larger deviations in granularity are possible with *vorbei*: the only criterion is that the distance between trajectory and Ground should be small enough to conceptualize both as being at a certain place. The discussion of *entlang*, in relation to *vorbei*, illustrates that the formal mechanisms introduced are expressive enough to characterize SHAPE-prepositions without recourse to the global shape of the trajectory. The next step should be to add the notion of direction inherent in *entlang* to the simplified characterization presented here, and to contrast *entlang* with other SHAPE-prepositions like *um* ('around').

In comparison to Nikanne and van der Zee (this volume), only two levels of representational granularity have been discussed: the representations of an object as extended or atomic. The case of atomic (or point-like) representation can be linked to their neutral or 'grain level 0' verbs, which can be seen as focusing on the SOURCE-places and GOAL-places of a path. The SHAPE-modifiers *entlang* and *vorbei* can naturally be linked to 'grain level 1', on which the global shape of the route is described. How to represent the level of local shape—'grain level 2' in the terminology of Nikanne and van der Zee—has not been addressed in this chapter. The question remains whether there are prepositions in languages such as German that require an even finer level of representational granularity, for which not only the shape but also the inner structure or texture of a Ground object would be important, or whether this level is encoded mainly in the lexical entries of verbs and nouns in these languages. A grain-size approach for representing this finest level of representational granularity has been discussed with respect to aggregation objects, such as are denoted by the term **forest** in Schmidtke (2005a).

11

The lexical representation of path curvature in motion expressions: a three-way path curvature distinction[1]

URPO NIKANNE, EMILE VAN DER ZEE

11.1 Introduction

Motion verbs can express path curvature. In the sentence *John zigzagged down the hill* the verb *to zigzag* expresses a fine-grained curvature (several iterations of angular path shapes), and the verb in combination with its adjunct indicates that there is a coarser-grained path along which John travels (a path of indeterminate shape) (van der Zee, 2000; see also section 5 below for an explanation of the meaning of this example). In this chapter we consider the different ways in which path curvature can be encoded by motion verbs in Finnish and Dutch. We will first introduce the path-curvature features and the Finnish and Dutch verbs expressing these distinctions. After that, we will show that Dutch and Finnish grammars are sensitive to these distinctions by discussing combinations of path-curvature verbs with other verbs, with adverbs and with PP- and infinitival adjuncts. Sometimes we also give English examples to illustrate our reasoning.

11.2 Path curvature representation in motion verbs

In this chapter we hypothesize that verbs encoding path curvature can represent this curvature at three different levels. (1) illustrates the three hypothesized levels with examples from Finnish:

[1] We want to thank Mila Vulchanova Liliana Martinez, and three anonymous reviewers for their comments. Earlier versions of the chapter were presented at the Second International Conference on Construction Grammar (6–8 September 2002, Helsinki, Finland) and the 21st Scandinavian Conference of Linguistics (1–4 June 2005, Trondheim, Norway). Any shortcomings it contains are, of course, our responsibility.

(1) Grain level 0 verbs, encoding neutral path curvature: *mennä* 'to go', *siirtyä* 'to change place'
Grain level 1 verbs, encoding global path curvature: *kaartaa* 'to go along a curved path; to make a curve'
Grain level 2 verbs, encoding local path curvature: *mutkitella* 'to go and make curves along a path; to zigzag/to slalom'

Grain level 0 verbs (GL0 verbs) do not make reference to the shape of a path in their lexical semantics. These verbs just express that a Figure moves from one location to another. Global path-curvature verbs (GL1 verbs) focus on the overall shape of the path of a Figure. And local path-curvature verbs (GL2 verbs) focus on the fine-grained aspects of a Figure's path of motion. It is the consequences of this three-way distinction that are the focus of this chapter (for an application of our framework to Akan see Apraku 2005, for an application to Bulgarian see Martinez 2007, and for an application to English language and iconic gesturing see van der Zee et al. 2010).

Verbs describing path curvature should be distinguished from verbs describing object axis curvature change. The following examples are taken from Dutch (van der Zee 2000):

(2) *buigen* 'to bend'
krullen 'to coil'
vouwen 'to fold'

The verbs in (2) describe changes in the curvature of objects, bodies, their parts, etc.

Some Dutch verbs, however, straddle both categories:

(3) *Zoë slalomde de heuvel af.* (PATH – Zoë moved with curves in her path)
'Zoe slalomed down the hill.'
Het pad slalomde tussen rotsen en struiken. (OBJECT – the path has curves in it)
'The path slalomed between rocks and bushes.'

In this chapter we focus on the path meaning of verbs that can refer to both path curvature and object curvature.

It is also not unusual for language users to indicate motion along a curved path by using Manner of Motion (MoM) verbs such as *to wriggle*, *to rock*, or *to swing*:

(4) *De slang kronkelde de heuvel af.*
'The snake twisted down the hill.'

We assume that in their lexical meanings these verbs do not express the shape of a path, but that they refer to the movements of the object causing and/or undergoing the motion, which in turn results in a path with a distinctive curvature. We will return to MoM verbs in section 11.3 and the encoding of manner in relation to path in section 11.7 (see Talmy 2000 for an elaborate discussion of both). But, let us first consider the three-way path-curvature distinction in more detail.

An example of the Finnish neutral path-curvature verb *mennä* 'to go' is given in (5):

(5) *X menee A:sta B:hen*
X go-3sg A-elative B-illative
'X goes from A to B'

Although we are likely to assume that the path described in (5) is straight by default, the path could be of any shape—slightly curved, straight, or even zigzag. Here are some examples of GLo verbs in both Finnish and Dutch:

(6) Finnish:
mennä 'to go'
tulla 'to come'
siirtyä 'to go'
kulkea 'to travel'
matkata 'to travel'
matkustaa 'to travel'

Dutch:
arriveren 'to arrive'
aankomen 'to arrive'
gaan 'to go'
komen 'to come'
naderen 'to approach'
reizen 'to travel'

The Finnish verbs *tulla* and *mennä* and the Dutch verbs *gaan* and *(aan)komen* contain lexicalized deictic information: *mennä* and *gaan* 'to go' indicate that the point of view is from the source of the path, and *tulla* and *komen* 'to come' indicate that the point of view is from the goal of the path. (For a detailed analysis of the deictic system of Finnish, see Larjavaara 1990, 2007.) *Siirtyä* 'to move, change place' emphasizes that a Figure changes its location; the motion between the original and the new location is not in focus. *Matkata*, *matkustaa*, and *reizen* 'to travel' are employed most naturally in relation to the use of a vehicle over a relatively long distance.

There seems only to be a handful of GLo verbs in either language. Although MoM verbs can also be used to express neutral path curvature (e.g. *Het paard galoppeerde naar London* 'The horse galloped to London'), MoM verbs can be used without a path complement (e.g. *The horse galloped*), whereas GLo verbs cannot be used

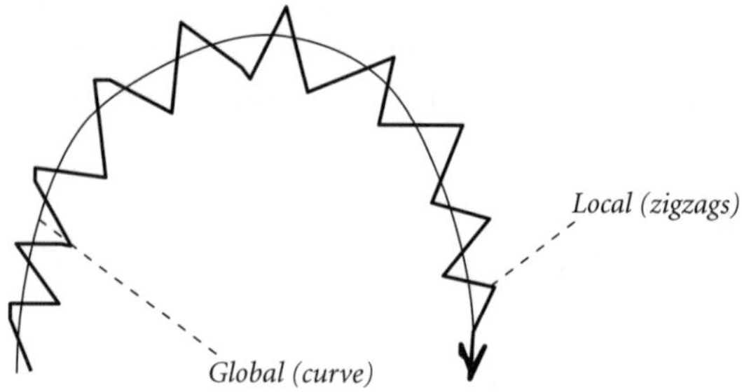

FIGURE 11.1 A combination of zigzags and a curve. The Finnish verb *kaartaa* refers to global curvature (ignoring local curvature), whereas the verb *mutkitella* refers to local curvature (ignoring global curvature).

without a path complement (**The horse went/came/travelled*). In this sense GL0 verbs are path verbs, whereas MoM verbs are not (see also section 11.3 below).

Global path-curvature verbs (or GL1 verbs) focus on the overall shape or the coarse grain of a path of motion. The Finnish verb *kaartaa* 'to go along a curved path' is an example of such a verb:

(7) *X kaartaa A:sta B:hen*
'X goes from A to B making a curve'

For the verb *kaartaa* to apply, the Figure may or may not also make smaller curves, as long as the global shape of the path can be interpreted as one curve (see Figure 11.1).

Here are some examples of Finnish GL1 verbs:

(8) *kaartaa* 'to make a curve'
kiertää 'to go along a curved path/go around smoothly'
koukata 'to make a hook-shaped curve'

Of these verbs, *kaartaa* is the clearest example of a GL1 verb. The verbs *kiertää* and *koukata* indicate in certain contexts going around some obstacle (see Sivonen 2005).

Dutch seems to have very few GL1 verbs, consisting of compounds constructed from motion verbs and adverbs:

(9) *af/inbuigen* 'to bend off/into'
af/indraaien 'to turn off/into'
af/inslaan 'to turn off/into'; (lit. off/in-hit.)

In the same fashion as the Finnish GL1 verbs, these verbs refer to paths whose overall shape is curved, but whose fine-grained structure can be anything. However, these verbs can only be used in restrictive contexts. *Afbuigen/inbuigen*, *af/indraaien*, and *af/inslaan* all seem to refer to means of transportation (cars, bikes, horses, carriages, boats) changing direction, while making use of a predetermined layout (a road system, a canal system, etc.). Whereas *af/inbuigen* refers to a smoothly curved path, *af/inslaan* refers to a more abrupt, non-smooth path shape. *Af/indraaien* seems neutral in relation to the smoothness of the path curvature. GL1 verbs thus allow Dutch speakers to make distinctions between smooth and non-smooth path curvatures (van der Zee 2000).

Local curvature verbs (or GL2 verbs) refer to fine-grained details of path curvature; relatively small curves that a Figure makes as it goes along its path.

The following example illustrates a Finnish verb expressing local path curvature:

(10) *X mutkittelee A:sta B:hen*
'X goes from A to B making small curves on the way'

The verb indicates that the path consists of several iterations of angular path shapes. GL2 verbs do not make any statements about global path shape. As can be seen in Figure 11.1, when using *mutkitella* 'to zigzag', the global path may be curved. However, the global path may also be straight, hook-shaped, etc.

Finnish GL2 verbs are, for instance:

(11) *mutkitella* 'to go and make curves'
sahata 'to go back and forth' (lit. 'saw')
puikkelehtia 'to wind in and out', 'to weave'
pujotella 'to go between several obstacles on one path',[2] 'to slalom'

The verb *mutkitella* can be used in any context in which the shape of the path includes local curves (the curves do not have to be a regular repetition of smooth or non-smooth curves, but can be a random collection of curves). *Sahata* is used if the Figure is going back and forth along the same path or if the angle of the local curves is very sharp (in which case the Figure is moving very close to the direction it was coming from). The data in Sivonen's study (2005) show that *mutkitella* emphasizes the non-straightness of the path. The root of the verb *mutk-i-tt-ele* is *mutka* 'curve', *i* is a continuative derivative suffix, *tt(A)* is a causative derivative suffix, and *ele* is a frequentative derivative suffix. The semantics of the derivative suffixes is not

[2] A possible path that can be referred to with the verb *pujotella*:

straightforward. But, as Sivonen points out, the verb indicates continuative motion, making curves repetitively. Sivonen also discusses other verbs that would be classified as GL2 verbs in the present study, e.g. *puikkelehtia* and *pujotella*, which are normally used when local curves are made in order to pass obstacles on the way. The curvature is a lexical feature of these verbs: if the Figure goes straight, one cannot refer to its motion with the verbs *pujotella* or *puikkelehtia*, even if it passes objects on its way.

Dutch seems to have very few GL2 verbs:

(12)[3] *zigzaggen* 'to zigzag'
slalommen 'to slalom'
slingeren 'to make curves while moving'
zwenken 'to go from left to right with short abrupt movements'
spiralen 'to spiral'
cirkelen 'to circle'

Zigzaggen refers to non-smooth curvature changes, whereas *spiralen*, *slingeren*, and *slalommen* refer to smooth curvature changes. *Zwenken* refers to a high frequency of relatively small smooth or non-smooth path curvatures and so seems to be neutral in relation to these two specific curvatures. GL2 verbs thus make it possible for Dutch speakers to make distinctions between non-smooth and smooth curvatures in path shapes.

It is important to notice that Dutch and Finnish do not possess all of the curvature verbs that are logically possible if we consider all possible qualitative curvature descriptions: smooth curvature, non-smooth curvature, and straight, plus all possible combinations of these curvatures.

To begin with, there are no GL1 or GL2 verbs that explicitly specify the straightness of a global or a local path. In Dutch and Finnish, path straightness at a global grain level is pragmatically inferred from GL0 verbs or MoM verbs in combination with path expressions, as in *The horse went/walked to the tree.*[4]

Verbs specifying path straightness at the local or GL2 level is impossible. Figure 11.2 illustrates why.

Suppose that there were a GL2 verb *to splum* which indicated local path straightness. When trying to use this verb to describe a part of dotted global Path 1 in Figure 11.2, it is not clear what part of the path *to splum* should refer to; part A, part B, or

[3] Although it would be possible to categorise slingeren and zwenken as MoM verbs since they can be used without a path PP, a Google search indicates that an MoM use of these verbs is extremely rare, and idiomatic. If anything, the category of GL2 verbs in Dutch is thus inflated here, confirming our point that these verbs are quite rare in Dutch.

[4] Finnish has the verb *suoria* (derived from the adjective *suora* 'straight'). This verb does not indicate path shape, but means that the Figure is taking the shortest possible route. e.g. *Hän suorii kotiin* [S/he suoria-3SG home-ILLATIVE] means that 'S/he takes the shortest possible way home'. (See also footnote 14 below.)

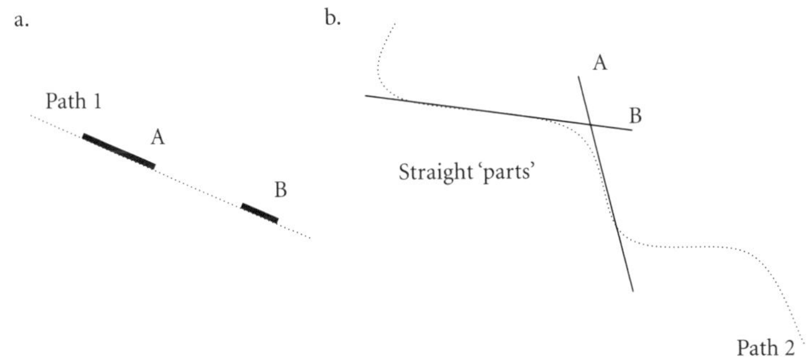

FIGURE 11.2 Two paths with an arbitrary number of straight path parts in them

another (local) part? This is even clearer when the path is not straight, as in Figure 11.2b. It is completely arbitrary whether *to splum* should apply to the local straight parts A or B, or to another local part of Path 2. This problem would be further enhanced if we zoom in on Path 2: the number of possible local path parts appearing to be straight would increase. So, whatever the global shape of a path, it is not possible to have a verb which refers to path straightness at a local level, since such a verb would not be able to select an identifiable path part or set of path parts as its referent.

It is not clear to us why there are no verbs in Dutch, Finnish, English (van der Zee et al. 2010), Bulgarian (Martinez 2007), or Akan (Apraku 2005) that specify global path straightness—other than that global path straightness is inferred from MoM verbs or GLo verbs in combination with path expressions. Why are there no verbs indicating a straight path to a goal or away from a source? Would this be an instance where an inference overrides an explicitly encoded feature? It would be necessary to look at many other languages even to start answering these questions.

Finally, Dutch and Finnish do not have path-curvature verbs that combine local and global curvature distinctions. For example, there are no path-curvature verbs that combine the following:

(13) a. local and global path curvatures alternatingly
b. local and global path curvatures occurring at the same time (a conflation of the paths in Figure 1)
c. two or more local path curvatures alternatingly
d. two or more local path curvatures occurring at the same time
e. two or more global path curvatures alternatingly
f. two or more global path curvatures occurring at the same time

Although some combinations are implausible (13a, 13c) or impossible (13d, 13f), there do not seem to be any a priori reasons why (13b) and (13e) are not present in Dutch or in Finnish. We thus have to conclude that in relation to path curvature, Dutch and Finnish verbs only specify first-order but not second-order or higher-order curvature distinctions.

As we have seen before, MoM verbs are able to encode path curvature. How it is possible for these verbs to do this is the subject of the next section.

11.3 Manner of Motion (MoM) verbs and path curvature

MoM verbs such as *to wriggle, to rock*, and *to swing* do not express the shape of a path in their lexical conceptual structure: a sentence such as *Ben rocks* does not express a path with a particular curvature along which Ben is travelling, but expresses a (rocking) motion of Ben. However, as indicated before, MoM verbs can be used to express motion along a path if combined with path expressions:[5]

(14) NP[SUBJ] – V[MoM] – PP[PATH][6]

a. *Mies horjuu töistä kotiin.*
man rock-3SG work-ELA home-ILL.
'The man goes rocking from work to home.'

b. *De man danste de berg af.*
The man dance-PAST the mountain off.
'The man danced down the mountain.' (i.e. 'came down dancing')

Examples such as those in (14) invite readings of a Figure going along a path, where the path is not entirely straight, but has some curves in it. These examples thus pose two challenges: if MoM verbs do not express the shape of a path in their lexical conceptual structure, what is the linguistic mechanism that explains how it is possible to arrive at a path interpretation for sentences as in (14), and, how is the notion of path curvature licensed by the verb and its satellite? Let us start with the latter issue.

The notion of path curvature is licensed pragmatically. We seem to know that a man who is rocking as he walks (14a) or who is dancing when he comes down a mountain (14b) tends to make characteristic curves along the path that he follows. The pragmatic reading is thus inferred from the linguistic expressions, and is not encoded as necessary information in the lexical meanings of the MoM verbs (see also

[5] We use the following abbreviations for the Finnish morphological categories: GEN = genitive case, PAR = partitive case, ESS = essive case, TRA = translative case, INE = inessive case, ELA = elative case, ILL = illative case, ADE = adessive case, ABL = ablative case, ALL = allative case, INF1 = 1st infinitive, INF2 = 2nd infinitive, INF3 = 3rd infinitive.

[6] Note that for constructions, syntactic categories are represented in capitals, and semantic categories are represented in capitals within square brackets.

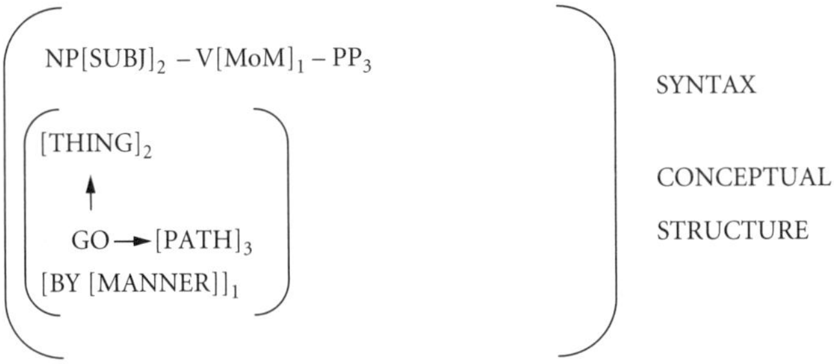

FIGURE 11.3 The Manner of Motion Construction in Finnish and Dutch

Östman 1986). This is confirmed by the fact that MoM verbs can be used without a path-complement, as in *John is dancing*.

We suggest that a path interpretation for the examples in (14) is explained by a construction which we call the Manner of Motion Construction. (We base our ideas on the work of Jackendoff 1990, and Fillmore and Kay 1996). This construction can be seen as the special case of a resultative construction. The Manner of Motion Construction, in which the main verb is a MoM verb and the event expressed is a non-causative motion along a path, can be formalized as follows: GO is a function indicating change or motion along a path. The function GO selects (i) a PATH and (ii) a Theme (i.e. the event structure participant being in motion) (see Jackendoff 1983, 1990).[7] The arrows indicate selection. BY is a subordinate function indicating the manner in which the matrix proposition ('the thing going along a path') expresses motion (see Jackendoff 1990). Subscript-indices stand for the linking between syntactic and semantic elements. For instance, the subject NP is marked with index 2, which indicates that it is linked to the Theme-argument (the THING that is selected by the function GO). Notice that the function GO is not linked to any element in the syntactic structure: GO is derived from combining a MoM verb with a path expression.

We have seen that GL0, GL1, GL2, and also MoM verbs are all able to express path curvature, and that path verbs and MoM verbs do this in different ways. The next

[7] In our chapter we sometimes refer to the entity in motion or the entity whose location is referred to as a 'Figure', or a 'Theme'. The first notion is a perceptual characterization (i.e. a Figure as distinguished from a background). The second notion is a semantic notion (i.e. an argument of a predicate describing the entities' motion or location).

section considers what the dominant lexical strategy is in Dutch and Finnish for expressing path curvature.

11.4 The ratio of path verbs to MoM verbs in Dutch and Finnish

Matsumoto (2003) suggests that there may be an inverse relation between the number of path verbs and the number of MoM verbs in a language. For example, he observes that English has more than one hundred MoM verbs but only twenty path verbs, whereas Japanese has only thirteen MoM verbs but thirty-three path verbs. In this section we will briefly consider the ratio between Finnish and Dutch path-curvature verbs on the one hand, and MoM verbs on the other, and we will give an explanation for this ratio in terms of the potential curvature distinctions expressed by these verb classes.

In Dutch and Finnish, MoM verbs seem to belong to an open class. For example, only considering verbs of Levin's (1993) *run* and *roll* types gives at least the following MoM verbs in Dutch:

(15) run-type verbs in Dutch: *bestijgen, dansen, dartelen, dobberen, draven, drijven, dribbelen, fietsen, fladderen, galopperen, glibberen, glijden, glippen, haasten, hinkelen, hollen, huppelen, jagen, jakkeren, joggen, kanoën, kruipen, klimmen, klauteren, kuieren, lopen, marcheren, paraderen, racen, razen, rennen, ritsen, roetsjen, scheren, scheuren, schuiven, schrijden, slenteren, slingeren, sluipen, snellen, snelwandelen, stappen, strompelen, springen, tippelen, trippelen, varen, vliegen, waden, wandelen, waggelen, zeilen, zwemmen, zwerven*, etc.

(16) roll-type verbs in Dutch: *buitelen, draaien, duikelen, kolken, krioelen, rollen, schommelen, tuimelen, tollen, wippen, wiebelen, wiegen, wemelen, wentelen, wervelen, zwenken, zwermen*, etc.

(15) and (16) can be further expanded, but it is not the purpose of the present chapter to define the full sets here (if at all possible); we merely want to illustrate that these classes contain more verbs than the path verb classes.

Finnish also contains many MoM verbs, and even seems to have productive devices for constructing such verbs. For example, it is possible in Finnish to derive motion verbs from nouns referring to vehicles with the derivative suffix *ile*:

(17) *auto : autoile-* 'car : to use a car as a vehicle'
pyörä : pyöräile- 'bicycle : to use a bicycle as a vehicle'
vene : veneile- 'boat : to use a boat as a vehicle'
lainelauta : lainelautaile- 'surf board : to use a surf board as a vehicle'
potkupyörä : potkupyöräile- 'kick bike : to use a kick bike as a vehicle'
etc.

Without further discussing productive strategies for MoM verbs in Finnish, here are some examples of Levin's (1993) *run* and *roll* types in Finnish:

(18) run-type verbs in Finnish: *kiivetä, tanssia, ajaa, kävellä, autoilla, veneillä, marssia, juosta, juoksennella, pinkoa, viilettää, viiletellä, hölkätä, hölkötellä, lönkytellä, hissutella, sipsuttaa, sipsutella, jolkottaa, jolkotella, jolkuttaa, jolkutella, laukata, ravata*, etc.

(19) roll-type verbs in Finnish: *liukua, valua, pudota, vieriä, upota*, etc.

Apart from the seventeen Dutch path verbs in (6), (9), and (12), and the thirteen Finnish path verbs in (6), (8), and (11), there do not seem to be many more Dutch or Finnish path-curvature verbs than we have listed here. These data thus seem to confirm Matsumoto's hypothesis of an inverse relation between the number of MoM verbs and the number of path verbs: in both Dutch and Finnish there are many more MoM verbs than path verbs. What then is the cause of this lexical dominance?

Given that GL0 verbs do not specify path shape, and that GL1 verbs and GL2 verbs provide a speaker with some very basic first-order path-curvature information (e.g. that there is one curve or that there are more curves in a path, and that these curvatures are smooth or angular), it is perhaps not surprising that there are only very few verbs in each of these categories. In theory, one only needs one GL0 verb to express neutral curvature, and only four verbs at a global or local level of path curvature to specify the presence of one curve with smooth or angular curvature or more curves that are smooth or angular. The fact that each of the path-curvature verb classes contains slightly more than four verbs seems to result from the inclusion of other features apart from this very basic curvature information. As we have seen, GL0 verbs can include deictic information (giving the antonyms *to come* and *to go*) and can include information about the Theme (i.e. that 'people' or 'vehicles of transportation' are the Theme in 'travel' verbs, and that the Theme is underspecified in 'go' verbs). In other words, the number of curvature verbs is only slightly higher than can be expected on the basis of the very basic curvature distinctions expressed by the three verb curvature classes, because only a few other features are encoded by these verbs.

Given that language users have a need to express refined curvature distinctions, the number of curvature verbs can only be low if there is another system for encoding such refined distinctions. Apart from encoding manner of motion, MoM verbs allow for the encoding of these refined distinctions. Both Finnish and Dutch speakers can pragmatically derive refined path curvature from MoM verbs when a path complement is used, thus sidestepping the necessity to explicitly encode this in the matrix verb; for example it is possible to derive a path with many irregular shapes from the description *The man staggered home.*[8] This might explain the observed

[8] In this process, the language user is relying on the spatial information of the verb and their knowledge or experience of the physical world: if a man staggers while moving from one place to another, he is bound to make curves on his way.

asymmetries between the number of MoM verbs and the number of path verbs. If the number of MoM verbs is high, allowing these verbs to express refined curvature distinctions, then why encode these distinctions in the path-curvature verbs? And conversely, if the number of MoM verbs is low, and refined curvature distinctions thus cannot be expressed by these verbs, then language users try to encode these distinctions in the path-curvature verbs. The asymmetry thus seems to be based on a language's choice to encode more basic curvature distinctions in one system (path-curvature verbs), and refined curvature distinctions by way of another system (MoM verbs), while avoiding an overlap of these features in both systems.[9]

We have, so far, considered the path-curvature verbs in isolation. In the next section we will consider how these verbs combine with PP adjuncts.

11.5 Path curvature representation in constructions

It is possible to express the presence of path curvature in several other ways in Finnish and Dutch grammars, apart from employing GL1 and GL2 verbs, or by pragmatically deriving it from MoM verbs in combination with a path expression. For example, in both Dutch and Finnish it is possible to use VERB[GL0]–VERB [GL1/GL2] combinations as in (20) and (21), or VERB[CAUSATIVE]–NP[GL1/GL2] combinations as in (22) and (23). In Dutch it is possible, in addition, to use VERB [GL0]–PP[GL1/GL2] combinations as in (24) and (25):[10]

(20) *De vlieg gaat zigzaggend door de lucht.*
The fly goes zigzagging through the air
'The fly zigzags through the sky.'

(21) *Käärme tuli kiven alle mutkitellen.*
Snake came stone-GEN under-ALL wind-INF2-INS
'The snake came winding from under the stone.'

(22) *De rat maakt een bocht/doet een zigzag, en rent over de tafel heen.*
The rat makes a bend/does a zigzag, and runs across the table
'The rat runs across the table in a curve/zigzag.'

(23) *Lentokone teki mutkan/täyden ympyrän ilmassa.*
Air-plane made curve-ACC/full-ACC circle-ACC air-INESSIVE
'The airplane made a curve/a full circle in the air.'

[9] Note that this hypothesis is an expansion of Grice's maxims of quantity and manner (i.e. avoiding making a contribution to a conversation that is too informative or longer than necessary, as for example when doubling up information by several lexical items in one sentence).

[10] Please note that these data were checked with Google for permissibility or non-permissibility. We also used Google to check our intuitions in relation to other examples.

(24) *Het vliegtuig gaat in een bocht/cirkel/spiraal/zigzag door de lucht.*
The airplane goes in a bend/circle/spiral/zigzag through the air
'The airplane goes through the air in a curve/spiral/zigzag.'

(25) *De auto gaat met een bocht/zigzag de garage in/uit.*
The car goes in a bend/zigzag the garage in/out
'The car curves/zigzags into/out of the garage.'

VERB[GL0]–Verb[GL1/GL2] combinations as in (20) and (21) will be considered in more detail in the next section. In this section we will consider the other two types: VERB[CAUSATIVE]–NP[GL1/GL2] and VERB[GL0]–PP(P NP[GL1/GL2]) combinations. Let us start with the latter.

Focusing on (24) and (25), it becomes clear that not every NP[GL1/GL2] is able to fill the PP(P NP[GL1/GL2]) frame:

(26) *Hij ging in cirkels/een cirkel/*(een) zigzag(-gen)/*(een) slalom(-men)/een rechte lijn het weiland door.*
'He went in circles/a circle/*a zigzag(s)/*(a) slalom(s)/a straight line through the pasture.'

V	$[_{PP1}$ *in* ?NP]	PP2	— syntactic categories
|	|	|	
GL0	GL1/GL2	VIA Path	— semantic categories

(26) shows that V[GL0] PP['in a straight line'] represents going along a straight global path, which GL1 verbs cannot encode, as we have seen before. Although not all nouns referring to path-curvature distinctions can be part of the VERB[GL0]–PP [GL1/GL2] structure, we leave the reasons for this being the case for future research. Here, we will focus on the properties of the structure itself.

(27) shows that not all prepositions can be part of the VERB[GL0]–PP[GL1/GL2] construction:

(27) *Hij ging in/met/*bij/*van een bocht/zigzag het weiland door.*
'He went in/with/*at/*from a curve/zigzag through the pasture.'

(27) entails that GL0 verbs can in principle be combined with a PP expressing global ('a curve') or local ('zigzag') curvatures, as well as a PP expressing a VIA path (see Jackendoff 1983 for a definition of VIA paths).[11] PP1 and PP2 can also be combined with the main verb in a different order (V–PP2–PP1), but whereas PP1 is optional, PP2 is obligatory.

[11] It seems only possible to combine the highly context-sensitive GL1 verbs with a PP2 that specifies a GOAL or a SOURCE path. Given the highly contextual nature of GL1 verbs, we will not go into any details about this here.

This thus reveals a construction that allows Dutch speakers to talk about GL1 or GL2 curvature using a GL0 verb, a PP1 expressing path curvature, and a PP2 expressing a GOAL, a SOURCE, or a VIA path:

(28) *Hij ging in/met een bocht/zigzag de straat in/uit/door.*
'He went in/with a curve/zigzag into/out of/through the street.'

V	[$_{PP1}$ *in/met* NP]	PP2	— syntactic categories
|	|	|	
GL0	GL1/GL2	GOAL/SOURCE/VIA Path	— semantic categories

This pattern is the same for GL2 verbs, the highly context sensitive GL1 verbs, and the MoM verbs:

(29) *Hij slalomde/draaide/liep in/met een bocht/zigzag de straat in/uit/door.*
'He slalomed/turned/walked in/with a curve/zigzag into/out of/through the street.'

V	([$_{PP1}$ *in/met* NP])	PP2	— syntactic categories
|	|	|	
MOTION	GL1/GL2	GOAL/SOURCE/VIA Path	— semantic categories

Based on the above examples, we can say that in Dutch it is possible to employ the following construction for expressing path curvature: V[MOTION]–($_{PP}$ *in/met* NP [GL1/GL2])–PP2[PATH] (where round brackets indicate optionality). Figure 11.4 is a more elaborate description of this construction, better taking into account the different levels of information representation involved. The subscript-indices stand for a linking between parts of the syntactic, conceptual, and spatial structures. Only the relevant parts of each representation are given. The schematic higher-order spatial structure is divided into two parts: motion and path. Motion has two parts: the Figure and the change of the Figure's location. The path is also divided into two parts: the direction and the shape of the path.

In Figure 11.4, PATH is a path-function with an argument (see Jackendoff, 1983, 1990). The shape of the path is linked with the predicate verb and PP1 in syntactic structure. If the predicate verb is a GL0 verb, then the shape of the path is only expressed by PP1, otherwise (e.g. in cases of a verb like *to zigzag*) path shape is also specified by the verb. It should be noticed that PP1 is not linked to anything in conceptual structure: only a link between the syntactic representation and the spatial representation is needed.[12]

[12] It seems to be the simplest solution to assume that there is a direct linking between the spatial and syntactic representations. This means that no conceptual structure representation is needed for the first PP. According to van der Zee and Nikanne (2000), not all linking between linguistic and extra-linguistic representations need to go through conceptual structure.

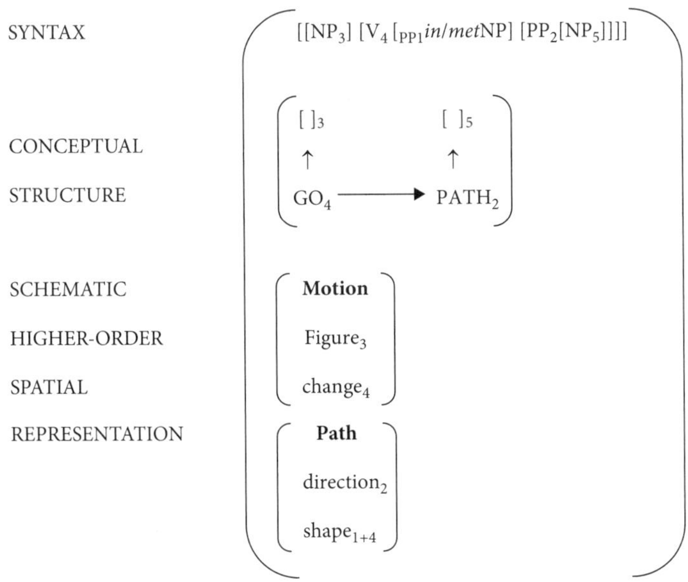

FIGURE 11.4 The V[MOTION]-(PP *in/met* NP[GL1/GL2])-PP2[PATH] construction in Dutch.

It should be noted that (29) and Figure 11.4 are also able to explain something that we observed in the Introduction to this chapter. In the Introduction we argued that in *John zigzagged down the hill*, the verb *to zigzag* expresses a fine-grained curvature (several iterations of angular path shapes), and that the verb in combination with its adjunct indicates that there is a coarser-grained path along which John travels (a path of indeterminate shape). (29) and Figure 11.4 motivate the latter part of this observation, in that the obligatory PATH (that we see with both GL0 verbs, but also GL2 verbs in Dutch),[13] does not have a specific curvature associated with it. The—possibly global—curvature of the PATH is underspecified; any defined curvature follows from the motion verb (V_4), or the non-obligatory prepositional phrase (PP_1).

In Finnish, unlike Dutch, the V[MOTION]-(PP *in/met* NP[GL1/GL2])-PP2 [PATH] construction does not work. It is not ungrammatical to combine a PP

[13] We have distinguished Dutch local curvature verbs from MoM verbs by the fact that the former need a path-PP complement:

(a) **De vogel/man/auto zigzagde/slalomde/slingerde/zwenkte/spiraalde/cirkelde.*
'*The bird/man/car zigzagged/slalommed/made curves/went from left to right/spiralled/circled.'

(b) *De vogel/man/auto zigzagde/slalomde/slingerde/zwenkte/spiraalde/cirkelde van links naar rechts/ door de lucht/door de straat.*
'The bird/man/car zigzagged/slalommed/made curves/went from left to right/spiralled/circled from left to right/through the air/through the street.'

expressing curvature with a motion verb, but the reading of this structure is not the same as in Dutch, as illustrated in (30a–c).[14]

(30) a. *Hän kulki mutkassa kotiin.*
S/he went curve + INE home + ILL
'S/he went home in a curve.'
(i.e. there was a concrete curve on the way; or s/he was in a twisted/bent position)

b. *Hän kulki suorassa kotiin.*
S/he went straight + INE home + ILL
'S/he went home in a straight position.'

c. *Hän kulki suoralla kotiin.*
S/he went straigh + ADE home + ILL
'S/he was on a straight part of the path going home.'

In Finnish, according to the so-called 'Relation rule' (Siro 1964), the locative PPs predicate the subject of an intransitive sentence and the object of the transitive sentence. According to that rule, in (30a) and (30b) the interpretation is that the subject of the intransitive verb *kulkea* 'to go' is curved or straight, and not the path. Another possibility for parsing is that *mutkassa* in (30a) and *suoralla* in (30c) are sentence adverbials with a scope over the whole sentence, i.e. the whole event expressed by the sentence is taking place in a curve or a straight part of the path. The word *suora* 'straight' is somewhat more complicated than the word *mutka* 'to curve', as *suora* can be either a noun 'a straight part of a path' or an adjective 'straight', whereas *mutka* can only be a noun. The external locative cases, e.g. the adessive in (30c),[15] are required with *suora* when it is used in an expression referring

[14] See also note 4. In order to express the meaning 'straight home', it is possible to use the adverb *suoraan*, which is a fossilized illative case form of *suora* 'straight'. Very much like in English, the word can, with certain verbs, refer to a straight or shortest path, and also express the temporal meaning 'immediately'. e.g.

Hän kulki suoraan kotiin.
S/he went straight home + ILL
'S/he went straight home.'

Hän lähti suoraan kotiin.
S/he left straight home + ILL
'She left home immediately.'

[15] Finnish has three sets of locative cases:

- general locative cases: translative '(in)to' and essive 'as';
- internal locative cases: inessive 'in', elative 'from (inside)', and illative '(in)to';
- external locative cases: adessive 'at/on', ablative 'from (the surface of)', and allative '(on)to'.

to a location on a straight part of the path. The Dutch construction for combining motion verbs and PPs thus leads to a different interpretation in Finnish.

As we have seen at the beginning of this section, also VERB[CAUSATIVE]–NP [GL1/GL2] combinations are able to encode path curvature. Curiously, the Dutch example in (22) and the Finnish example in (23) do not contain motion verbs, but the examples do refer to path motion, and even specify path curvature. In what follows below we will consider some more examples in Dutch to investigate this idea, while these examples also cover similar Finnish distinctions.

As can be seen in (31), the role of the motion verb seems to have been taken over by the functional semantic structure of the subject NP (i.e. the subject NP is an entity that tends to move when potentially causing a particularly shaped path-part):

(31) *De schoonspringster/het vliegtuig/de kunstrijder maakt/doet een spiraal/looping.*
The (female)diver/the airplane/the ice skater makes/does a spiral/loop
'The (female)diver/the airplane/the ice skater moves in a spiral/loop.'

(32) confirms that the functional semantic structure of the subject NP should license a motion interpretation:

(32) ?*De man maakt/doet een spiral/looping.*
?The man makes/does a spiral/loop
'The man moves in a spiral/loop.'

(32) sounds odd, since there is nothing (contextually, or within the sentence) that licenses a motion or path interpretation. We do not want to go into the details of how a VERB[CAUSATIVE]–NP[GL1/GL2] structure is licensed here, but we merely want to observe that for a structure like this, it is possible to express path curvature. Figure 11.5 explains how a path-motion interpretation can be derived, if correctly licensed.

The interesting thing about this construction is that there is no correspondence in syntax with the GO and PATH functions and also the PATH argument at conceptual level, nor is anything known at either the spatial or conceptual levels of information representation about the direction of the path, or the change of location of the Figure. All we know is that a Figure is in motion, and that it is linked to a particular path shape.

Other external locative cases can be used with the word *suora* in a context close to that in (8c), for instance:

Hän tuli suoralle.
S/he came straight + ALLATIVE
'S/he came to the straight part of the path.'

Hän tuli suoralta.
S/he came straight + ABLATIVE
'S/he came from the straight part of the path.'

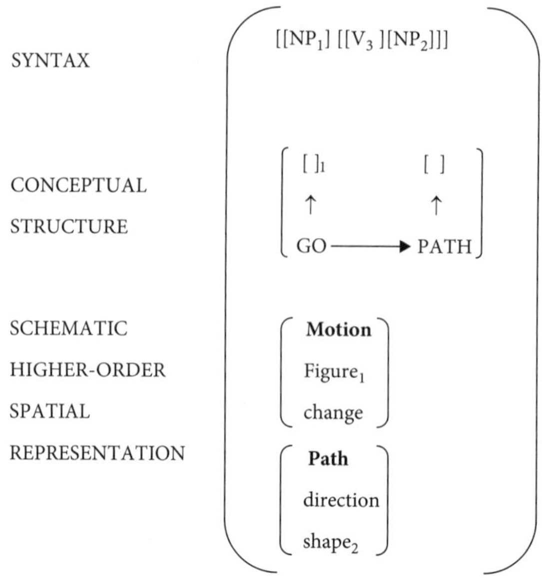

FIGURE 11.5 The VERB[CAUSATIVE]–NP[GL1/GL2] constructions in Dutch and Finnish

In the next section we will consider how motion verbs referring to path curvature can be combined, based on the distinctions that we have made here.

11.6 Constraints on combinations of path-curvature verbs, GL0 verbs, and MoM verbs

It is possible to combine GL0 verbs with GL1 and GL2 verbs in order to specify distinctions in distance, speed, deixis, etc. while also expressing global or local path curvature. For instance, in Finnish:

(33) a. *Mies tuli mutkitellen (GL2)/kaartaen(GL1) mäkeä alas.*
Man came make-curves/make-a-curve-INF2-INS hill-PAR down
'The man came down the hill making curves/making one curve on his way.'

b. *Mies viiletti mutkitellen(GL2)/kaartaen(GL1) mäkeä alas.*
Man moved-fast make-curves/make-a-curve-INF2-INS hill-PAR down
'The man moved fast down the hill making curves/making one curve on his way.'

As the grammatical system allows this kind of combination, it is not necessary to lexicalize all kinds of information in all verb groups. We will consider more elaborately below what combinations of GL0, GL1, GL2, and MoM verbs are possible, and what possible constraints on these combinations exist. We are by no means trying to give an exhaustive description of all possible infinitival complements and adjuncts in Finnish and Dutch. That will be an interesting topic for future research.

Finnish has a rich system of infinitival verb forms, which opens up possibilities for combining verbs with each other; different grain levels, path shapes, and manner of motions may be combined using an infinitival phrase. We will discuss one of these possibilities, in which the infinitival verb is in the so-called second infinitive (marker *-Te*) instructive case form. This infinitival form is to some extent similar to the Germanic gerundive adjunct (in English marked with the suffix *-ing*, see below), indicating that the subject argument of both the predicate and the infinitival verb is the same and the events expressed by the predicate and the infinitival verb take place simultaneously, cf.:

English: *Bill walked home* ***sing-ing***
Finnish: *Bill käveli kotiin* ***laula-e-n***
Bill walked home-ILLATIVE sing-INF2-INSTRUCTIVE
'Bill walked home singing.'

The INF2 + INSTRUCTIVE adjunct can also be used in order to specify the form of the path of motion, e.g.:

(34)

Hän	*meni*	*kotiin*	*mutkitellen*
S/he	went	home + ILL	zigzag + INF2 + INS
|	|	|	
V	PP	INF2 + INS	— syntactic categories
|	|	|	
GL0	Path Goal	GL2	— semantic categories

'She went home zigzagging'.

We will now go through different combinations of a predicate verb and an INF2 + INS adjunct verb. It turns out that there are some interesting restrictions on such combinations. In the following list, the marking 'GL0 GL1' indicates a combination of two motion verbs, the predicate verb being a GL0 verb and the INF2 + INS adjunct being a GL1 verb. Grammatical combinations of such verbs in Finnish are:

(35) GL0 GL1
Kivi/mies meni/tuli mäkeä alas kaartaen.
Stone/man went/came hill-PAR down make-a-curve-INF2 INS
'The stone/the man went/came down the hill rolling.'

(36) GL0 GL2
Käärme tuli kiven alle mutkitellen.
Snake came stone-GEN under-ALL wind-INF2-INS
'The snake came under the stone winding.'

(37) GL0 MoM
Käärme tuli kiven alle kiemurrellen.
Snake came stone-GEN under-ALL wriggle-INF2-INS
'The snake came under the stone wriggling.'

(38) GL1 GL2
Lentopallo kaartoi mutkitellen ulos kentältä.
Volley-ball curved zigzagging out court-ABL
'The volley ball curved out of the court zigzagging.'

(39) GL1 MoM
Mies mutkitteli kotiin horjuen.
Man zigzagged home + ILL rock + INF2 + INS
'The man zigzagged home rocking.'

(40) GL2 GL1
Käärme mutkitteli kiven alle kaartaen.
Snake wound stone-GEN under-ALL curve-INF2-INS
'The snake wound under the stone curving.'

(41) GL2 MoM
Käärme mutkitteli kiven alle kiemurrellen.
Snake wound stone-GEN under-ALL wriggle-INF2-INS
'The snake wound under the stone wriggling.'

(42) MoM GL1
Käärme kiemurteli kiven alle kaartaen.
Snake wriggled stone + GEN under + ALL make-a-curve + INF2-INS
'The snake wriggled under the stone on a curved path.'

(43) MoM GL2
Käärme kiemurteli kiven alle mutkitellen.
Snake wriggled stone + GEN under + ALL curve + INF2 + INS
zigzag-INF2-INS
'The snake wriggled under the stone zigzagging.'

(44) MoM MoM
Käärme kiemurteli kiven alle täristen.
Snake wriggled stone-GEN under-ALL tremble + INF2 + INS
'The snake wriggled under the stone trembling.'

Ungrammatical or unnatural combinations in Finnish are:

(45) GL0 GL0
??Poika tuli mäkeä alas kulkien.
??Boy came hill + PAR down move + INF2 + INS

(46) GL1 GL0
**Kivi kaarsi mäkeä alas mennen/tullen.*
*Stone rolled hill-PAR down go-/come + INF2 + INS

(47) GL2 GL0
**Käärme mutkitteli kiven alle mennen.*
*Snake zigzagged stone + GEN under + ALL go + INF2 + INS

(48) MoM GL0
**Käärme kiemurteli kiven alle mennen.*
*Snake wriggled stone-GEN under-ALL go + INF2-INS

(49) GL1 GL1 (Conflict: two different shapes)
??Mies kaartoi kotiin koukaten.
??Man curved home-ILL make.hook-shaped turn-INF2-INS
'The man curved home making a hook-shaped turn.'

(50) GL2 GL2 (Conflict: two different shapes)
??Käärme mutkitteli kiven alle sahaten.
??Snake zigzagged stone-GEN under-ALL "saw"-INF2-INS
'The snake wound under the stone "zigzagging".'

As it seems that not all combinations are possible, we suggest that the following constraint works for the Finnish INF2 + INS adjuncts:

No Infinitival GL0-Adjuncts Constraint
*V[motion]–V[motion GL0] + INF2 + INS

The constraint states that a motion verb cannot be combined with a second infinitive instructive adjunct if the adjunct is a motion verb and the curvature is neutral (GL0).

It is easier to combine a non-motion predicate verb with an INF2 + INS GL0-verb.

(51) (?)*Poika lauloi mäkeä alas tullen.*
(?)Boy sang hill + PAR down come + INF2 + ILL
'The boy was singing as he was coming down the hill.'

The sentence becomes more natural if the word order is changed so that the adjunct verb precedes the PP:

(52) *Poika lauloi tullen mäkeä alas.*
Boy sang come + INF2 + ILL hill + PAR down
'The boy was singing as he was coming down the hill.'

This word order change has to do with focusing on the path ('down the hill'). A similar change does not, however, make other ungrammatical combinations (45)–(50) any better. Actually, the GL0 GL0 combination becomes very strange with such a word order, cf. (45):

(53) ??*Poika tuli kulkien mäkeä alas.*
??Boy came move + INF2 + INS hill + PAR down

We will not go deeper into the word order effects. In Finnish, the word order is expressing the information structure (topicality, focus, etc.) (see Vilkuna, 1989), and the above-mentioned effects are most likely to find their explanation there.

In Dutch, the acceptable combinations of verbs and gerundive adjuncts is different compared to similar syntactic patterns in Finnish. The No Infinitival GL0-Adjunct Constraint, however, also applies in Dutch with gerundive adjuncts. Consider:

(54) GL2 GL0
**Hij zigzagde gaand de berg af.*
*He zigzagged going the mountain off.

(55) GL1 GL0
**Hij draaide gaand de straat in.*
*He turned going the street into.

(56) MoM GL0
**Hij danste gaand.*
*He danced going.

Other combinations of curvature verbs are allowed in Dutch:

(57) GL0 GL2
Hij ging zigzaggend de berg af.
He went zigzagging the mountain off.
'He went zigzagging down the mountain.'

(58) GL0 MoM
Hij ging trillend de berg af.
He went trembling the mountain off.
'He went trembling down the mountain.'

(59) GL1 GL2
Hij draaide zigzaggend de straat in.
He turned zigzagging the street into.
'He turned into the street zigzagging.'

(60) GL1 MoM
Hij draaide dansend de straat in.
He turned dancing the street into
'He turned into the street dancing.'

(61) GL1 MoM
Hij zigzagde dansend de berg af.
He zigzagged dancing the mountain off.
'He zigzagged down the mountain dancing.'

(62) MoM GL2
Hij danste zigzaggend de berg af.
He danced zigzagging the mountain off.
'He danced down the mountain zigzagging.'

(63) MoM MoM
Hij danste trillend de berg af.
He danced trembling the mountain off
'He danced down the mountain trembling.'

Ungrammatical or unnatural combinations in Dutch are:

(64) GL0 GL1
**Hij ging indraaiend/afslaand/inbuigend de straat in.*
'He went turning in/turning off/bending into the street.'

(65) GL2 GL1
**Hij zigzagde indraaiend/afslaand/inbuigend de straat in.*
'He zigzagged turning into the street.'

(66) MoM GL1
**Hij danste indraaiend/afslaand/inbuigend de straat in.*
'He danced into the street while following a path with a bend in it.'

These examples show that in Dutch it is not possible to have the highly context sensitive GL1 (compound) verbs as gerundive adjuncts. This means that it is possible to formulate a constraint on the use of Dutch gerundive adjuncts on the basis of the three curvature level hypothesis formulated above:

Gerundive GL1 Adjunct Constraint:
*V[motion]–V-ing[motion GL1]

Just like in Finnish, a combination of two GL0, GL1, or GL2 verbs is impossible in Dutch, as these combinations are either tautological, or give a conflict relating to path shapes:

(67) GL0 GL0 (tautological)
??*Hij ging reisde/reizend de berg af.*
'He went travelled/travelling down the mountain.'

(68) GL1 GL1 (tautological)
??*Hij draaide sloeg/slaand de straat in.*
'He turned hit/hitting into the street.'

(69) GL2 GL2 (contradiction)
??*Hij zigzagde slalomde/slalommend de berg af.*
'He zigzagged slalomed/slaloming down the mountain.'

The same-curvature-level constraint is more of a pragmatic nature, since it leads to tautologies or contradictions. The combination of two neutral verbs GLo GLo may, however, be acceptable if the PP indicating the direction of the path—in (45), *mäkeä alas* down the hill—is focused and the infinitival verb is unstressed. The Manner of Motion verbs do not express any path shape and can therefore be combined without leading to conflicts.

11.7 The verb-framed vs. satellite-framed path-curvature hypothesis

In this chapter we have considered several ways in which path curvature can be encoded. We have seen that the first way in which path curvature can be encoded is that it is lexically conflated with motion in path-curvature verbs, such as *to curve* (GL1) and *to zigzag* (GL2). The second way in which path curvature can be encoded is in special constructions. In such cases, path curvature encoded in an NP can be combined with a causative verb in Dutch or Finnish, or path curvature is encoded in the NP part of a PP (headed by *in/met*; only in Dutch). This PP can then be combined with GLo verbs (like *to go*) or with certain MoM verbs (like *to walk*), both of which are neutral in relation to path curvature specification. Thirdly, we have seen that path curvature can be derived pragmatically from certain MoM verbs (such as *to swagger*, or *to hike*), leading to characteristic path curvatures if such verbs are combined with path expressions.

These observations lead to two interesting conclusions. In the first place, MoM verbs seem to fall into two different classes, depending on whether they pragmatically invite a straight—or rather, an underspecified—path curvature, or whether they pragmatically invite a path curvature of a particular nature (e.g. we seem to know that the path curvature invited by *to swagger* is different from the path curvature invited by *to hike*). We leave the investigation of this non-lexical difference based on pragmatic inference to future research. The second thing of interest, however, is that motion and curvature appear to behave in a fashion similar to the lexicalization of motion and manner (Talmy 2000). According to Talmy, Spanish for example usually conflates motion and path in the main verb, and puts manner in what he calls a satellite:

(70) *La botella entró a la cueva flotando.*
'The bottle entered the cave floating.'

| | |
Figure Motion + Path Manner

On the other hand, English conflates motion and manner in the main verb, and puts the path in a satellite:

(71)

The bottle	*floated*	*into the cave.*
|	|	|
Figure	Motion + Manner	Path

Based on the distribution of motion, path, and manner, Talmy refers to Spanish as a verb-framed language (since the path is lexically encoded in the verb), and refers to English as a satellite-framed language (since it puts the path in a verb-satellite).

As we have seen, motion and path curvature are either conflated in the main verb, or motion and path curvature are encoded separately (motion in the verb, and path curvature in an NP as part of a construction):

(72) *Hij cirkelde het weiland door.*
'He went in a circle through the pasture.'

V	PP	— syntactic categories
|	|	
Motion + Curvature	Path	— semantic categories
(GL2)		

(73) *Hij ging/liep in een cirkel het weiland door.*
'He went in a circle through the pasture.'

V	[$_{\mathrm{PP1}}$ *in* NP]	PP2	— syntactic categories
|	|	|	
Motion	Curvature	Path	— semantic categories
(GL0 or MoM)		(GL2)	

(74) *De danser maakte een cirkel op het podium.*
'The dancer made a circle on stage.'

V	[NP]	— syntactic categories
|	|	
Causative	Curvature	— semantic categories
	(GL1)	

One can refer to the representation in (72) as verb-framed path curvature representation, and to path curvature representation in (73) and (74) as (construction-based) satellite-framed path curvature representation. Dutch and Finnish appear to allow for both kinds of path curvature representation (although Finnish—as we have seen in section 11.5—does not allow constructions as in (73)). It remains to be seen whether the verb-framed and (construction-based) satellite-framed path-curvature distinction corresponds to an interesting typological difference in the lexical representation of motion, or whether it is merely a convenient means to describe the two different ways in which path curvature is represented in the lexicon. We leave this to be investigated in the future.

11.8 Conclusions

In this chapter we have seen that distinguishing three levels of path curvature representation in the lexical conceptual structure of motion verbs referring to paths leads to new insights in the Dutch and Finnish grammars: it is not possible to have infinitival/gerundive Neutral Curvature-Adjuncts in either Finnish or Dutch; it is not possible to have a gerundive Global Curvature-Adjunct in Dutch; in both languages it is possible to have a causative verb + curvature noun combination expressing path curvature; but only in Dutch is it possible to have a PP-Adjunct expressing path curvature in combination with a Neutral Curvature verb. Furthermore, both languages apply the pragmatic same-curvature-level constraint (making it sound strange if the same level of curvature representation is expressed more than once in the same clause), and both languages allow the pragmatic inference of path curvature on the basis of Manner of Motion verbs (whether the path is globally straight, or whether the path locally has a distinctive curvature). What follows from these observations is that path curvature can be lexically represented in a verb or in a noun (in which case constructions are employed to express path curvature), or that path curvature can be systematically inferred. We have discussed examples of all of these.

Although our work is based on Dutch (Indo-European, Germanic), and Finnish (Finno-Ugric, Finnic), it has been demonstrated that our system can in principle be generalized to other languages (for Akan see Apraku 2005; for Bulgarian see Martinez 2007; and for English see van der Zee et al. 2010). Other typologically different languages must be studied in order to determine whether the three curvature levels are universal, and whether the verb-framed versus satellite-framed lexical encoding strategies allow for a typological division.

References

Abbott, V., Black, J. H., and Smith, E. E. (1985), The representation of scripts in memory. *Journal of Memory and Language* 24: 179–99.

Alexander, R. M. (1982), *Locomotion of Animals*. New York: Chapman & Hall.

Alexander, R. M. (1989), *Dynamics of Dinosaurs and Other Extinct Giants*. New York: Columbia University Press.

Alexander, R. M. (1991), Energy-saving mechanisms in walking and running. *Journal of Experimental Biology* 160: 55–69.

Alexander, R. M. (1996), Chapter 3. In *Optima for Animals*. Princeton, NJ: Princeton University Press, 45–64.

Alexander, R. (1999), One price to run, swim or fly? *Nature* 397: 651–3.

Allen, G. L. (1997), From knowledge to words to wayfinding: issues in the production and comprehension of route directions. In S. C. Hirtle and A. U. Frank (eds), *Spatial Information Theory: a Theoretical Basis for GIS*. Berlin: Springer, 363–72.

Ameka, F. and Essegbey, J. (2001), Serializing languages: verb-framed, satellite-framed or neither? In *Proceedings of the 32nd Annual Conference on African Linguistics. University of California, Berkeley*. Trenton, NJ: Africa World Press.

Ameka, F. and Levinson, S. (2007), *Positional and Postural Verbs*. Special issue of *Linguistics*.

Apraku, P. (2005), Conceptual structures of motion events in Akan as compared to English. Unpublished MPhil thesis, Department of Modern and Foreign Languages, Faculty of Arts, NTNU, Trondheim, Norway.

Arad, M. (2007), Some aspects of the Hebrew verb *saxah* 'swim'. In Maisak and Rakhilina (eds), 2007.

Arkadiev, P. M. (2007), Glagoly peremeščenija v vode v litovskom jazyke. (Aquamotion verbs in Lithuanian.) In Maisak and Rakhilina (eds), 2007.

Barker, R. G. and Wright, H. F. (1954), *Midwest and its Children: the Psychological Ecology of an American Town*. Evanston: Row, Peterson & Co.

Barsalou, L. W. (1999), Perceptual symbol systems. *Behavioral and Brain Sciences* 22: 577–660.

Batoréo, H. J. (2008), Cognitive and lexical characteristics of motion in liquid medium: aquamotion verbs in typologically different languages. *Psychology of Language and Communication* 12(2), 3–15.

Beavers, J., Levin, B., and Tham, S. (2010), The typology of motion expressions revisited. *Journal of Linguistics* 46: 331–77.

Bennett, D. (1975), *Spatial and Temporal Uses of English Prepositions*. London: Longman.

Bennett, L. B. and Cristani, V. M. (2003), Editorial. *Spatial Cognition and Computation*, 33, issues: 2 and 3, 93–6, http://www.informaworld.com/smpp/title~content=t775653698~db=all~tab=issueslist~branches=3

Bethell-Fox, C. E. and Shepard, R. N. (1988), Mental rotation: effects of stimulus complexity and familiarity. *Journal of Experimental Psychology: Human Perception and Performance* 13: 12–23.

Bloomfield, L. (1957), *Eastern Ojibwa: Grammatical Sketch, Texts, and Word List*. Ann Arbor: University of Michigan Press.

Bohnemeyer, J. (1999), Some Primordial Soup for the Evolution of a Research Project on Event Representation in Language and Cognition. Unpublished manuscript, Max Planck Institute for Psycholinguistics.

Bohnemeyer, J. (2003), The unique vector constraint: the impact of direction changes on the linguistic segmentation of motion events. In E. van der Zee and J. Slack (eds), *Representing Direction in Language and Space*. Oxford: Oxford University Press, 86–110.

Bohnemeyer, J. and Brown, P. (2007), Standing divided: dispositional verbs and locative predications in two Mayan languages. *Linguistics* 45(5/5): 1105–52.

Bohnemeyer, J., Eisenbeiss, S., and Narasimhan, B. (2006), Ways to go: methodological considerations in Whorfian studies on motion events. In S. Eissenbeiss (ed.), *Essex Research Reports in Linguistics* 50.

Bos, J., Klein, E., and Oka, T. (2003), Meaningful conversation with a mobile robot. In *Proceedings of the 10th Conference of the European Chapter of the Association for Computational Linguistics (EACL10)*: 71–4, Budapest, April 2003.

Brown, P. (1994), The INs and ONs of Tzeltal locative expressions: the semantics of static descriptions of location. *Linguistics* 32: 743–90.

Bryant, D. J. and Tversky, B. (1999), Mental representations of perspective and spatial relations from diagrams and models. *Journal of Experimental Psychology: Learning, Memory, and Cognition* 25(1): 137–56.

Bryant, D. J., Tversky, B., and Franklin, N. (1992), Internal and external spatial frameworks for representing described scenes. *Journal of Memory and Language* 31(1): 74–98.

Burigo, M. and Coventry, K. (2010), Context affects scale selection for proximity terms. *Spatial Cognition and Computation* 10(4): 292–312.

Burkhard, H.-D., Düffert, U., Hoffmann, J., Jüngel, M., Lötzsch, M., Brunn, R., Kallnik, M., Kuntze, N., Kunz, M., Petters, S., Risler, M., v. Stryk, O., Koschmieder, N., Laue, T., Röfer, T., Spiess, Cesarz A., Dahm, I., Hebbel, M., Nowak, W., and Ziegler, J. (2002), *GermanTeam 2002*. Technical Report (178 pages), Universität Bremen, http://www.informatik.uni-bremen.de/kogrob/papers/GermanTeam2002.pdf

Byrne, R. W. (2002), Seeing actions as hierarchically organized structures: great ape manual skills. In A. N. Meltzoff and W. Prinz (eds), *The Imitative Mind: Development, Evolution, and Brain Bases*. Cambridge: Cambridge University Press, 122–40.

Cadierno, T. and Ruiz, L. (2006), Motion events in Spanish L2 acquisition. *Annual Review of Cognitive Linguistics* 4: 183–216.

Carlson L. A. (2010), Encoding space in spatial language. In K. S. Mix, L. B. Smith and M. Graesser (eds), *Spatial Foundations of Cognition and Language*. Oxford: Oxford University Press, 157–87.

Carlson, L. A. and Covey, E. S. (2005), How far is near? Inferring distance from spatial descriptions. *Language and Cognitive Processes* 20: 617–32.

Carlson, L. and Logan, G. D. (2001), Using spatial terms to select an object. *Memory and Cognition* 29: 883–92.

Carlson, L. A. and van der Zee, E. (2005). *Functional Features in Language and Space: Insights from Perception, Categorization and Development.* Oxford: Oxford University Press.

Carlson-Radvansky, L. A. and Logan, G. D. (1997), The influence of reference frame selection on spatial template construction. *Journal of Memory and Language* 37: 411–37.

Clark, H. H. (1973), Space, time, semantics, and the child. In T. E. Moore (ed.), *Cognitive Development and the Acquisition of Language.* New York: Academic Press.

Conway, M. A. and Rubin, D. C. (1993), The structure of autobiographical memory. In A. F. Collins, S. E. Gathercole, M. A. Conway, and P. E. Morris (eds), *Theories of Memory* 1. Hillsdale, NJ: Lawrence Erlbaum Associates, 103–37.

Coventry, K. R. and Garrod, S. C. (2004), *Saying, Seeing, and Acting: The Psychological Semantics of Spatial Prepositions.* Hove: Psychology Press.

Crawford, L. E., Regier, T., and Huttenlocher, J. (2000), Linguistic and non-linguistic spatial categorization. *Cognition* 75: 209–35.

Croft, W., Barðdal, J., Hollman, W., Sotirova, V., and Taoka, C. (2010), Revisiting Talmy's typological classification of complex events. In H. Boas (ed.), *Contrastive Construction Grammar.* Amsterdam/Philadelphia: John Benjamins.

Dale, R., Geldof, S., and Prost, J.-P. (2005), Using natural language generation in automatic route description. *Journal of Research and Practice in Information Technology* 37: 89–105.

Daniel, M. P. and Denis, M. (1998), Spatial descriptions as navigational aids: a cognitive analysis of route directions. *Kognitionswissenschaft* 7: 45–52.

Davies, C. and Pederson, E. (2001), Grid patterns and cultural expectations in urban wayfinding. In D. R. Montello (ed.), *Spatial Information Theory: Foundations of Geographic Information Science.* Berlin: Springer, 400–14.

de Vries, L. J. (2005), Towards a typology of tail-head linkage in Papuan languages. *Studies in Language* 29(2): 363–84.

Denis, M. (1997). The description of routes: a cognitive approach to the production of spatial discourse. *Cahier de Psychologie Cognitive* 16: 409–58.

Denis, M., Pazzaglia, F., Cornoldi, C., and Bertolo, L. (1999), Spatial discourse and navigation: an analysis of route directions in the city of Venice. *Applied Cognitive Psychology* 13: 145–74.

Di Meola, C. (1998). Semantisch relevante und irrelevante Kasusalternation am Beispiel von 'entlang'. *Zeitschrift für Sprachwissenschaft* 17: 204–35.

Dimitrova-Vulchanova, M. (1999), *Verb Semantics, Diathesis and Aspect.* München/Newcastle: LINCOM EUROPA.

Dimitrova-Vulchanova, M. (2003), On two types of result: resultatives revisited. In http://www.ling.hf.ntnu.no/tross/TROSS03-toc.html

Dimitrova-Vulchanova, M. (2004a), Verbs of motion and their conceptual structure. Motion Encoding Workshop, Åbo Akademi, Turku.

Dimitrova-Vulchanova, M. (2004b), Paths in verbs of motion. Invited talk at Argument Structure CASTL Conference, Tromsø University, Tromsø.

Dimitrova-Vulchanova, M. (2009), Going Balkan: convergence in the Balkan lexicon. Talk given at the workshop 'Spatial Cognition, Spatial Language and the Balkan Spatial Lexicon', Brussels.

Dimitrova-Vulchanova, M. and Weisgerber, M. (2007), Integrating context in semantic representation. Workshop 'Formal Approaches to Language as a Cognitive System', Tampere, Finland.

Dimitrova-Vulchanova, M., Martinez, L. and Edsberg, O. (in press), A basic level for the encoding of motion. In J. Hudson, U. Magnusson, and C. Paradis (eds), *The Construal of Spatial Meaning: Windows into Conceptual Space*. Oxford: Oxford University Press.

Dimitrova-Vulchanova, M., Martinez, L., Eshuis, R., and Listhaug, K. (under revision), No evidence of L1 path encoding strategies in the L2 in advanced Bulgarian speakers of Norwegian. In *First and Second Language Acquisition of Spatial Language*, special edition of *Spatial Cognition and Computation*.

Divjak, D. and Lemmens, M. (2007), Lexical conflation patterns in Dutch aquamotion verbs. In Maisak and Rakhilina (eds), 2007.

Dowell, R., Martin, B. A., and Tversky, B. (2004), Segmenting Everyday Actions: an Object Bias? *Proceedings of the 26th Annual Meeting of the Cognitive Science Society*. Chicago, IL.

Du Bois, J. (1985), Competing Motivations. In J. Haiman (ed.), *Iconicity in Syntax*. Amsterdam: John Benjamins, 343–65.

Du Bois, J. (1987), The discourse basis of ergativity. *Language* 63: 805–55.

Dzidzorm, G. (2007), Motion verbs in Ewe. Unpublished manuscript, Norwegian University of Science and Technology.

Egenhofer M. J. and Mark D. M. (1995), Naïve Geography. In A. U. Franck and W. Kuhn (eds), *Spatial Information Theory: A Theoretical Basis for GIS*, Lecture Notes in Computer Sciences No. 988. Berlin: Springer, 1–15.

Egg, M. (1994), *Aktionsart und Kompositionalität. Zur kompositionellen Ableitung der Aktionsart komplexer Kategorien*. Berlin: Akademie Verlag.

Erelt, M. (2003), Syntax. In M. Erelt (ed.), *Estonian Language* (Linguistica Uralica. Supplementary Series). Tallinn: Estonian Academy Publishers, 93–129.

Erelt, M., Kasik, R., Metslang, H., Rajandi, H., Ross, K., Saari, H., Tael, K., and Vare, S. (1993), *Eesti keele grammatika* (Grammar of the Estonian Language). Tallinn: Keele ja Kirjanduse Instituut.

Eschenbach, C. (2005), Contextual, functional, and geometric components in the semantics of projective terms. In L. Carlson and E. van der Zee (eds), *Functional Features in Language and Space: Insights from Perception, Categorization, and Development*. Oxford: Oxford University Press, 71–91.

Eschenbach, C., Habel, C., and Kulik, L. (1999), Representing simple trajectories as oriented curves. In A. Kumar and I. Russell (eds), *Proceedings of the 12th International FLAIRS Conference*. Menlo Park, CA: AAAI Press, 431–6.

Eschenbach, C., Tschander, L., Habel, C., and Kulik, L. (2000), Lexical specifications of paths. In C. Freksa, W. Brauer, C. Habel, and K. Wender (eds), *Spatial Cognition II*. Berlin: Springer, 127–44.

Evans, G. W. (1980), Environmental cognition. *Psychological Bulletin* 88: 259–87.

Evans V. (2003), *The Structure of Time: Language, Meaning and Temporal Cognition*. Amsterdam/Philadelphia: John Benjamins.

Fellbaum, C. (1990), English verbs as a semantic net. *International Journal of Lexicography* 3(4): 278–301.

Filipović, L. (2007), *Talking about Motion: a Cross-linguistic Investigation of Lexicalization Patterns*. Amsterdam: John Benjamins.

Fillmore, C. and Kay, P. (1996), *Construction Grammar*. CSLI Lecture Notes 5. Linguistics X 20. University of California, Berkeley.

Fillmore, C. J. (1977), The case for case reopened. In *Grammatical Relations. Syntax and Semantics 8*, 59–82. New York: Academic Press.

Fillmore, C. J. (1983), How to know whether you're *coming* or *going*. In Gisa Rauh (ed.), *Essays on Deixis*. Tübingen: Narr.

Fillmore, C. J. (1997), *Lectures on Deixis*. Stanford: CSLI Publications.

Fischer, K. (2003), Linguistic methods for investigating concepts in use. In Th. Stolz and K. Kolbe (eds), *Methodologie in der Linguistik*. Frankfurt am Main: Peter Lang.

Fischer, K. and Moratz, R. (2001), From communicative strategies to cognitive modelling. *Workshop Epigenetic Robotics*, Lund.

Foote, I. (1967), Verbs of motion. In D. Ward (ed.), *Studies in the Modern Russian Language*. Cambridge: Cambridge University Press.

Frank, A. U. (1996), Qualitative spatial reasoning: cardinal directions as an example. *International Journal of Geographical Information Systems* 10: 269–90.

Franklin, N. and Tversky, B. (1990), Searching imagined environments. *Journal of Experimental Psychology: General* 119(1): 63–76.

Franklin, N., Tversky, B., and Coon, V. (1992), Switching points of view in spatial mental models. *Memory and Cognition* 20: 507–18.

Freundschuh S. M. and Egenhofer M. J. (1997), Human conceptions of spaces: implications for geographic information systems, *Transactions in GIS* 2(4): 361–75.

Fried, M. and Östman, J.-O. (2004), Construction grammar. A thumbnail sketch. In M. Fried and J.-O. Östman (eds), *Construction Grammar in a Cross-Language Perspective*. Amsterdam and Philadelphia: John Benjamins, 11–86. (Constructional Approaches to Language, 2).

Galambos, J. A. (1983), Normative studies of six characteristics of our knowledge of common activities. *Behavior Research Methods and Instrumentation* 15(3): 327–40.

Geuder, W. and Weisgerber, M. (2006), Manner and causation in movement verbs. In C. Ebert and C. Endriss (eds), *Proceedings from Sinn und Bedeutung 10, Berlin, ZAS Papers in Linguistics*, 125–38.

Giese, M. A. and Poggio, T. (2003), Neural mechanisms for the recognition of biological movements and action. *Nature Reviews Neuroscience* 4: 179–92.

Goddard, C. and Wierzbicka, A. (eds) (1994), *Semantic and Lexical Universals—theory and Empirical Findings*. Amsterdam: John Benjamins.

Goldberg, A. (2006), *Constructions at Work: the nature of Generalization in Language*. Oxford: Oxford University Press.

Grice, H. P. (1975), Logic and conversation. In P. Cole and J. Morgan (eds), *Syntax and Semantics, 3: Speech Acts*, 41–58. New York: Academic Press. Reprinted in H. P. Grice (ed.), *Studies in the Way of Words*, 22–40.

Grice, H. P. (ed.) (1989), *Studies in the Way of Words*. Cambridge, MA: Harvard University Press.

Gries, S. (2006), Corpus-based methods in cognitive semantics: the many meanings of 'to run'. In S. Gries and A. Stefanowitsch (eds), *Corpora in Cognitive Linguistics: Corpus-Based Approaches to Syntax and Lexis*. Berlin: Mouton de Gruyter, 57–99.

Gruber, J. (1965), Studies in lexical relations. Doctoral dissertation, MIT.

Gryl, A., Moulin, B., and Kettani, B. (2002), A conceptual model for representing verbal expressions used in route descriptions. In K. R. Coventry and P. Olivier (eds), *Spatial Language: Cognitive and Computational Perspectives*. Dordrecht: Kluwer Academic Publishers, 19–42.

Gullberg, M. (2011), Language-specific encoding of placement events in gestures. In J. Bohnemeyer and E. Pederson (eds), *Events Representations in Language and Cognition*. Cambridge: Cambridge University Press.

Habel, C. (1988), Prozedurale Aspekte der Wegplanung und Wegbeschreibung. In H. Schnelle and G. Rickheit (eds), *Sprache in Mensch und Computer*. Opladen: Westdeutscher Verlag, 107–33.

Habel, C. (1999), Drehsinn und Reorientierung—Modus und Richtung beim Bewegungsverb *drehen*. In G. Rickheit (hrsg.), *Richtungen im Raum*. Opladen: Westdeutscher Verlag.

Hanson, C. and Hirst, W. (1989), On the representation of events: a study of orientation, recall, and recognition. *Journal of Experimental Psychology: General* 118(2): 136–47.

Hanson, C. and Hirst, W. (1991), Recognizing differences in recognition tasks: a reply to Lassiter and Slaw. *Journal of Experimental Psychology: General* 120(2): 211–12.

Heeschen, V. (1998), *An Ethnographic Grammar of the Eipo Language*. Berlin: Dittrich Reimer.

Heine, B. and Kuteva, T. (2002), *World Lexicon of Grammaticalization*. Cambridge: Cambridge University Press.

Herrmann, T. and Deutsch, W. (1976), *Psychologie der Objektbenennung*. Bern: Huber Verlag.

Herrmann, T., Schweizer, K., Janzen, G., and Katz, S. (1998), Routen- und Überblickswissen – Konzeptuelle Überlegungen. *Kognitionswissenschaft* 7: 145–59.

Herskovits, A. (1986). *Language and Spatial Cognition: an Interdisciplinary Study of the Representation of the Prepositions in English*. Cambridge: Cambridge University Press.

Herskovits, A. (1997), Language, spatial cognition, and vision. In O. Stock (ed.), *Spatial and Temporal Reasoning*. Dordrecht: Kluwer Academic Publishers, 155–202.

Hildebrand, M. Bramble, D. M., Liem, K. F., and Wake, D. B. (eds), (1985), *Functional Vertebrate Morphology*. Cambridge, MA: Harvard University Press.

Holland, B., Bateman, R., and Gordy, B. (1964), *Please Mr. Postman* (The Beatles' second album). Capitol.

Hook, P. E. (1991), The emergence of perfective aspect in Indo-Aryan languages. In E. Traugott and B. Heine (eds), *Approaches to Grammaticalization*. Amsterdam: John Benjamins, 59–89.

Huang S. and Tanangkingsing, M. (2005), Reference to motion events in six Western Austronesian languages: toward a semantic typology. *Oceanic Linguistics* 44(2).

Huddleston R. and Pullum G. K. (2005), *A Student's Introduction to English Grammar*. Cambridge: Cambridge University Press.

Huumo, T. (2010), Suomen väyläadpositioiden prepositio- ja postpositiokäyttöjen merkityseroista. (On meaning differences between prepositional and postpositional uses of Finnish path adpositions). *Virittäjä* 4: 531–61.

Huumo, T. (in press), Väylä, liike ja 'skannaus': suomen väyläadpositioiden prepositio- ja postpositiokäyttöjen merkityseroista. *Virittäjä*.

Iacobini, C. (2009), The number and use of manner verbs as a cue for typological change in the strategies of motion event encoding. *Proceedings from the Space in Language Conference*, 8–10 October 2009. Pisa, Italy.

Ibarretxe-Antuñano, I. (in press), Cuestiones pendientes de la tipología semántica para el análisis de los eventos de movimento. In J. F. Val Álvaro and M. C. Horno Chéliz (eds), *La gramática del sentído: léxico y sintaxis en la encrucijada*. Zaragoza: PUZ.

Jackendoff, R. (1983), *Semantics and Cognition*. Cambridge, MA: MIT Press.

Jackendoff, R. (1990), *Semantic Structures*. Cambridge, MA: MIT Press.

Jackendoff, R. (1997), *The Architecture of the Language Faculty*. Cambridge, MA: MIT Press.

Jackendoff, R. (2002), *Foundations of Language*. Oxford: Oxford University Press.

Jackendoff, R. (2003), *Foundations of Language: Brain, Meaning, Grammar, Evolution*. Oxford: Oxford University Press.

Jackendoff. R. (2010), *Meaning and the Lexicon: the Parallel Architecture 1975–2010*. Oxford: Oxford University Press.

Jastorff, J., Kourtzi, Z., and Giese, M. (2006), Learning to discriminate complex movements: biological versus artificial trajectories. *Journal of Vision* 6: 791–804.

Jellema, T. and Perrett, D. I. (2003). Cells in monkey STS responsive to articulated body motions and consequent static posture: a case of implied motion? *Neuropsychologia* 41: 1728–37.

Johansson, G. (1973). Visual perception of biological motion and a model for its analysis. *Perception and Psychophysics* 14: 201–11.

Johnson, M. (1987), *The Body in the Mind: the Bodily Basis of Meaning, Imagination, and Reason*. Chicago, IL: University of Chicago Press.

Khetarpal, N., Majid, A., and Regier, T. (2009), Spatial terms reflect near-optimal spatial categories. In N. Taatgen and H. van Rijn (eds), *Proceedings of the 31st Annual Meeting of the Cognitive Science Society*.

Khetarpal, N., Majid, A., Malt, B., Sloman, S., and Regier, T. (2010), Similarity judgments reflect both language and cross-language tendencies: evidence from two semantic domains. In S. Ohlsson and R. Catrambone (eds), *Proceedings of the 32nd Annual Meeting of the Cognitive Science Society*.

Khokhlova, L. V. and Singh C. (2007), Glagoly peremeščenija v židkoj srede i dviženija židkosti v zapadnyx indoarijskix jazykax. (The verbs of motion in liquid medium and motion of liquid in Western Indo-Aryan languages.) In Maisak and Rakhilina (eds), 2007.

Kita, S. and Özyürek, A. (2003), What does cross-linguistic variation in semantic coordination of speech and reveal?: Evidence for an interface representation of spatial thinking and speaking. *Journal of Memory and Language*, 48, 16–32.

Klavan, J. (in press), *Evidence in Linguistics: Corpus-linguistic and Experimental Methods for Studying Grammatical Synonymy*. Tartu: Tartu University Press.

Klavan, J., Kesküla, K., and Ojava, L. (2011), The division of labour between synonymous locative cases and adpositions: the Estonian adessive and the adposition *peal* 'on'. In S. Kittilä, K. Västi, J. Ylikoski (eds), *Studies on Case, Animacy and Semantic Roles*. Amsterdam: John Benjamins, 1–19.

Klein, W. (1979), Wegauskünfte. *Zeitschrift für Literaturwissenschaft und Linguistik* 33: 9–57.

Klippel, A. (2003), Wayfinding choremes. In W. Kuhn, M. Worboys, and S. Timpf (eds), *Spatial Information Theory: Foundations of Geographic Information Science Proceedings of International Conference COSIT 2003*, September 24–28, 2003, Hingen, Switzerland. Berlin: Springer, 320–34.

Klippel, A., Dewey, C., Knauff, M., Richter, K. F., Montello, D. R., Freksa, C., and Loeliger, E. A. (2004), Direction concepts in wayfinding assistance systems. In J. Baus, C. Kray, and R. Porzel (eds), *Workshop on Artificial Intelligence in Mobile Systems (AIMS'04), Proceedings SFB 378 Memo 84*, Saarbrücken, 1–8.

Klippel, A., Hansen, S., Davies, J., and Winter, S. (2005), A high-level cognitive framework for route directions. In *Proceedings of the SSC 2005 Spatial Intelligence, Innovation and Praxis: The National Biennial Conference of the Spatial Science Institute*, September 2005. Melbourne.

Klippel, A. and Montello, D. R. (2004), On the robustness of mental conceptualizations of turn direction concepts. In M. J. Egenhofer, C. Freksa, and H. Miller (eds), *GIScience 2004. The Third International Conference on Geographic Information Science*, October 20–23, 2004, University of Maryland. Adelphi, MD, USA, 139–41 (Extended Abstract).

Klippel, A., Richter, K.-F., and Hansen, S. (2005), Structural salience as a landmark. In *MOBILE MAPS 2005—Interactivity and Usability of Map-based Mobile Services.* Workshop at MobileHCI, Salzburg, 2005.

Klippel, A., Tappe, H., and Habel, C. (2003), Pictorial representations of routes: chunking route segments during comprehension. In C. Freksa, W. Brauer, C. Habel, and K. F. Wender (eds), *Spatial Cognition III: Routes and Navigation, Human Memory and Learning, Spatial Representation and Spatial Learning*. Berlin: Springer, 11–33.

Klippel, A., Tappe, H., Kulik, L., and Lee, P. U. (2005), Wayfinding choremes: a language for modeling conceptual route knowledge. *Journal of Visual Languages and Computing* 16: 311–29.

Klippel, A. and Winter, S. (2005), Structural salience of landmarks for route directions. In A. G. Cohn and D. M. Mark (eds), *Spatial Information Theory*. Berlin: Springer, 347–62.

Koenig, J.-P., Mauner, G. and Bienvenue, B. (2003), Arguments for adjuncts. *Cognition* 89: 67–103.

Koptjevskaja-Tamm, Maria (2008), Approaching lexical typology. In M. Vanhove (ed.), *From Polysemy to Semantic Change. Towards a Typology of Lexical Semantic Associations.* Amsterdam: John Benjamins.

Koptjevskaja-Tamm, M., Divjak, D., and Rakhilina E. V. (2010), Aquamotion verbs in Slavic and Germanic: a case study in lexical typology. In V. Hasko and R. Perelmutter (eds), *New Approaches to Slavic Verbs of Motion*. Amsterdam: John Benjamins.

Korhonen, A. (2002), Assigning verbs to semantic classes via Wordnet. *Proceedings of the Coling 2002 Workshop SemaNet'02: Building and Using Semantic Network*, August 2002. Taipei.

Kosslyn, S. (1980), *Image and Mind.* Cambridge, MA: MIT Press.

Kosslyn, S. (1994), *Image and Brain: The Resolution of the Imagery Debate.* Cambridge, MA: MIT Press.

Kray, C., Baus, J., Zimmer, H., Speiser, H., and Krüger, A. (2001), Two path prepositions: *along* and *past*. In D. Montello (ed.), *International Conference on Spatial Information Theory*. Berlin. Springer, 263–77.

Krüger, A. and Maaß, W. (1997), Towards a computational semantics of path relations. *Proceedings of the Workshop 'Language and Space, AAAI '97'*. Providence, RI, 101–9.

Kruijff, G.-J. M., Zender, H., Jensfelt, P., and Christensen, H. I. (2007), Situated dialogue and spatial organization: what, where... and why? *International Journal of Advanced Robotic Systems, Special Issue on Human and Robot Interactive Communication* 4(2).

Kuznetsova, J. (2007), Glagoly peremeščenija v vode v persidskom jazyke. (Aquamotion verbs in Persian.) In Maisak and Rakhilina (eds), 2007.

Lakoff, G. (1973), Hedges: a study in meaning criteria and the logic of fuzzy concepts. *Journal of Philosophical Logic* 2: 458–508.

Lakoff, G. (1987), *Women, Fire, and Dangerous Things: What Categories Reveal about the Mind*. Chicago, IL: University of Chicago Press.

Lakoff, G. and Johnson, M. (1980), *Metaphors We Live By*. Chicago IL: University of Chicago Press.

Lander, Y. A. (2008), Indonezijskie glagoly plavanija i principy organizacii glagol'nogo leksikona. (Indonesian aquamotion verbs and the principles of verbal lexicon organization.) In: N. F. Alieva et al. (eds), *Malajsko-indonezijskie Issledovanija*. Vyp. 18. Moscow: Kluch-C.

Lander, Y. A. and Kramarova, S. G. (2007), Indonezijskie glagoly plavanija i ix sistema. (Indonesian aquamotion verbs and their system.) In Maisak and Rakhilina (eds), 2007.

Langacker, R. W. (1987), *Foundations of Cognitive Grammar. Vol. 1: Theoretical Prerequisites*. Stanford CA: Stanford University Press

Larjavaara, M. (1990), *Suomen Deiksis*. Helsinki: Finnish Literature Society.

Larjavaara, M. (2007), *Pragmasemantiikka*. Helsinki: Finnish Literature Society.

Lassiter, G. D. and Slaw, R. D. (1991), The unitization and memory of events. *Journal of Experimental Psychology: General* 120(1): 80–2.

Lassiter, G. D., Stone, J. I., and Rogers, S. L. (1988), Memorial consequences of variation in behavior perception. *Journal of Experimental Social Psychology* 24(3): 222–39.

Lee S. H. and Maisak T. A. (2007), Glagoly peremeščenija v vode v korejskom jazyke. (Aquamotion verbs in Korean.) In Maisak and Rakhilina (eds), 2007.

Lemmens, M. (2002), The semantic network of Dutch posture verbs. In J. Newman (ed.), *The Linguistics of Sitting, Standing, and Lying* (*Typological Studies in Language*, 51). Amsterdam and Philadelphia: John Benjamins, 103–39.

Lemmens M. (2006), Caused posture: experiential patterns emerging from corpus research. In A. Stefanowitsch and S. Gries (eds), *Corpora in Cognitive Linguistics. Vol. II: The Syntax-Lexis Interface*. Berlin: Mouton de Gruyter.

Letuchiy, A. B. (2007), Glagoly plavanija v arabskom jazyke. (Aquamotion verbs in Arabic.) In Maisak and Rakhilina (eds), 2007.

Levelt, W. J. M. (1989), *Speaking: from Intention to Articulation*. Cambridge, MA: MIT Press.

Levin, B. (1993), *English Verb Classes and Alternations: a Preliminary Investigation* (Vol. XVIII). Chicago, IL.: University of Chicago Press.

Levinson, S. C. (1996), Frames of reference and Molyneux's question: cross-linguistic evidence. In P. Bloom, M. A. Petersen, L. Nadel, and M. F. Garrett (eds), *Language and Space*. Cambridge, MA: MIT Press, 109–491.

Levinson, S. C. (2003), *Space in Language and Cognition. Explorations in Cognitive Diversity*. Cambridge: Cambridge University Press.

Levinson, S. C. and Wilkins, D. (2006), *Grammars of Space*. Cambridge: Cambridge University Press.

Ligozat, G. (2000), From language to motion, and back: generating and using route descriptions. In D. N. Christodoulakis (ed.), *Natural Language Processing—NLP 2000: Second International Conference, Patras, Greece, June 2000. Proceedings*. Berlin: Springer, 328–45.

Logan, G. D. and Sadler, D. D. (1999), A computational analysis of the apprehension of spatial relations. In P. Bloom, M. A. Peterson, L. Nadel, and M. F. Garrett (eds), *Language and Space*. Cambridge, MMA: MIT Press, 493–529.

Loucks, J. and Baldwin, D. (2009), Sources of information for discriminating dynamic human actions. *Cognition* 111: 84–97.

Lovelace, K., Hegarty, M., and Montello, D. R. (1999), Elements of good route directions in familiar and unfamiliar environments. In C. Freksa and D. M. Mark (eds), *Spatial Information Theory: Cognitive and Computational Foundations of Geographic Information Science*. Berlin: Springer, 65–82.

Lynch, K. (1960), *The Image of the City*. Cambridge, MMA.: MIT Press.

Maisak, T. A. and Rakhilina E. V. (eds) (2007), *Glagoly Dviženija v Vode: Leksičeskaja Tipologija*. (Aquamotion verbs: a study in lexical typology.) Moscow: Indrik.

Maisak, T. A. and Rakhilina E. V. (2007), Glagoly dviženija i naxoždenija v vode: leksičeskie sistemy i semantičeskie parametry. (The verbs of motion and staying in water: lexical systems and semantic parameters.) In Maisak and Rakhilina (eds), 2007.

Maisak, T. A., Rostovtsev-Popiel, A. A., and Khurshudian V. G. (2007), Sistemy glagolov plavanija v kavkazskix jazykax. (The systems of aquamotion verbs in Caucasian languages.) In Maisak and Rakhilina (eds), 2007.

Majid, A., Bowerman, M., van Staden, M., and Boster, J. S. (2007), The semantic categories of cutting and breaking events: a cross-linguistic perspective. *Cognitive Linguistics* 18: 133–52.

Majid, A., Boster, J. S., and Bowerman M. (2008), The cross-linguistic categorization of everyday events: a study of cutting and breaking. *Cognition* 109: 235–50.

Makeeva, I. I. and Rakhilina E.V.(2004), Semantika russkogo *plyt'* ~ *plavat'*: sinxronija i diaxronija. (The semantics of Russian *plyt'* ~ *plavat'*: synchrony and diachrony.) In Ju. D. Apresian (ed.), *Sokrovennye smysly: Slovo. Tekst. Kul'tura. Sbornik statej v čest' N.D. Arutjunovoj*. Moscow: Jazyki slavjanskoj kul'tury.

Mallot, H. (1999), Spatial cognition: behavioural competences, neural mechanisms, and evolutionary scaling. *Kognitionswissenschaft* 8: 40–8.

Malt, B., Gennari, S., and Imai, M. (2010), Lexicalization patterns and the world-to-word mapping. In B. Malt and P. Wolff (eds), 2010, 29–57.

Malt, B., Gennari, S., Imai, M., Ameel, E., Tsuda, N., and Majid, A. (2008), Talking about walking: biomechanics and the language of locomotion. *Psychological Science* 19(3): 232–40.

Malt, B. and Wolff, P. (eds) (2010), *Words and the Mind. How Words Capture Human Experience*. Oxford: Oxford University Press.

Mandler, J. (2004), *The Foundations of Mind: the Origins of Conceptual Thought*. New York: Oxford University Press.

Mark, D. M., Comas, D., Egenhofer, M. J., Freundschuh, S. M., Gould, M. D., and Nunes, J. (1995), Evaluating and refining computational models of spatial relations through cross-linguistic human-subjects testing. In A. U. Frank and W. Kuhn (eds), *Spatial Information Theory: a Theoretical Basis for GIS*. Berlin: Springer, 553–68.

Martinez, L. (2007), Path shape verbs in Bulgarian. In *Proceedings of the 2nd Scandinavian Ph.D. Conference in Linguistics and Philology*, Bergen, June 2007.

Martinez, L. (2009), Attention to locomotion pattern vs. trajectory in motion event description. Talk given at the workshop 'Spatial Cognition, Spatial Language and the Balkan Spatial Lexicon'. Brussels.

Martinez, L. (in preparation), *Conceptualization and Linguistic Encoding of Path Curvature* (working title). Trondheim: Norwegian University of Science and Technology.

Matsumoto, Y. (2003), Typologies of lexicalization patterns and event integration: clarifications and reformulations. In S. Chiba (ed.), *Empirical and Theoretical Investigations into Language. A Festschrift for Masaru Kajita*. Tokyo: Kaitakusha, 403–18.

Matsumura, K. (1994), Is the Estonian adessive really a local case? *Journal of Asian and African Studies* 46/47: 223–35.

McCartney, P. (1967), *Your Mother Should Know (Magical Mystery Tour)*. Capitol.

McMahon, T. (1984), *Muscles, Reflexes, and Locomotion*. Princeton, NJ: Princeton University Press.

Mervis, C. B. and Rosch, E. (1981), Categorization of natural objects. *Annual Review of Psychology* 32: 89–115.

Metslang, H. (1993), Kas eesti keeles on olemas progressiiv? (Is there a progressive in Estonian?) *Keel ja Kirjandus* 6, 7, 8: 326–34, 410–16, 468–76.

Metslang, H. (1994), Temporal relations in the predicate and the grammatical system of Estonian and Finnish. Dissertation. Oulu: Oulun yliopiston suomen ja saamen kielen laitoksen tutkimusraportteja 39.

Metslang, H. (1995), The progressive in Estonian. In M. Squartini (ed.), *Temporal Reference, Aspect*. Turin: Rosenberg & Seller, 169–83.

Metslang, H. (2001), On the developments of the Estonian aspect the verbal particle *ära*. In D. Östen and M. Koptjevskaja-Tamm (eds), *The Circum-Baltic Languages: Typology and Contact: Grammar and Typology*. Amsterdam and Philadelphia: John Benjamins, 443–79.

Miller, G. A., Beckwith, R., Fellbaum, Ch., Gross, D., and Miller K. J. (1990), Introduction to WordNet: an on-line lexical database. *International Journal of Lexicography* 3: 235–44.

Miller, G. A. (1995), Wordnet: A lexical database for English. *Communications of ACM*, 38(11), 39–41.

Miller, G. A. and Johnson-Laird, P. N. (1976), *Language and Perception*. Cambridge, MMA: Harvard University Press.

Moar, I. and Bower, G. H. (1983), Inconsistency in spatial knowledge. *Memory and Cognition* 11: 107–13.

Montello D. R. (1993), Scale and multiple psychologies of space. In A. U. Franck and I. Campari (eds), *Spatial Information Theory: a Theoretical Basis for GIS, Proceedings of COSIT '93. Lecture Notes in Computer Science 716*. Berlin: Springer, 312–21.

Montello, D. R. (2005), Navigation. In P. Shah and A. Miyake (eds), *Cambridge Handbook of Visuospatial Thinking*. Cambridge: Cambridge University Press, 257–94.

Moratz, R. and Tenbrink T. (2006), Spatial reference in linguistic human–robot interaction: iterative, empirically supported development of a model of projective relations. *Spatial Cognition and Computation* 6(1): 63–106.

Moratz, R. and Tenbrink T. (2008), Affordance-based human–robot interaction. In E. Rome, J. Hertzberg, and G. Dorffner (eds), *Towards Affordance-based Robot Control, LNAI 4760*. Berlin: Springer, 63–76.

Moratz, R., Fischer, K., and Tenbrink T. (2001), Cognitive modeling of spatial reference for human–robot interaction. *International Journal on Artificial Intelligence Tools* 10(4): 589–611.

Morris, M. W. and Murphy, G. L. (1990), Converging operations on a basic level in event taxonomies. *Memory and Cognition* 18: 407–18.

Morrow, D. G. and Clark, H. H. (1988), Interpreting words in spatial descriptions. *Language and Cognitive Processes* 3(4): 275–91.

Narasimhan B. and Cablitz G. (2002), Granularity in the cross-linguistic encoding of motion and location. Talk given at the 3rd Annual Workshop on Language and Space, University of Bielefeld, July 2002.

Narasimhan, B. (forthcoming), Putting and taking in Tamil and Hindi. To appear in A. Kopecka and B. Narasimhan (eds), *Events of 'putting' and 'taking': a Crosslinguistic Perspective'* (working title).

Ndiwalana, M. (2003), Verbs of movement in Luganda: a frame semantics and sign model perspective. MA thesis, NTNU.

Newman, John (ed). (1997), *The Linguistics of Giving*. Amsterdam: John Benjamins.

Newman, John (ed). (2002), *The Linguistics of Sitting, Standing and Lying*. Amsterdam: John Benjamins.

Newman, John (ed). (2009), *The Linguistics of Eating and Drinking*. Amsterdam: John Benjamins.

Newtson, D. (1973), Attribution and the unit of perception of ongoing behavior. *Journal of Personality and Social Psychology* 28(1): 28–38.

Newtson, D., Engquist, G., and Bois, J. (1977), The objective basis of behavior units. *Journal of Personality and Social Psychology* 35(12): 847–62.

Nikanne, U. (1990), *Zones and Tiers: a Study of Thematic Structure*. Helsinki: Finnish Literature Society.

Nikanne, U. (2002), Kerrokset ja kytkennät: konseptuaalisen semantiikan perusteet, http://www.abo.fi/fak/hf/fin/kurssit/KONSEM/index.htm. (Searched 18 June 2007.)

Nikanne, U. (2005), Constructions in conceptual semantics. In J.-O. Östman and M. Fried (eds), *Construction Grammars: Cognitive Grounding and Theoretical Extensions*. (Constructional Approaches to Language, 3). Amsterdam and Philadelphia: John Benjamins, 191–242.

Nikitina, T. (2008). Pragmatic factors and variation in the expression of spatial goals: the case of *into* vs. *in*. In A. Asbury, J. Dotlačil, B. Gehrke, and R. Nouwen (eds), *Syntax and Semantics of Spatial P*. Amsterdam: John Benjamins, 175–95.

Õim, H., Orav, H., Kahusk, N., and Taremaa P. (2010), Semantic analysis of sentences: the Estonian experience. In *Baltic HLT Proceedings: Human Language Technologies—the Baltic Perspective*, Riga, Latvia, 7–8 October 2010. IOS Press, 2010 (Frontiers in Artificial Intelligence and Applications), 208–13.

Olsen, S. (1996), Pleonastische Direktionale. In *Wenn die Semantik arbeitet. Klaus Baumgärtner zum 65. Geburtstag*. Tübingen: Niemeyer, 303–29.

O'Neill, M. J. (1992), Effects of familiarity and plan complexity on wayfinding in simulated buildings. *Journal of Environmental Psychology* 12: 319–27.

Orav, H. and Vider, K. (2005), Estonian Wordnet and lexicography. In *Symposium on Lexicography XI. Proceedings*. Tübingen: Niemeyer, 549–55.

Orav, H., Õim, H., Kerner K., and Kahusk N. (2010), Main trends in semantic research in Estonian language technology. In *Baltic HLT Proceedings: Human Language Technologies—the Baltic Perspective*, Riga, Latvia, 7–8 October 2010. IOS Press (Frontiers in Artificial Intelligence and Applications), 201–7.

Östman J.-O. (1986), Pragmatics as implicitness: an analysis of question particles in Solf Swedish, with implications of passive clauses and the language persuasion. Ph.D. thesis, University of California, Berkeley. Ann Arbor, MI: University Microfilms International, 86-24885.

Pajusalu, R. (2001), The polysemy of *seisma* 'to stand': multiple motivations for multiple meanings. In I. Tragel (ed.), *Papers in Estonian Cognitive Linguistics. Publications of the Department of General Linguistics* 2. Tartu: Tartu Ülikooli kirjastus, 170–91.

Pajusalu, R. and Orav, H. (2008), Supiinid koha väljendajana: liikumissündmuse keelendamise asümmeetriast. (Supine constructions encoding spatial entities: asymmetry in expressing motion event). *Emakeele Seltsi Aastaraamat* (The Estonian Mother Tongue Society Year Book, 2008), 104–21.

Panina, A. S. (2007), Vyraženie peremeščenija i naxoždenija v vode v japonskom jazyke. (The expression of motion and being in water in Japanese.) In Maisak and Rakhilina (eds), 2007.

Parsons, L. M. (1987), Imagined spatial transformation of one's body. *Journal of Experimental Psychology: General* 116(2): 172–91.

Pawley, A. (1987), Encoding events in Kalam and English: different logics for reporting experience. In R. S. Tomlin (ed.), *Coherence and Grounding in Discourse* (Vol. 11). Amsterdam and Philadelphia: John Benjamins, 129–361.

Pourcel, S. (2010), Motion: a conceptual typology. In V. Evans and P. Chilton (eds), *Language, Cognition and Space: the State of the Art and New Directions*. London, Oakville: Equinox, 419–50.

Pourcel, S. and Kopecka, A. (2005), Motion expression in French: typological diversity. *Durham and Newcastle Working Papers in Linguistics* 11: 139–53.

Presson, C. C. and Montello, D. R. (1988), Points of reference in spatial cognition: stalking the elusive landmark. *British Journal of Developmental Psychology* 6: 378–81.

Rakhilina, E. V. (2007), Tipy metaforičeskix upotreblenij glagolov plavanija. (Types of metaphorical uses of aquamotion verbs.) In Maisak and Rakhilina (eds), 2007.

Reed, C. L., Stone, V. E., Bozova, S., and Tanaka, J. (2003), The body-inversion effect. *Psychological Science* 14: 302–8.

Regier, T. (1996), *The Human Semantic Potential: Spatial Language and Constraint Connectionism*. Cambridge, MMA: MIT Press.

Regier, T. and Carlson, L. A. (2001), Grounding spatial language in perception: an empirical and computational investigation. *Journal of Experimental Psychology: General* 130: 272–98.

Retz-Schmidt, Gudula (1988), Various views on spatial prepositions. *AI Magazine* 9(2), 95–105.

Rice, S. and Newman, J. (1994), Aspect in the making: a corpus analysis of English aspect-marking prepositions. In M. Archard and S. Kemmer (eds), *Language, Culture, and Mind*. Stanford CA: CSLI Publications.

Richardson, D. and Matlock, T. (2007), The integration of figurative language and static depictions: an eye movement study of fictive motion. *Cognition* 102: 129–38.

Rosch, E. and Lloyd, B. B. (eds) (1978), *Cognition and Categorization*. Hillsdale, NJ: Erlbaum.

Rosch, E., Mervis, C. B., Gray, W. D., Johnson, D. M., and Boyes-Braem, P. (1976), Basic objects in natural categories. *Cognitive Psychology* 8: 382–439.

Rukodelnikova, M. B. (2007), Glagoly peremeščenija v vode v kitajskom jazyke. (Verbs of aquamotion in Chinese.) In Maisak and Rakhilina (eds), 2007.

Sampaio, W., Sinha, C., and da Silva Sinha, V. (2009), Mixing and mapping: motion, path and manner in Amondawa. In J. Guo, E. Lieven, N. Budwig, S. Ervin-Tripp, K. Nakamura, and S. Özçaliskan (eds), *Crosslinguistic Approaches to the Study of Language: Research in the Tradition of Dan Isaac Slobin*. London and New York: Psychology Press, 427–39.

Sasse, H.-J. (1987), The thetic/categorical distinction revisited. *Linguistics* 25: 511–80.

Schank, R. C. and Abelson, R. P. (1977), *Scripts, Plans, Goals, and Understanding. An Inquiry into Human Knowledge Structures*. Hillsdale, NJ: Erlbaum.

Schegloff, E. (2000), On granularity. *Annual Review of Sociology* 26: 715–20.

Schlieder, C. (1995), Reasoning about ordering. In A. U. Frank and W. Kuhn (eds), *Spatial Information Theory: a Theoretical Basis for GIS*. Berlin: Springer, 341–9.

Schmidtke, H. R. (2003), A geometry for places: representing extension and extended objects. In W. Kuhn, M. Worboys, and S. Timpf (eds), *International Conference on Spatial Information Theory*. Berlin: Springer, LNCS 2825, 235–52.

Schmidtke, H. R. (2005a), Aggregations and constituents: geometric specification of multi-granular objects. *Journal of Visual Languages and Computing* 16(4): 289–309.

Schmidtke, H. R. (2005b), Eine axiomatische Charakterisierung räumlicher Granularität: formale Grundlagen detailgrad-abhängiger Objekt- und Raumrepräsentation. Doctoral dissertation, Universität Hamburg, Fachbereich Informatik.

Schmidtke, H. R. and Beigl, M. (2010), Positions, regions, and clusters. In *Proceedings of KI 2010*. Berlin: Springer, LNAI 6359, 272–9.

Schmidtke, H. R., Tschander, L., Eschenbach, C., and Habel, C. (2003), Change of orientation. In E. van der Zee and J. Slack (eds), *Representing Direction in Language and Space*. Oxford: Oxford University Press, 166–90.

Schmidtke, H. R. and Woo, W. (2007), A size-based qualitative approach to the representation of spatial granularity. In M. M. Veloso (ed.), *Twentieth International Joint Conference on Artificial Intelligence*, 563–8.

Senft, G. (ed.) (forthcoming), *Serial Verb Constructions in Austronesian and Papuan Languages*. Canberra: Pacific Linguistics.

Senft, G. (forthcoming), Event conceptualization and event report in serial verb constructions in Kilivila: towards a new approach to research a new phenomenon. To appear in G. Senft (ed.), *Serial Verb Constructions in Austronesian and Papuan Languages*.

Shelton, A. L. and Zacks, J. M. (in press), Spatial transformations of scene stimuli: its's an upright world. In J. S. Gero (ed.), *Studying Visual and Spatial Reasoning for Design Creativity*. Berlin: Springer.

Shemanaeva, O. Y. (2007), Vyraženie peremeščenija v vode v nemeckom jazyke. (The expression of aquamotion in German.) In Maisak and Rakhilina (eds), 2007.

Shepard, R. N. and Metzler, J. (1971), Mental rotation of three-dimensional objects. *Science* 171: 701–3.

Shipley, T. F. (2003), The effect of object and event orientation on perception of biological motion. *Psychological Science* 14(4): 377–80.

Sigala, R., Serre, T., Poggio, T., and Giese, M. (2005), Learning as principle of action recognition in visual cortex. Lecture Notes in Computer Science, Volume 3696/2005, 241–6.

Sinha, C. and Kuteva, T. (1995), Distributed spatial semantics. *Nordic Journal of Linguistics* 18: 167–99, Cambridge: Cambridge University Press.

Siro, P. (1964), *Suomen kielen lauseoppi*. Helsinki: Tietosanakirja oy.

Sivonen J. (2005), *Mutkia matkassa. Nykysuomen epäsuoraa reittiä ilmaisevien verbien kognitiivista semantiikkaa*. Helsinki: Finnish Literature Society.

Slobin, D. (1985), The language making capacity. In D. Slobin (ed.), *The Cross-linguistic Study of Language Acquisition*. New York: Erlbaum, 1157–256.

Slobin, D. (1987), Thinking for speaking, *Proceedings of the Thirteenth Annual Meeting of the Berkeley Linguistics Society*, 435–45.

Slobin, D. (1991), Learning to think for speaking: native language, cognition, and rhetorical style. *Pragmatics* 1: 7–26.

Slobin, D. (1996a), From 'thought and language' to 'thinking for speaking'. In J. J. Gumperz and S. C. Levinson (eds), *Rethinking Linguistic Relativity*. (Studies in the Social and Cultural Foundation of Language (17). Cambridge: Cambridge University Press, 70–96.

Slobin, D. (1996b), Two ways to travel: verbs of motion in Spanish and English. In M. S. Shibatani and S. A. Thompson (eds), *Grammatical Constructions: Their Form and Meaning*. Oxford: Clarendon Press, 195–220.

Slobin, D. (2000), Verbalized events: a dynamic approach to linguistic relativity and determinism. In S. Niemeier, R. Dirven, and J. A. Lucy (eds), *Evidence for Linguistic Relativity*. Amsterdam: John Benjamins, 107–38.

Slobin, D. (2001), Form-function relations: how do children find out what they are? In M. Bowerman and S. Levinson (eds), *Language Acquisition and Conceptual Development*. Cambridge: Cambridge University Press, 406–49.

Slobin, D. (2004), The many ways to search for a frog: Linguistic typology and the expression of motion events. In S. S. and L. V. (eds), *Relating Events in Narrative. Vol. 2: Typological and Contextual Perspectives*. Mahwah, NJ: Erlbaum, 219–57.

Slobin, D. (2006), Typology and usage: explorations of motion events across languages. Paper given at the V International Conference of the Spanish Cognitive Linguistics Association, Universidad de Murcia, Spain.

Smith, T. (2006), Bulgarian motion verbs: manner and path in a Balkan context. Talk given at the First Meeting of the Slavic Linguistic Society, Indiana University, Bloomington, Indiana.

Spexard, T., Li, S., Wrede, B., Fritsch, J., Sagerer, G., Booij, O., Zivkovic, Z., Terwijn, B., and Kröse, B. (2006), BIRON, where are you? Enabling a robot to learn new places in a real home environment by integrating spoken dialog and visual localization. In *Proceedings of the IEEE/RSJ International Conference on Intelligent Robots and Systems (IROS).*

Stavrou, M. and Horrocks, G. (2003), Actions and their results in Greek and English: the complementarity of morphologically encoded (viewpoint) aspect and syntactic resultative predication. *Journal of Semantics* 20: 297–327.

Stefanowitsch, A. (2008), Covarying manner–path collexemes in German and Spanish motion clauses. Invited talk presented at the Workshop 'Human Locomotion Across Languages', Max Planck Institute for Psycholinguistics, Nijmegen.

Strömquist, S. and Verhoeven, L. (eds) (2004), *Relating Events in Narrative: Typological and Contextual Perspectives.* Mahwah, NJ: Erlbaum.

Talmy, L. (1983), How language structures space. In J. H. L. Pick and L. P. Acredolo (eds), *Spatial Orientation: Theory, Research and Application.* New York: Plenum Press.

Talmy, L. (1985), Lexicalization patterns: semantic structure in lexical forms. In T. Shopen (ed.), *Language Typology and Syntactic Description. Volume III: Grammatical Categories and the Lexicon.* Cambridge: Cambridge University Press, 57–149.

Talmy, L. (1988), Force dynamics in language and cognition. *Cognitive Science* 12: 49–100.

Talmy L. (1991), Path to realization: a typology of event conflation, *Proceedings of the Seventh Annual Meeting of the Berkeley Linguistics Society*, 480–519.

Talmy, L. (1996), Fictive motion in language and 'ception'. In P. Bloom, M. A. Peterson, L. Nadel and M. F. Garrett (eds), *Language and Space.* Cambridge, MA: MIT Press, 211–76.

Talmy, L. (2000), *Toward a Cognitive Semantics, Vol. I & II.* Cambridge, MA: MIT Press.

Talmy, L. (2003). The representation of spatial structure in spoken and signed language. In K. Emmorey (ed.), *Perspectives in Classifier Constructions in Sign Language.* Mahwah, NJ: Erlbaum, 169–95.

Tappe, H. (1999), Schichten konzeptueller Repräsentationen: Integration und Separierung. In I. Wachsmuth and B. Jung (eds), *KogWis99—Proceedings der 4. Fachtagung der Gesellschaft für Kognitionswissenschaft, Bielefeld, 28. September—1. Oktober 1999.* Sankt Augustin: Infix, 104–10.

Taylor, H. A. and Tversky, B. (1992a), Descriptions and depictions of environments. *Memory and Cognition* 20(5): 483–96.

Taylor, H. A. and Tversky, B. (1992b), Spatial mental models derived from survey and route descriptions. *Journal of Memory and Language* 31(2): 261–92.

Taylor, H. A. and Tversky, B. (1996), Perspective in spatial descriptions. *Journal of Memory and Language* 35(3): 371–91.

Tenbrink, T. (2005), Identifying objects on the basis of spatial contrast: an empirical study. In C. Freksa, M. Knauff, and B. Krieg-Brueckner (eds), *Spatial Cognition IV: Reasoning,*

Action, and Interaction. International Conference Spatial Cognition 2004, Frauenchiemsee, Germany, October 11–13, 2004, Revised Selected Papers. Berlin: Springer, 124–46.

Tenbrink, T. (2006), Localising objects and events: discoursal applicability conditions for spatiotemporal expressions in English and German. Dissertation, University of Bremen, 2005. Mikrofiche, Staats- und Universitätsbibliothek Bremen, ej 6922/E03.

Tenbrink, T. (2007), *Space, Time, and the Use of Language: an Investigation of Relationships*. Berlin: Mouton de Gruyter.

Tenbrink, T. (2009), Identifying objects in English and German: a contrastive linguistic analysis of spatial reference. In K. Coventery, T. Tenbrink, and J. Bateman (eds), *Spatial Language and Dialogue*. Oxford: Oxford University Press, 104–18.

Tenbrink, T. (2011), Reference frames of space and time in language. *Journal of Pragmatics*, 43(3), 704–22.

Tenbrink, T. and Winter, S. (2009), Granularity in route directions. *Spatial Cognition and Computation* 9(1): 64–9.

Thornton, I., Resnik, R., and Shiffrar, M. (2002), Active versus passive processing of biological motion. *Perception* 31: 837–53.

Thornton, I. and Vuong, Q. C. (2004), Incidental processing of biological motion. *Current Biology*.

Tom, A. and Denis, M. (2003), Referring to landmark or street information in route directions: what difference does it make? In W. Kuhn, M. Worboys, and S. Timpf (eds), *Spatial Information Theory: Foundations of Geographic Information Science*. Berlin: Springer, 362–74.

Trouvain, B. A., Schneider, F. E., and Wildermuth, D. (2001), Integrating a multimodal human–robot interaction method into a multi-robot control station. *IEEE International Workshop on Robot and Human Interactive Communication, ROMAN 2001*, 468–72.

Trullier, O., Wiener, S., Berthoz, A., and Meyer, J.-A. (1997). Biologically based artificial navigation systems: review and prospects. *Progress in Neurobiology* 51: 483–544.

Tschander, L., Schmidtke, H. R., Eschenbach, C., Habel, C., and Kulik, L. (2003), A geometric agent following route instructions. In C. Freksa, W. Brauer, C. Habel, and K. Wender (eds), *Spatial Cognition III*. Berlin: Springer, LNCS 2685, 89–111.

Tsuji, T. and Tanaka, Y. (2005), Tracking control properties of human-robotic systems based on impedance control. *IEEE Trans. on Sys., Man, and Cybern., Part A: Systems and Humans* 35(4): 523–34.

Tversky, A. (1977), Features of similarity. *Psychological Review*, 84(4), 327–52.

Tversky, B. (2005), Functional significance of visuospatial representations. In P. Shah and A. Miyake (eds), *The Cambridge Handbook of Visuospatial Thinking*. Cambridge: Cambridge University Press.

Tversky, B. and Hemenway, K. (1983), Categories of environmental scenes. *Cognitive Psychology* 15: 121–49.

Tversky, B. and Hemenway, K. (1984), Objects, parts, and categories. *Journal of Experimental Psychology: General* 113(2): 169–93.

Tversky, B., Kim, J., and Cohen, A. (1999), Mental models of spatial relations and transformations from language advances in psychology 128. In G. Rickheit and C. Habel (eds), *Mental Models in Discourse Processing and Reasoning*. Amsterdam: North-Holland/ Elsevier Science Publishers, 239–58.

Tversky, B. and Lee, P. U. (1999), Pictorial and verbal tools for conveying routes. In C. Freksa and D. M. Mark (eds), *Spatial Information Theory: Cognitive and Computational Foundations of Geographic Information Science*. Berlin: Springer, 51–64.

Tversky, B., Morrison, J. B., Franklin, N., and Bryant, D. J. (1999), Three spaces of spatial cognition. *Professional Geographer* 51: 516–24.

Tyler A. and Evans V. (2003), *The Semantics of English Prepositions*. Cambridge: Cambridge University Press.

Vainik, E. (1995), *Eesti keele väliskohakäänete semantika kognitiivse grammatika vaatenurgast*. (The semantics of Estonian external locative cases from the viewpoint of cognitive grammar.) Tallinn: Eesti Teaduste Akadeemia Eesti keele instituut.

Vandeloise C. (1986), *L'espace en français*. Paris: Éditions du Seuil.

van der Zee, E. (2000), Why we can talk about bulging barrels and spinning spirals: curvature representation in the lexical interface. In E. van der Zee and U. Nikanne (eds), *Cognitive Interfaces: Constraints on Linking Cognitive Information*. Oxford: Oxford University Press, 143–82.

van der Zee, E., Adams, K., and Niemi, J. (2009), The influence of geometrical and non-geometrical features on the use of the lexical concepts NEAR and FAR in English and Finnish. *Spatial Cognition and Computation* 9: 305–17.

van der Zee, E. and Eshuis, R. (2003), Directions from shape: how spatial features determine reference axis categorization. In E. van der Zee and J. Slack (eds), *Representing Direction in Language and Space*. Oxford: Oxford University Press, 209–25.

van der Zee, E. and Nikanne, U. (2000), Introducing cognitive interfaces and constraints on linking cognitive information. In E. van der Zee and U. Nikanne (eds), *Cognitive Interfaces*. Oxford: Oxford University Press, 1–17.

van der Zee, E., Nikanne, U., and Sassenberg, U. (2010), Grain levels in English path curvature descriptions and accompanying iconic gestures. *Journal of Spatial Information Science* 1: 95–113.

van der Zee, E. and Slack, J. (2003), *Representing Direction in Language and Space*. Oxford: Oxford University Press.

van Staden, M., Bowerman, M., and Verhelst, M. (2006), Some properties of spatial description in Dutch. In S. C. Levinson and D. Wilkins (eds) 2006, 477–513.

van Staden, M. and Reesink, G. P. (2008), Serial verb constructions in a linguistic area. To appear in G. Senft (ed.), forthcoming.

van Staden, M. and Senft, G. (2001), Event report and serial verb constructions in Austronesian and Papuan languages. Poster presented for the Fachbeirat at the Max Planck Institute for Psycholinguistics in Nijmegen.

Veismann, A. (2004), Sõna *üle* tähendusest. (On the meaning of 'üle'.) *Keel ja Kirjandus* 10: 762–77.

Veismann, A. and Tragel, I. (2008), *Kuidas horisontaalne ja vertikaalne liikumissuund eesti keeles aspektiks kehastuvad*. (Embodiment of the horizontal and vertical dimensions in Estonian aspect.) *Keel ja Kirjandus* 7: 515–30.

Viitso, T.-R. (2003), Structure of Estonian Language. Phonology, morphology and word formation. In M. Erelt (ed.), *Linguistica Uralica. Supplementary series: Vol. 1. Estonian Language*. Tallinn: Estonian Academy Publishers, 9–92.

Vilkuna, M. (1989), *Free Word Order in Finnish: its Syntax and Discourse Functions*. Helsinki: Finnish Literature Society.

von Stutterheim, C., Nüse, R. and Murcia-Serra, J. (2002), Cross-linguistic differences in the conceptualisation of events. In H. Hasselgård, S. Johansson, B. Behrens, and C. Fabricius-Hansen (eds), *Information Structure in a Cross-linguistic Perspective*. Amsterdam and New York: Rodopi, 179–98.

Vorwerg, C. (2001), *Raumrelationen in Wahrnehmung und Sprache: Kategorisierungsprozesse bei der Benennung visueller Richtungsrelationen*. Wiesbaden: DUV.

Vorwerg, C. (2003), Use of reference directions in spatial encoding. In C. Freksa, W. Brauer, and C. Habel (eds), *Spatial Cognition III: Routes and Navigation, Human Memory and Learning, Spatial Representation and Spatial Learning*. Berlin: Springer, 321–47.

Vorwerg, C. and Tenbrink, T. (2007), Discourse factors influencing spatial descriptions in English and German. In T. Barkowsky, M. Knauff, G. Ligozat, and D. Montello (eds), *Spatial Cognition V: Reasoning, Action, Interaction*. Berlin: Springer.

Vostrikova, N. V. (2007), Glagoly peremeščenija v vode v sel'kupskom, komi i udmurtskom jazykax. (Aquamotion verbs in Selkup, Komi, and Udmurt.) In Maisak and Rakhilina (eds), 2007.

Vydrine, V. F. (2007), Glagoly peremeščenija v vode v jazuke maninka. (Aquamotion verbs in Maninka.) In Maisak and Rakhilina (eds), 2007.

Wahlster, W., Blocher, A., Baus, J., Stopp, E., and Speiser, H. (1998), Resourcenadaptierende Objectlokalisation: Sprachliche Raumbeschreibung unter Zeitdruck. *Kognitionswissenschaft* 7: 111–17.

Weisgerber, M. (2008), Where lexical semantics meets physics: towards a three-level framework of modelling ROUTE. Manuscript, Konstanz University.

Weisgerber, M. and Geuder, W. (2007), Force antagonism in the semantics of movement verbs. Talk given at the conference 'FiGS 2007: Forces in Grammatical Structures'. Paris, France.

Weisman, G. D. (1987), Improving way-finding and architectural legibility in housing for the elderly. In V. Regnier and J. Pynoos (eds), *Housing the Aged: Design Directives and Policy Considerations*. New York: Elsevier, 441–64.

Werner, S., Krieg-Brückner, B., and Herrmann, T. (2000), Modelling navigational knowledge by route graphs. In C. Freksa, W. Brauer, C. Habel, and K. Wender (eds), *Spatial Cognition II*. Berlin: Springer, 295–316.

Winterboer, A. (2004), Sprachschnittstellen für die Robotersteuerung und deren empirische Validierung. Diploma thesis, Universität Bremen.

Worboys, M. F. (2001), Nearness relations in environmental space. *International Journal of Geographical Information Science* 15(7): 633–51.

Wunderlich, D. and Herweg, M. (1991), Lokale und Direktionale. In A. von Stechow and D. Wunderlich (eds), *Handbuch der Semantik*. Berlin: De Gruyter, 758–85.

Wunderlich, D. and Reinelt, R. (1982), How to get from here to there. In R. Jarvella and W. Klein (eds), *Speech, Place, and Action*. Chichester: Wiley, 183–201.

Yao, X. and Thill, J.-C. (2005), How far is too far? A statistical approach to context-contingent proximity modeling. *Transactions in GIS* 9: 157–78.

Zacks, J. M. (2004), Using movement and intentions to understand simple events. *Cognitive Science* 28(6): 979–1008.

Zacks, J. M., Braver, T. S., Sheridan, M. A., Donaldson, D. I., Snyder, A. Z., Ollinger, J. M., Buckner, R. L., and Raichle, M. E. (2001), Human brain activity time-locked to perceptual event boundaries. *Neuroscience* 4(6): 651–5.

Zacks, J. M. and Michelon, P. (2005), Transformations of visuospatial images. *Behavioral and Cognitive Neuroscience Reviews* 4, 96–118.

Zacks, J. M. and Tversky, B. (2001a), Event structure in perception and conception. *Psychological Bulletin* 127(1): 3–21.

Zacks, J. M. and Tversky, B. (2001b), Perceiving, remembering, and communicating structure in events. *Journal of Experimental Psychology: General* 130(1): 29–58.

Zacks, J. M. and Tversky, B. (2005), Multiple systems for spatial imagery: transformations of objects and bodies. *Spatial Cognition and Computation*, 5, 271–306.

Zacks, J. M., Tversky, B., and Iyer, G. (2001), Perceiving, remembering, and communicating structure in events. *Journal of Experimental Psychology: General* 130(1): 29–58.

Zakay, D. and Block, R. A. (1997), Temporal cognition. *Current Directions in Psychological Science* 6(1): 12–16.

Zimmer, H. D., Speiser, H. R., Baus, J., Blocher, A., and Stopp, E. (1998), The use of locative expressions in dependence of the spatial relation between target and reference object in two-dimensional layouts. In C. Freksa, C. Habel, and K. F. Wender (eds), *Spatial Cognition: An Interdisciplinary Approach to Representing and Processing Spatial Knowledge*. Berlin: Springer, 223–40.

Zlatev, J., Blomberg, J., and David, C. (2010), Translocation, language and the categorization of experience. In V. Evans and P. Chilton (eds.), *Language, Cognition and Space: the State of the Art and New Directions*. London, Oakville: Equinox, 389–418.

Zlatev, J. and Yangklang, P. (2004), A third way to travel: the place of Thai in motion-event typology. In S. Strömqvist and L. Verhoeven (eds), *Relating Events in Narrative: Vol. 2. Typological and Contextual Perspectives*. Mahwah, NJ: Erlbaum, 219–57.

Zwaan, R. A. and Radvansky, G. A. (1998), Situation models in language comprehension and memory. *Psychological Bulletin* 123: 162–85.

Zwarts, J. (2003), Vectors across spatial domains: from place to size, orientation, shape and parts. In E. van der Zee and J. Slack (eds), *Representing Direction in Language and Space*. Oxford: Oxford University Press, 39–68.

Zwarts, J. (2005). Prepositional aspect and the algebra of paths. *Linguistics and Philosophy* 28(6): 739–79.

Index

Adjective 193, 202
Adposition 4, 51, 53–4, 56, 63, 65–6, 181–2
Adverb 50, 52–4, 57–8, 61, 63, 65–6, 86, 88, 181, 187, 190, 202
adverbial: 4, 7, 35, 45, 47, 49, 53–5, 57–62, 64, 86, 138, 140–1, 202; *see also* Adverb
affordance 224
agent 20, 39, 45–7, 57, 62, 66, 89, 149, 151, 163, 155–6, 158, 161–4, 167–85
attention 2, 4, 5, 17, 20, 162
axial system, *see* reference (frame)
axis 12–13, 18, 34, 37–8, 86–8, 102–3, 106, 109, 112, 145, 160, 169–71, 188

Bulgarian 2–3, 11, 13–14, 19–21, 23–5, 27–8, 30, 35–8, 71, 188, 193, 212

Case 4, 45–6, 50–66, 143, 194, 202, 205
categorization 11, 12, 14–18, 20, 36–8, 44, 69, 79, 103, 167
caused motion, *see* motion
comprehension 129
coordinate system, *see* reference (frame)

development 85, 90, 97–9
dialogue 107, 170
dimension 45–6, 51, 54–5, 57, 59–61, 65–6
direction 2–5, 12–13, 17, 23, 25, 30, 34–7, 54, 57, 81, 84–100, 102–19, 142–5, 147, 151, 154, 156, 158–9, 161–2, 168, 170, 175, 180, 185, 191, 200, 201, 203, 204, 210
directional 3–4, 13, 30, 54, 84–100, 102, 107, 144, 168
directionality: *see* direction
distance 7, 12, 21, 25, 28, 29, 34, 43, 86–7, 90, 93, 97, 99, 123–4, 126, 149, 156–64, 167–9, 178, 181–5, 189, 204
Dutch 7, 71, 80–1, 137, 145, 151, 187–212

end point 17, 46, 54, 58, 63–4, 139, 172
English 1–3, 5, 11, 13–14, 19, 21, 27–8, 35–8, 48, 50, 54, 68–72, 75, 78, 80, 88, 107, 108, 118, 135–9, 143–7, 153, 163, 187–8, 193, 196, 202, 205, 211–12
episode 135
Estonian 2, 4, 44–9, 51, 53–8, 61, 63–6
events 6, 19, 23, 35, 44–7, 51–3, 56–8, 60–6, 103, 124, 126–9, 132, 134–48, 150–3, 158, 162, 164–5, 184, 205

feature 2–7, 11–12, 14–24, 27–33, 35–9, 135, 138–40, 149–64
Figure 2–5, 11–12, 16–20, 35, 38, 68, 71, 73–5, 80–2, 88, 135, 138–40, 142–3, 145–6, 149, 151–64, 168–72, 176–8, 181, 188–92, 195, 200–4, 211
Finnish 7, 63, 71, 187–98, 201–5, 207–12
French 71, 127, 150–1, 157–8
function 6, 11–12, 35, 44, 47, 52–5, 57, 63, 102, 104–5, 109–10, 113–15, 117–19, 126–7, 138, 140, 147, 149–50, 152, 157, 158, 164, 177–8, 195, 201, 203

German 2, 4, 7, 71, 76, 85, 88, 93, 138–9, 166, 168, 176, 181, 186
Gesture 2, 89, 107
Goal 2, 4–5, 19, 45–7, 53–7, 61–6, 85–7, 89–91, 93–5, 97–9, 110, 119, 129, 138, 142, 143, 146–7, 168–9, 172, 175, 177, 179–82, 185, 189, 193, 199–200, 205
grain 2–7, 60, 123, 126, 128–9, 132, 137, 142, 151, 163–4, 166, 167, 171–5, 177, 179, 184–5, 188, 190, 192, 205
granularity 3–7, 13, 39, 122, 123, 134–9, 141–2, 145, 147–53, 162–4, 166–8, 170–1, 173–80, 182–6
Ground 2–3, 5, 12–13, 18, 20, 24, 26, 32, 59, 68–9, 85, 135, 139–40, 142–3, 145–7, 149, 153–64, 168–71, 176–8, 181–6

Hindi 71, 79, 137, 140–1, 143–5, 147

Indonesian 4, 68, 71–5, 77, 78, 80–1, 83

information 13, 16–17, 22, 25, 70, 84, 92, 102–7, 109, 111–19, 124–6, 128, 135–7, 144–7, 149, 151, 153, 163, 168, 171, 175, 189, 194, 197–8, 201, 203, 204, 208
Italian 2–3, 11, 14, 19, 21, 28–32, 35–8, 71, 123

Kalam 137, 139
Kilivila 134, 137, 139–41

landmark 35, 51, 64, 103–4, 106–7, 109–10, 112–19, 154–5, 158, 160–3, 166, 175–6, 181, 184
Lexical Conceptual Structure 194, 212
location 2–7, 13, 35, 45–7, 51–2, 54–5, 57–66, 68–9, 75–6, 80–1, 86, 90, 93, 95, 106, 108, 110, 112, 114, 116, 132, 134–5, 137, 139–45, 147, 149, 153–65, 167, 170–5, 180, 182, 184, 188–9, 195, 201–3

Manner of motion 2–3, 12, 47, 53, 135, 136, 143, 150–1, 188, 193, 195, 197, 204, 210, 211
Map 5, 107–8, 113, 115, 119, 129, 132, 152, 167, 175–7
meaning 2, 23, 25, 29, 32, 35, 45–51, 54, 56–7, 59–64, 67, 70, 80, 105, 154, 160, 173, 176–7, 179–81, 183–5, 187–9, 194, 202

nominal 48, 64, 73, 143
Norwegian 2–3, 11, 14, 19, 21–22, 26, 30–2, 35–8
Noun 48, 52, 54–56, 78, 80, 88, 128, 135, 139, 143–4, 147, 178, 186, 196, 199, 202, 212

object 2, 5–7, 12, 14, 17–18, 21, 45, 47, 52–3, 55, 57–8, 60, 63, 66, 85–6, 88–90, 93–4, 102, 106, 111, 115, 118, 119, 123–32, 138–43, 145–7, 149–50, 152–64, 166–75, 177–8, 183–6, 188–9, 192, 202
orientation 4, 11, 13, 17–20, 27, 34–9, 87–8, 91, 102, 129–32, 144, 146, 149, 154, 163–4, 179

parameters 2–4, 7, 11–12, 14–15, 19, 36, 68–9, 83, 102
partonomy 125
partonomic level 134–5
partonomic hierarchy 135–7, 142, 147
path 2–7, 11–13, 15–20, 25, 27, 30, 37–8, 44, 46, 63, 68, 86–8, 91, 95, 104, 105, 117, 132, 135, 139, 140, 142, 149, 153–6, 158–4, 166, 168–9, 172–3, 175–7, 179–82, 185, 187, 212
perception 11, 15–17, 125, 127, 134, 138, 141, 147, 151, 153, 156, 162, 164, 165, 172
Persian 2, 4, 71, 77, 82
perspective 2, 4, 7, 15, 16, 61, 64, 68, 79, 83–4, 89, 104, 112, 129–31, 168, 171–2, 175
point 1, 5, 7, 12–13, 16–18, 24, 27, 35, 36, 46, 49, 51–2, 54, 57–9, 61–2, 63, 64, 68, 70–1, 78, 82, 89–71, 78, 82, 89, 95, 99, 103–5, 107–10, 113–19, 135, 151, 154–5, 158–61, 164, 166–73, 175
Postposition 46, 50, 52, 56, 60–1, 63–5, 181–2
Preposition 2, 4–7, 46, 50, 65, 69, 86, 135, 139, 143–4, 149–50, 153–9, 161–6, 168–9, 172, 174, 176–8, 180–1, 183, 185–6, 199, 201
  Projective (e.g., in front of, behind) 149–65, 169
Production 119
Pronoun 53, 62, 128
properties 5–6, 12, 17, 22, 33–4, 36, 82, 98, 102, 114, 123, 145–7, 151–2, 154–5, 157, 159, 162–3, 199

reference frame / frame of reference 85, 130, 149, 155
  absolute / environment centered 106
  intrinsic / object centered 130, 155, 156
  relative 153, 155, 161, 163
reference system, *see* reference frame
relations 1, 3–5, 12, 17, 48, 66, 68, 85–6, 90, 102, 104, 111, 115, 117, 126, 131, 136, 138, 145, 149–51, 153–4, 156, 158–65, 172–4, 176, 178–81
representation 2–3, 5, 7, 15, 21, 32, 46, 68–9, 103, 112, 126–7, 129, 135, 147, 150, 166–8, 170–2, 175–7, 185, 187–8, 198, 200–1, 203–4, 211–12

route 2, 5, 7, 46–47, 52–3, 63–4, 66, 87, 98, 103–19, 129, 132, 156, 166, 172–3, 175–6, 179–80, 182–5, 192
route descriptions 175
route perspective 172
Russian 2–4, 11, 14, 19, 21–2, 32–8, 65, 67, 69, 71, 75–6, 82
satellite-framed 3, 19, 44, 210–12
scale 2, 5–6, 15, 32, 123–30, 132, 135, 150, 152–3, 158–9, 161, 163–4, 167, 172, 180, 184
script 135, 138, 142
shape 2, 4, 12–13, 16, 18, 20, 25, 30, 36, 38, 87, 109, 124, 127, 146–7, 168–70, 172–4, 176, 180–1, 185–94, 197, 200–1, 203–5, 207, 209, 210
size 5, 7, 86, 93, 95, 105, 123, 126, 132, 146–7, 152–5, 157–9, 161, 163–4, 167–71, 173–9, 182–5
Source 1–2, 4, 15, 21, 45–7, 49, 51–4, 61–3, 65–6, 69–70, 86, 141–2, 169, 178–80, 185, 189, 193, 199–200
Space 1–2, 5, 17, 30, 38, 44–6, 50–2, 55, 59–61, 66, 68, 72, 81, 103, 123–5, 129–31, 146, 149–50, 152–6, 158–64, 167, 170–2, 175, 177, 185
spatial 1–7, 12, 14, 44, 46–7, 51, 53, 56–7, 62, 64–6, 84–7, 89–90, 98–100, 102–9, 111–19, 123–6, 129–32, 143, 145–6, 149–57, 159, 161–4, 166, 168, 171–3, 175, 179, 181, 184–5, 187, 200–1, 203–4
spatial
  directional 84
  relations 66, 85–6, 102, 104, 111, 115, 117, 164, 172, 176
  representation 5, 175, 201
  template 86–7, 102
starting point 17, 46, 49, 51–2, 70, 107, 175
survey perspective 129, 168, 172

Swedish 71

Tamil 3–4, 71, 77
taxonomy 5, 123, 125–6
Tidore 137, 139–41, 143–7
Tzeltal 134, 137, 146–7

Verb 2–7, 12–14, 17–38, 43–5, 47–50, 52–3, 55, 57–8, 60–83, 92, 94–5, 108–10, 112, 116, 118, 128, 135–6, 138–47, 150–1, 153, 157, 161–2, 176, 178–9, 183–205, 207–12
participial verb 140–141
Verb of motion (motion verb) 4, 7, 12–14, 19, 21–3, 25–30, 32–3, 35, 38, 44–5, 48–9, 55, 58, 63–4, 66, 68–9, 72, 74–5, 79, 82, 91, 94–5, 150, 187–9, 196, 201–3, 205, 207, 210, 212
verb-framed 3–4, 19, 44, 210–12